A VIETNAM VET'S
REMARKABLE LIFE

Published by Brolga Publishing Pty Ltd
PO Box 12544 A'Beckett St Melbourne Australia 8006
ABN 46 063 962 443
email: admin@brolgapublishing.com.au
web: www.brolgapublishing.com.au
All rights reserved. No part of this publication may be reproduced, stored in a retrieval system or transmitted in any form or by any means electronic, mechanical, photocopying, recording or otherwise without prior permission from the publisher.
Copyright 2012 © John 'Jethro' Thompson

National Library of Australia Cataloguing-in-Publication entry

Author:	Thompson, John
Title:	A Vietnam Vet's Remarkable Life
ISBN:	9781922036148

National Library of Australia Cataloguing-in-Publication entry:
Printed in China
Cover design by David Khan
Typesetting by Takiri Nia

BE PUBLISHED

Publish Through a Successful Australian Publisher
National Distribution
Enquiries to Brolga Publishing
Email: admin@brolgapublishing.com.au
markzocchi@brolgapublishing.com.au

A Vietnam Vet's Remarkable Life

The True Meaning of Mateship

John *'JETHRO'* Thompson

FOREWORD

Since my time in Vietnam, I have shared snippets about my experiences with my family, friends and journalists, skirting around the real story. In 2007 family and mates regularly gathered at my bedside to support me once again while undergoing and recovering from open-heart surgery. I was so overwhelmed by their support that I felt compelled to share my true story with them – warts and all.

There are many fine stories recorded and books published about Australians involved in the Vietnam War already. My story is not a war story. It is about what happens after a soldier is removed from the field. I have no doubt that many civilian patients have also experienced similar difficulties and frustrations.

To minimise the possibility of embarrassing individuals who I had to mention, I have changed some names and deliberately omitted the surname of others. My army medical file and Repatriation Hospital file provided detailed information about daily events that occurred over forty years ago and supported my own recollection of a very significant period in my life.

Relying on one's memory however, can be fraught with danger, I sought out friends who allowed me to delve deeply into their memories, some as painful as my own.

DEDICATION

My story is dedicated to the following:

The memory of Glen T Bartholomew, Gregory V Brady, Dennis L Brooks, Ray J Deed, John L O'Hara and Terry J Renshaw. Six Sappers who perished while laying the Barrier Minefield.

The crew of 9 Squadron RAAF aircraft No 1025 and 1021 who responded to the Dustoff call on the morning of 9 May 1967 and conveyed my colleagues and I so swiftly to hospital.

The doctors, nurses and all staff of the US Army 36 Evacuation Hospital Vung Tau Vietnam. Their skill, professionalism and dedication kept me alive against the odds and returned me to my family. The doctors, nurses and all who contributed to my recovery at the Repatriation General Hospital. Heidelberg, Victoria, Australia.

Over the last forty-five years as a patient in a number of hospitals, I have received wonderful care and my admiration for all who choose to work in the medical profession has not wavered. I remain grateful to the staff at the Department of Veterans' Affairs who have ensured my access to high standard medical care continues.

Mark Zocchi, my publisher, who responded so enthusiastically to my unsolicited manuscript and Julie Capaldo, who edited my manuscript and guided me in the right direction . They have helped make it possible for my story to be published.

HAPPINESS

"Reflect upon your present blessings, of which every man has many; not on your past misfortunes, of which all men have some."

– **Charles Dickens**

PROLOGUE

9 May 1967

Whoompa! I'm catapulted into the air with enormous force, then crash down on my back. A cloud of debris slowly rains over me. I can hear the gentle rhythmic sound of soil landing around me despite the noise of the explosion still ringing in my ears. I close my eyes against the gritty, sandy soil as it covers me. I feel no pain. I look at my hands. Some fingers are missing; others are hanging loosely. My arms are red with blood gushing from many wounds. I attempt to sit up, but I can't feel my legs.

'Call Dustoff!'

I can hear someone moaning. I don't know who it is. Someone else is calling for the safety pins to be replaced in the mines.

'We can't replace them.'

'Why not?'

'Jethro has them in his pocket.'

Sergeant Brett Nolen is ripping open shell dressings. He kneels beside me, shielding me from the sun. He looks at me silently for a moment then starts sticking shell dressings into my guts. I feel his hands pressing down hard onto my stomach. He tears open more dressings. They look terribly small in his bloodied hands. I still feel no pain, but blood is running into my eyes. It's warm and sticky. Lieutenant Joe Cazey and Nolen are telling me about the lovely nurses who'll look after me once the Dustoff chopper gets me to hospital. The thought of pretty nurses distracts me for a while as I lie in the minefield, not wanting to think about my life-blood soaking into the ground around me.

1.
Heading to South Vietnam

November 1966

Exercise *Barrawinga* was over and most of the squadron personnel had returned to Enoggera Army Camp from Shoalwater Bay. Christmas leave and resurrecting a local social life occupied my thoughts. I was unaware that the Army had immediate plans for me: the war in South Vietnam. Within days a large number of squadron personnel were ordered to move to the School of Military Engineering (SME) at Casula near Liverpool New South Wales. We were to join the Royal Australian Engineer (RAE) reinforcement pool. I would be in South Vietnam before Christmas.

Ray Hiddlestone asked Charlie Lynn and me to accompany him on the drive south to SME in his Ford Customline. The combined travelling allowance paid by the Army would easily cover the cost of fuel and refreshments along the way. With a twelve-hour overnight drive ahead of us we wasted no time obtaining a clearance from camp and saying goodbye to the few mates still around the barracks. Three of us were sitting on the large front bench seat as we left Enoggera and headed west towards Ipswich and the New England Highway. Traffic was light and the weather pleasant as we covered mile after mile. Sitting between Charlie and Ray I was thinking about friends back at Enoggera. Would I ever see them again? Many of the blokes in the squadron were National Servicemen and most had chosen not to extend their time in the Army to serve in South Vietnam. Other mates were reaching the end of their period of enlistment and would also be discharged before I returned. The close environment of military life has a natural tendency to accelerate the bonds of friendship as you share experiences not normally encountered in civilian life. Your peers quickly identify and assess your character. Qualities most looked for are loyalty, honesty and reliability. If these three basics exist other flaws in your personality will be tolerated. An affinity will develop into friendship regardless of the brevity of your time together. From the beginning of my army service in June 1964 I had developed a number of sound friendships. A six-month tour of service in Borneo in 1965 intensified some relationships and generated even more.

Ray, driving into the night, asked that at least one of us remain awake ensuring he would not fall asleep. In the interest of self-preservation I was more than willing to stay awake. However, the need to make conversation was an intrusion on my moments of reflection. Ray said he was feeling good behind the wheel and had declined my offer to relieve him for a while. A little after dawn the gourmet delights purchased at an all-night petrol station: steamed dim sims, chiko roll, chips and coke were playing havoc with my guts. I farted quietly and waited for the reaction. It stunk. Charlie quickly wound down the window. One would think that was sufficient remedial action but not Charlie. Foolishly, he climbed out through the window and sat in the window space hanging on for dear life. Only his feet hooked under the seat kept him from falling out of the car. He put on a great act of gasping for fresh air. As we rounded a sweeping bend, a motorcycle cop came towards us and seeing Charlie hanging out of the car, he did a U-turn and indicated for Ray to pull over. The cop walked towards our car so Charlie leaped out and started talking at a hundred miles an hour telling the cop how I had farted and he suspected I'd shit myself. Maintaining he had no alternative but to take desperate action, Charlie then audaciously invited the cop, if he had any doubts, to sit in the car and take a deep breath. While the cop scratched his nuts and pondered about the three guys in front of him, Charlie spun a yarn about how we were heading off to South Vietnam immediately when we arrived in Sydney to perform a specialist task. With all our gear stashed on the back seat as well as in the boot, the cop fell for it. He gave us a stern warning about acting the goat while driving and then waved us on our way. Reaching SME without further incident about 0600 hours, we parked near the camp guardhouse. Ray and I settled for a nap. Charlie went off for an early morning jog.

As we were not required to report in at the Orderly Room until 1000 hours, we opted to drive into Liverpool for breakfast. Shops were starting to open and few people were on the streets. Charlie thought it would be nice to buy his wife a present. A ladies dress shop was opening its doors as we strolled by and after a brief look in the window we followed Charlie as he made his way towards a young shop assistant. With a straight face he explained how he was going to South Vietnam but first he would have one week pre-embarkation leave at home with his wife Jill and he wanted to buy a very nice going away present. The girl made a variety of suggestions then asked Charlie what he thought would be suitable.

'Bras, yes bras would be ideal.'

'What size would your wife be?' the girl asked.

Taking everyone by surprise, Charlie placed his hand over the girl's breast and said, 'Yes, that's about the size. What size do you take?'

Fearing the worse, Ray and I stood silently as the red-faced girl blurted out her size and went looking for the appropriate item.

With the bra gift wrapped, we headed straight back to SME.

About 60 sappers of all ranks had arrived by the end of the day. We had no idea when we would leave or whether we would have pre-embarkation leave. Medical checks, inoculations and dental inspections were performed within days of our arrival. We listened to a corporal recently returned from a year in Vietnam give a presentation on the sappers' role in the war. Although he endeavoured to the best of his ability, he failed to hold our attention. The days passed slowly with little, if any, worthwhile information forwarded to the assembled troops. Many were becoming bored. We played squash daily and went for long runs to maintain our fitness and tried to avoid drinking too much beer. Then the news we were waiting for finally arrived: we would be flying to South Vietnam in the first week of January. Combined pre-embarkation and Christmas leave would give me two weeks at home.

I headed into Liverpool with Sapper Brian Kalisperis who was also going to Sydney airport. Despite the cost we agreed that a taxi would be the least difficult way to the airport. The crowd queuing for a taxi was rather long. After about 30 minutes we made it to the front of the queue. As we started to load our bags into the taxi the driver asked where we were heading. 'The airport' we said. We were taken by surprise when he told us to get our bags out of his taxi and go by train. We fired up immediately, refusing to step back and insisting he drive us to the airport. After being in the queue for so long we were not about to take much crap from the driver. I could see a punch-up looming. The crowd waiting at the rank became a little noisy; impatient customers started telling us to move on and stop holding them up. Others agreed with us and verbally supported our stand. Brian spotted two motorcycle cops cruising past on the other side of the road. His shrieking whistle startled them so much that one turned his bike into the other and both fell off. I really felt we were about to get the arse from the taxi. Most likely agitated by their spill and a little embarrassed, the cops demanded to know who was next in line. We answered that we were. The driver was told to take us where we wanted to go. Our ride to the airport was hair-raising to say the least. From occasional glances via the rear view mirror it was obvious the driver's rage towards us never diminished, despite the lengthy drive.

Christmas 1966

Being home in time for Christmas pleased my mother immensely. Her son and three daughters were together again. As a child food was never in abundance in our house apart from Christmas and Easter when the dinner table would be straining to support the amount of food available to gorge ourselves on. This Christmas was the same. I set out to see what social activity might be available. Surprisingly, the result was not too good. Most mates were involved with steady girlfriends and not interested in spending time with me. The only offer I received for a night out was from a neighbour across the road.

Blue Lisle, a World War Two veteran who still served in the Citizens Military Forces (CMF), was eager to take me to the Sergeants' Mess at the Broadmeadows camp for a few beers and a talk. Blue told me not to mention that I was in the Army as I was not a sergeant. A quick look around the near empty mess convinced me a quiet beer in the backyard would have been the better option. Blue must have had the same thought as he said, 'Always is quiet on a Friday night.' I emptied my glass and declined another beer. We headed back to the car and I felt a little sorry for Blue who, apart from a bit of showing off, was obviously eager to have a few beers with me. Driving home along Sydney Road we could hear the music blaring from the Boundary Hotel. We turned right into Boundary Road and Blue pulled into the car park. We headed towards vacant seats next to two rather drunk looking ladies in the lounge bar. Both were much older than I was, but younger than Blue. They had obviously put in a big effort in front of their mirrors titivating before stepping out that evening, unquestionably mutton dressed up as lamb. Blue asked the ladies what they would like to drink and gave me a stab in the ribs and a wink. After another beer I started to go along with Blue, chatting them up. Then to my horror the lady next to me stood up to go to the 'ladies'. As she moved away I saw a large puddle on her seat. I told Blue it was time to move on.

My two weeks was up and I was to head back to Sydney on the overnight train from Spencer Street Station. Enjoying my last Sunday lunch with Mum and Dad and my two younger sisters before I headed off to war, I mentioned to my mother that I would appreciate her not coming to the station later in the afternoon, preferring to endure her emotional display in the privacy of our family home. I love my mother dearly but from an early age I have been embarrassed by the way she demonstrates her feelings, gesticulating wildly and repeating religious phrases, loudly in Maltese. I could never see a need for such a performance.

Dressed in my best summer uniform, I had a solitary medal ribbon for service in Borneo proudly displayed on my chest, the engineer corps dark blue lanyard on my right shoulder, and parachute wings on my right arm. Looking in the mirror I was happy with my appearance. Leaving my room I felt twelve feet tall and tremendously proud. I was a twenty-one year old Australian soldier going off to war. Dad drove me to the inter state station at Spencer Street and my two younger sisters, Sue and Patricia, came along to wave me off. As the train slowly pulled out I was left alone with my thoughts.

Speculation about what unit we might be posted to was the main topic of discussion once I made it back to SME. Naturally, I was prepared to serve wherever the Army sent me but 17 Construction Squadron RAE with the Australian Logistic Support Group at Vung Tau was my preference. The role of a construction squadron is primarily the development of main base establishments and all relevant infrastructure required by a task force. Construction squadrons are equipped with superior heavy earthmoving equipment. Opportunities to improve my skill as a plant operator would be plentiful.

January 1967

Our posting and departure date were placed on the notice board. I was to fly out on Friday, 6 January. I was pleased with the date but a little disappointed with my posting: 1 Field Squadron RAE at the Australian Task Force, at Nui Dat. The main role of the squadron was to work in close support of the infantry. After dinner I got to bed early, only to be woken when Charlie and Ray returned from the camp movie theatre full of booze and loudly discussing the merits of the movie. Eventually they got into bed but left the light on.

'Will one of you pricks turn out the bloody light?' I yelled at them. They started arguing about who was last in bed. Seeing no end to their alcohol induced gibbering, I said, 'I'll soon turn it out.' Reaching down beside my bed, I took hold of one of my boots and with a swift flick propelled the boot towards the naked light bulb. *What a shot!* I struck the globe, shattering it. From the darkness of the room a muffled voice said, 'Light's out.'

Thursday evening my last night in Australia, Ray and I headed into Kings Cross. At the 'Jungle Bar' we spotted two girls sitting alone. We moved closer and started chatting them up. Drinking, cuddling and smooching was soon going well. In need of a pee, I headed to the gents. As I stood at the urinal, the fellow beside me said, 'G'Day' and asked if I'd been or was going to Vietnam. He started to tell me about his brother who was a *Qantas* flight attendant flying out to Manila in the morning with a load of troops heading to Vietnam. 'I could be on that plane.' I said. The bloke asked for my name and told me he'd have his brother look after me.

The girl I had been chatting up lived nearby with her parents and Ray's new girlfriend was staying with her tonight, we suggested we take them home. After a short taxi ride we were stepping quietly through the front garden. Ray and his girlfriend went off into the shadows. My girl pointed out her bedroom window. I suggested that if she went inside and opened it, I'd be able to climb through the window. She agreed and went in while I stood alone in the garden anxiously waiting for the window to open. As the minutes passed I started to think I'd bombed out. To my delight the window opened. Quietly, I scampered up the wall into her bedroom. All was going good for a while, but fearing her parents sleeping in the next room might discover me became a distraction. Leaving the same way I had entered, I slipped and fell into the garden below. As I brushed myself down, Ray appeared and we headed off in search of a taxi to take us back to SME.

Next morning when we arrived at the airport the draft checked kit bags and weapons in, minus the bolt. The rifle bolt was to stay in our possession at all times. Sitting between Jack Campbell and Butch Carman I settled in for the flight to Manila. Once we were airborne a flight steward came looking for 'Jethro'. 'Here I am,' I said. He introduced himself as the brother of the bloke I had briefly shared a urinal with about twelve hours previously. Before long, beer and little bottles of Johnny Walker Red Label whisky were appearing regularly. *It's good to have friends in the right places,* I thought. Happily drinking our endless supply of grog, Jack, Butch and I talked about where we would like to go for Rest and Recreation Leave (R&R). We had been to Singapore a year ago so it was off the list. Thailand, Taiwan and Hong Kong appealed to Butch and me.

2
Manila

Arriving over Manila, my head was telling me we had stopped drinking not a minute too soon. In the hot afternoon sun we formed up and marched smartly to the baggage trolleys to retrieve our kit bags and weapons. It soon became obvious that all was not well with the local authorities. Despite the hot sun and heat radiating off the concrete surrounds, we were herded into a tight formation outside the international terminal building. An armed squad of Philippine Police formed a line that emphatically stated we were going nowhere fast. An official from the Australian Embassy arrived on the scene and began speaking with local officials and our Draft Conducting Officer. Without a word of explanation we remained in our position, sweltering outside the terminal building. The diplomatic discussion eventually found a solution to the problem. Local authorities had objected to foreign soldiers entering their country carrying weapons. We were to store the weapons in a room within the terminal but retain the bolts. The room would be locked and guarded overnight. After complying with the demand we were split into two groups. One group went to the USAF Clark airbase for the night. The second group went to the Hotel Timberland. Butch and I were in the hotel. Jack went to the airbase.

At the hotel I paired up with Brian 'Toby' Tobin, originally a Nasho who had been conscripted to serve two years in the army a year earlier. Like many other twenty year olds he had chosen to join the regular army so that he could go to Vietnam. As we settled into our room we realised that neither of us had been given a key. Inquiries revealed that all doors were to remain unlocked. We were grateful that our weapons were not in our possession. With enough time to have a beer before dinner, we headed down to the hotel bar. Sappers were hanging around the bar bitching about having ice cubes put in their beer to cool it down. We were happy to pass on the beer. I decided that a haircut and shave would be a nice treat before dinner. The soothing effect of the hot towels draped over my face was appreciated immediately. As the barber manoeuvred his cutthroat razor across my face, I felt totally relaxed and on the cusp of dozing off when I heard him asking if I would like a nice clean girl. With his razor just under my nose the barber had my full attention. Was it the position of the razor or the mention of a clean girl? As I thought about answering I heard, 'Jethro, we are going to be late for dinner'. Toby was standing in front of me. I scampered out of the barber's chair without answering and headed for dinner. Although I cleaned my plate all the blokes sitting at the table agreed that the steak must have come from the carcass of an aged water buffalo that had perished from exhaustion.

With my ravenous appetite satisfied for a while by the very ordinary meal I joined Toby, Butch Carman and Brian Kalisperis in a clapped out Mercedes and an equally shoddy looking driver who promised to show us a little of the Manila night life. Sleazy nightclubs, with near naked bar girls was all we saw. With a mid-morning bus ride back to the airport scheduled to continue our journey to Vietnam we returned to our hotel rather early. Next morning after breakfast Toby and I noticed a crowd forming around a doorway. We stopped to see what the attraction was: *holy hell!* One of our blokes was in bed with a girl and she was dressed only in an army green singlet. The two of them looked like they were trying to emulate every position in the 'Kama Sutra'. Neither party showed the slightest inhibition as the room filled with onlookers. Unashamedly the bloke justified his behaviour on the grounds he could be dead by the end of the week. He wasn't far out! *He was killed in action a few months later.*

3
Vietnam / Nui Dat

Standing on the hot concrete tarmac of Saigon's Tan Son Nhut International Airport, we waited for transport to Camp Alpha, a major staging camp for US Australian and New Zealand troops moving in or out of the country by air. Everywhere we looked were heavily armed South Vietnamese soldiers and US military police wearing helmets and flak jackets: grenades hanging nonchalantly like Christmas tree baubles from their webbing and belts of ammunition dangling from M60 machine guns. US Army jeeps were racing around with blaring horns muscling their way through the local traffic. We had definitely arrived in a war zone. A short bus ride delivered us to Camp Alpha. We were directed towards a number of accommodation buildings and advised to find a bed and secure our weapons. We read signs on the walls warning that we should retain our valuables in our possession at all times. Selecting a bed, that had a cleaner looking mattress than most, I deposited my kit. Although the sun was setting, the heat and humidity continued to sap my energy. I joined a group of blokes heading to the mess hall. What a delight! Copious amounts of food with an abundance of choice and the freedom to return for more appealed to me.

With my belly full, I looked around for a quiet corner in a beer hall. US servicemen of all ranks were present. While enjoying a beer with a few mates I heard a group of Diggers had ventured out of camp and tangled with some US military police. At least one of our guys had a swollen eye that would be as black as the ace of spades in the morning.

Two US Army officers sat at a nearby table looking rather bored. Their collar tags identified one as an infantry officer and the other, a medical officer. We invited them to join our little group. They told us that they had been on R&R and were waiting for transport back to their units. The two had only met each other over dinner. The medical officer was a doctor completing his obligation to his country as a draftee. The infantry officer was a regular soldier with an impressive collection of uniform embellishments. Silver parachute wings and Infantry Combat Badge, were the only two I recognised. In comparison, our uniforms were outstanding for their paucity of embellishment.

With several other sappers, I adjourned to the infantry officer's quarters. We were all listening enthusiastically to his experience in Vietnam and the significance of his badges and medals. From the moment I first heard 'The Ballad of the Green Beret' I was eager to souvenir a pair of silver wings. Whether it was the beer he had drunk or my persuasive argument, the officer removed his wings and handed them to me. In return I handed over an embroidered parachute patch. I was delighted having been in the country only a matter of hours and already I had inveigled a much sought after souvenir. Over breakfast, the last time we would all be together as a draft of reinforcements, I was disappointed to learn that our mate with the black eye had stolen a crossed rifles badge from the officer's collection.

Those posted to 1 Field Squadron were assembled and transported back to the airport to board a RAAF 35 Squadron *Wallaby Airline*

Caribou for a 30 minute flight to Luscombe Field, at Nui Dat. This was the moment of reality; we were now part of an army on active service in a foreign land. A truck was waiting to take us to the squadron's lines. Within minutes we were assembled next to squadron headquarters and welcomed to the unit by the duty officer. We were made aware of a number of standing orders such as: carrying weapons at all times and malaria control procedure. We were told that Major Brian Florence, the officer commanding the squadron (OC) would interview each man personally in the morning. Toby and Jack were marched off to 21 Support Troop lines, which were on the base perimeter. The rest of us were marched off to a marquee at the rear of 1 Troop lines and told to make ourselves comfortable. We would be allocated to a section over the next few days.

Troop Staff Sergeant Blair Parsons informed us that ammunition would be issued after roll call in the morning. In the meantime we should familiarise ourselves with the squadron layout. We were told that our Troop Commander was Captain Graham Moon, the Troop Officer was Lieutenant Colin Browne, and the Troop Sergeant was Allan West. We would meet them all in the morning. Most of the squadron personnel were having a rest day and many sappers had gone to Vung Tau by truck for the afternoon. Rest days, I learnt, were few and far between. After stashing my kitbag on a bed frame, I made my way to the unit boozer, where most of the blokes who had not gone to Vung Tau were enjoying a cold beer. Greetings between old friends were exchanged, with the degree of crudeness determined by the amount of beer the greeter had consumed.

After a couple beers, Toby and I went for a walk around the squadron lines. At the rear of 1 Troop we found a weapon pit with overhead protection. In the pit was an automatic rifle (AR L2A1), with its bipod resting on sandbags. American M26 fragmentation grenades were in a box beside it. The view from the pit looked out over an area of ground between squadron lines and the base of Nui Dat Hill. Slightly to the left we could see the area used by helicopters to refuel. The area to the right emerged from a depression in what looked like an unoccupied section of the base perimeter with little, if any, defensive positions that we could see. Back at the boozer we were told that two sappers manned the weapon pit over night.

Although I was tired, artillery fire throughout the night made sleeping difficult. However, I was eager to start my first working day. It was nearly two months since I had last operated any plant equipment. After morning parade all the new blokes made their way to squadron headquarters. Casually standing around talking about our first impressions of Vietnam, we did not notice Major Florence approach our group. Without fuss he requested that the senior soldier present take charge and have the group assemble in order of rank and alphabetically. Corporal Tony Evans, a national serviceman recently promoted before leaving Australia, set about sorting the group into order. Responding to my name I placed my weapon at the entrance to the office and marched in towards Major Florence. He was seated behind a desk. I saluted and remained standing at attention.

'Stand at ease,' he said.

A vacant chair was on my side of the desk but I was not invited to sit. Major Florence looked me up and down, as if he was trying to remember me. I remembered him; a shortish but solidly built man, with a red complexion to match his reddish hair. He had been OC of 7 Field Squadron at Enoggera, which shared the same barracks as 24 Construction Squadron. I listened as I was told, that in addition to developing base facilities, the squadron had the additional role of working in close support of the infantry. Sappers accompanied the infantry on almost every operation in search of the enemy.

'Vietnam will be a lot more demanding than your time in Borneo,' he said. Questions about my family life followed and he stressed the importance of writing home. As I listened I was thinking he sounded like a reasonable sort of bloke, not the ogre I had imagined him to be based on the opinions of some who had run foul of him in the past.

'Have you a girlfriend back home?' he asked.

I intended to write to at least four girls to ensure I received a steady flow of mail while in Vietnam so I replied, 'Several Sir.'

'A serious girlfriend I mean,' he said in a voice that strongly disapproved of my boastful reply.

Regretting my response, I wondered what to say next.

'Have you any questions you would like to ask me?' he asked.

Believing my willingness to start work, as a plant operator would impress him I seized the opportunity.

'How soon will it be before I'm assigned to a machine?'

His response had me reeling back in shock and rapidly changing my opinion of him.

'What do you know about an M79 grenade launcher? Have you ever fired an M16? When did you last carry a loaded weapon? Don't you think you should learn about the weapons you may well be expected to use before worrying about when you'll start operating plant equipment?'

'Yes, yes,' I uttered in response. My confidence shattered. I was feeling rather bewildered.

'Yes 'Sir,' you mean,' he said.

Hearing the word 'dismissed' was the most pleasant word I had heard in a long time. I saluted, about turned and marched out. My mates Butch and Brian, both plant operators, were interviewed also but I did not ask them if they had the same experience. As I lay on my bed that evening, I concluded that the OC was in fact, trying to help me appreciate my responsibility to the troop. I no longer viewed him as an ogre to be avoided.

A fresh day dawned and I was determined to acquire the knowledge Major Florence had stressed I should have. Before I could however, I was sent out on a patrol along the northern perimeter of the task force base. By mid-morning the heat was sapping my energy and my clothing was soaked in perspiration and had turned black. Like others in the patrol, I was constantly reaching for a water bottle. When the patrol arrived at the eastern boundary of the base we returned to our start point. My first patrol over, I made it back to Troop lines in time for lunch. After lunch, all reinforcements were allocated to a section. As the official Plant Operator replacement for Sapper Rodger Solomon, I scored all the ones: 1 section, 1 troop of 1 Field Squadron.

'Who likes operating D Pull scrapers?' Staff Sergeant Parsons asked.

'I do,' I said before anyone else could answer.

'Get over to the plant parking area and take the scraper out to the by-pass road,' he said. The road was being constructed to enable the flow of civilian traffic to travel north of Hoa Long towards Binh Ba without passing through the 1 ATF position along the original alignment of National Route 2. I was off in a flash. After a quick check of the machine and securing my rifle, I was racing along at top speed. I sucked in the exhilaration created by the satisfaction of operating a machine. A week after leaving home I was doing what I had come to Vietnam for.

Each day the road progressed closer towards the southern edge of Hoa Long village. My ability as an operator continued to improve as I gained experience. Everything was going great and my confidence was soaring.

I was invited to Corporal Lofty Harvey's going home party at the US artillery battery. Showering and dressing in clean greens, I reached for a jar of Old Spice hair cream that a girlfriend back in Brisbane had given me. It had remained unopened, but to my surprise I now discovered the jar had been opened and was bone dry. Barry, one of my three tent mates was lying on his bed, black hair slicked down as was his style, guilt was written all over his face. He had been helping himself – not a major crime but the breaking of mutual trust certainly was! Trust is so important when living in close quarters. I hurled myself over the wooden boxes between our beds and pummelled him with punches and abuse. Sapper Kevin Smith heard the commotion and rushed in to investigate. He grabbed me in a headlock and pulled me away from Barry. The fight was never mentioned to anyone else however, I regularly checked my kit and personal possessions.

One afternoon in late February, I was sitting outside my tent when I noticed a fellow loaded down with equipment heading towards me. As he got closer, I recognised Brett Nolen whom I had met back at SME in December. He had Sergeant Stripes on his sleeve. Two months earlier he had been the sports store corporal. He stopped near me and said, 'G'day Jethro.' Then he told me he was Sergeant West's replacement. I had only known Brett briefly but I was pleased he was to be my troop sergeant. Staff Sergeant George Biddlecome, whom I remembered from 7 Field Squadron at Enoggera, arrived a few days later as the replacement for Blair Parsons.

I thought it about time to familiarise myself with the weapons mentioned by Major Florence. On the base perimeter next to our plant parking area was a large observation bunker named *Kamikaze*. It stood out like a beacon to enemy observers, hence its name. Three sappers manned it over night and I was rostered for duty that evening. I asked one of the other two blokes on duty to familiarise me with the weapons and equipment in the bunker: two M60 machine guns, a M79 grenade launcher, the control box to detonate 'Foo-Gas' canisters and claymore mines that were positioned in front of the perimeter barbed wire fence, a starlight scope for night vision and a VHF 25 radio set.

Together we went through the sighting, firing and loading procedure of the weapons and discussed the merits of each. He talked and I listened and learnt.

4
The Sixth Battalion Royal Australian Regiment

21 March – 16 April 1967

The two battalions in the task force were each supported by one of the two engineer field troops in the squadron. 1 Troop regularly supported 6 Battalion and 2 Troop supported 5 Battalion. On *Operation Portsea* my section was tasked to support Charlie Company of 6 Battalion RAR. A two-man mini team was allocated to each platoon. Mini teams had been developed to provide immediate assistance to the infantry, while actively patrolling in search of the enemy. Team members had the wherewithal to destroy unexploded aerial bombs, artillery shells and disarm enemy booby-traps. They were also required to enter and search tunnels and bunkers when found. Barry and I were attached to 7 Platoon. We waited our turn to be lifted by helicopter from Luscombe airstrip to our destination. We were going on a Search and Destroy Operation to the east of Nui Dat and south towards the coast.

My equipment load consisted of: 24 hour combat ration packs for a week, hexamine stove and fuel tablets, six water bottles, weapon cleaning kit, personal hygiene items, a spare pair of socks and a bedroll. Believing I would have some spare time to read. Two books were also included. *Reach for the Sky* by Paul Brickhill, a biography of Douglas Bader the World War Two double leg amputee who became a flying ace of the Battle of Britain; and a novel *My Brother Jack* by George Johnston. Added to this lot was twenty half sticks of gelignite, ten sticks of plastic explosive, safety fuse, fuse instantaneous and detonators. One hundred and sixty rounds of ammunition, a little more than stipulated – just in case! Owing to the size of our packs, my load was easily in excess of 90 pounds (40kg) more than half my body weight. Barry and I were instructed to board last and sit on the floor.

Flying out on my first major operation, hyped up most likely from an adrenaline rush, I experienced a feeling of immortality. Regardless, I had every intention of maintaining a good grip, holding my weapon with my right hand and clutching at the pilot's seat structure tightly with the other. As the chopper roared up and away from the ground, I looked towards other choppers in the flight. They reminded me of frisky young stallions rearing up on their hind legs before galloping away. A company of infantrymen, who had flown out earlier, had secured the landing zone we were heading for. When we landed Barry and I was ensconced within 7 Platoon's Headquarters section that consisted of the platoon commander, platoon sergeant, radio operator, medic and two or three other infantry soldiers. The platoon sergeant, Jock Reid had introduced himself and suggested we stay close to him until we were needed elsewhere. He explained that we were to adopt a blocking position along the west bank of the Song Rai River and search for signs of enemy activity. A large enemy force was believed to be trying to escape to the north after a failed attack on a popular forces post at Lo Gom early the previous morning.

Not long after we started moving through heavy jungle, a

small enemy camp was located and signs of recent occupation were evident. After a search for weapons and anything that might indicate who the occupants were, the camp was enthusiastically demolished. Machetes hacked and chopped into smaller structures and brute force was required to push over larger structures. Legalised vandalism at its best. A second camp was located about a hundred metres further along the track. It was a fishing camp, most probably an additional food source for the occupants of the first camp. Newly erected fish traps showed signs of successful catches however, the camp had been hurriedly abandoned. Damage from either aerial bombs or artillery was evident. We set about demolishing the traps and camp structures, slashing and hacking away at very long thick bamboo poles with our machetes. Back on patrol, a small group of Viet Cong were spotted on the opposite bank of the river. I took cover behind a large tree as the shooting started. It ended as suddenly as it had begun.

Patrolling into the early part of the evening with failing light, a much larger enemy camp was discovered. Charlie Company formed a protective circle around the enemy camp as the sappers searched the area. I followed Corporal Tony Evans down a relatively short shaft, and through an equally short connecting tunnel into a large open space. In the centre a crude but efficient table had been sculptured by leaving a mound of soil in place. Although we had discovered a relatively innocuous underground complex, until it had been entered and cautiously searched, it had to be viewed as a hazardous environment with the potential to inflict serious injury or death if extreme caution was not exercised.

My first underground experience was completed and I was feeling as nervous as a virgin bride on her wedding night. I desperately needed to pee. I stepped behind a large tree with huge buttresses around its base to relieve myself. A repulsive odour was noticeable. Looking over the nearest buttress I saw a pile of bloodied bandages, soiled clothing covered in gore and a pile of very messy dressings. There was no doubt that this was a recently used aid post. Wounded Viet Cong from an earlier engagement had most probably been treated here before moving north. We placed explosives strategically around the structure and successfully collapsed the roof and the short connecting tunnel. We had added that 'little extra' to make a bigger bang – surreptitiously reducing the weight of our packs.

The company made camp for the night and immediately adopted a 'stand-to' position, in readiness for an attack that might occur with the failing light. I was advised that I would be doing the 0200–0400 hours shift on the machine gun. Self-doubt started to have an immediate effect on me. The burden of responsibility for the safety of others had never been placed almost exclusively on my shoulders before. On previous picket duty I was either in the troop weapon pit situated well back from the base perimeter or occasionally, with two other sappers in *Kamikaze,* on the perimeter. My first night outside the wire in enemy territory was going to be very different. All that stood between the enemy and me were four well-positioned machine guns, a number of claymore mines and alert sentries.

While there was still sufficient light I located the grunt (a friendly but slightly derogatory term for our infantrymen) I would be required to wake on the completion of my shift. I laid out my groundsheet very close to him, limiting my need to move around in the dark any more than necessary. Although my body was screaming out for a rest, sleep was not going to be easy. I had forgotten how noisy a jungle actually was at night. Most of the platoon members around me appeared to be sleeping. Many of them had survived almost twelve months in these demanding conditions. As my first day in the bush was ending I was developing an admiration for the infantry soldier.

I was woken by a voice whispering 'Holdfast' (the code name for engineers). It was time to take my place on the gun. Settling in beside the grunt, who still had an hour to go, I quietly said, 'G'Day Mate,' he replied with a similar greeting and then asked what I was like on the gun. Although I could not see his face clearly in the dark I gathered he was not impressed when I told him that I had never fired an M60 machine gun. After a short silence he suggested it would be best if I stay off the gun but, if I must fire, just squeeze the trigger until someone got to me. Then with a remark designed to cheer me up he said, 'One of our blokes will get to you… or the enemy.'

Although I carried an M60 machine gun when undergoing training at the Jungle Training Centre Canungra in southern Queensland, I had never fired one. We yelled 'bang-bang or rat-a-tat-tat' simulating gunfire, as we practiced immediate responses to a variety of combat situations. The infantry reclaimed the gun whenever we gathered on the firing range, denying me the opportunity to fire off a few rounds. The course concluded with a week of heavy bush work in the Wiangaree State Forest, over the border in northern New South Wales. Once again I had to carry the M60, yelling 'rat-a-tat-tat,' day after day. On the last day we simulated an early morning attack on an imaginary enemy camp.

After sitting silently for twelve hours on the side of a hill suffering from a lack of sleep, hungry and rapidly developing a dislike for infantry procedures, I was well out of rat-a-tat-tats and incurred the wrath of one of the accompanying instructors, who had noticed my lack of enthusiasm. As we assembled for our bus ride back to Canungra, my mate Rod McClennan came along and asked what I had been doing. Foolishly, I displayed my pissed off attitude by kicking the M60 at my feet saying, 'I've been carrying this bloody thing around all week.' Corporal Gabby Hayes (killed in action in August 1967) an experienced infantry soldier witnessed my kick and gave me a real tongue-lashing.

Hearing the call to 'stand-to' just before dawn was a surprisingly welcome relief from tossing and turning on my ground sheet as I tried to capture a few hours of elusive sleep. My first day and night out in enemy territory had ended peacefully.

Not long into the second day the forward scout observed a large naval shell lying out in open ground. We waited while a section of grunts made a cautionary patrol around the area to be certain it was not bait set to ambush our patrol. Then Barry and I, with a small protection party, moved cautiously towards the shell. Satisfied it had not been booby-trapped we set about preparing its destruction. We would blow it up with gelignite. Not that we had any other choice, our knowledge of demolitions was very limited. While I was retrieving a box of matches from my shirt pocket, I noticed our protection party hurriedly moving off, leaving Barry and I alone like shags on a rock. We were feeling very vulnerable alone with our '5-inch shell'. Sweating profusely, I tried to light the fuse. The match broke. Then the matchbox became soggy. My first real job as a member of a mini-team was rapidly going sour on me. Barry, who was on his last operation, calmly lit the fuse. We walked away from the charge, as we had been trained to do, however each step was instinctively getting faster and faster until we were running.

Whenever a suspicious vine was noticed standing out from the surrounding bush I was required to move up to the forward scout. Vines could be used to trigger booby traps positioned further back along the track triggering a devastating explosion. Suspicious vines had to be traced back to their source of origin. Invariably, the vine would be nothing more sinister than wayward foliage that had been displaced by either pedestrian traffic or the elements.

The alert forward scout indicated by hand signal for the platoon to stop. An artillery shell had been spotted wedged in a tree trunk about shoulder height from the ground. As we had previously done, Barry and I approached the tree cautiously. Gelignite was very gingerly placed above the shell, ensuring we did not disturb it. The combined explosion reduced the tree to fragments only suitable for fuelling a hot water chip heater.

The platoon had settled down after another hard day foot slogging its way through dense jungle. Looking forward to a few hours sleep before taking my turn on picket I had wasted no time locating the grunt I would relieve and made myself as comfortable as was possible and waited for the sleep fairies to carry me away. A loud *whoosh, crash, bang* had everyone awake and voices could be heard asking what the hell was going on. In the dark, we all waited for an answer. One of the grunts on picket reported that a limb had fallen out of a tree and landed on the M60 machine gun. He and the other grunt had heard the snap, followed by the whoosh of the falling branch and managed to roll out of the way. Unfortunately, the gun was now banana shaped. Not much could be done about the situation until daylight. A replacement gun would be required as the damaged machine gun was well and truly stuffed. To everyone's surprise the attached sappers were able to quickly remedy the situation. Kevin Smith had been issued with a M60 machine gun prior to leaving our troop lines. Arrangements were swiftly made to relieve him of his gun in exchange for a much lighter M16 to carry as his personal weapon.

Around midday 8 Platoon discovered a very large rice cache. The company deployed into a defensive position as the sappers made a thorough search for booby-traps. Many modified bright yellow cluster bomb units (CBU) and grenades were located in nearby trees but fortunately no trip wires had been attached. The enemy had bolted as we approached. Many more booby-traps in the area were discovered and neutralised. The rice cache consisted of two large camouflaged shelters with old corrugated iron roofs, chicken wire sides and rough floorboards. Each shelter contained hundreds of bags of unpolished rice. More booby traps were discovered strategically placed around each shelter. We were confident that even more would be found concealed in the stacks. The iron roof and camouflage was cautiously cleared away. Crude but deadly booby-traps were concealed in or under many bags. The trigger fuse was cunningly placed in one bag and linked by a thin piece of copper wire to the bomb in an adjoining bag, removing either bag would trigger a deadly explosion.

A protective wall was hastily constructed from bags of rice already searched and removed from the stack. As we had no grappling hook we used the pick point on an entrenching tool tied to toggle ropes to safely hook and pull the bags clear of the stack, while we sheltered behind the wall. A Chinook chopper brought in a Land Rover and trailer, additional men, and sling equipment to transport the rice away from the jungle camp. Although we were rather buggered, we were satisfied with our efforts – approximately thirty thousand kilograms of rice had been captured by the end of another extremely tiring day.

Early the next morning the Battalion Commanding Officer (CO) Lieutenant Colonel CM Townsend arrived by Sioux chopper, and strolled along towards our group. He asked if we were the blokes responsible for all the good work. The CO was particular complementary about our ability to locate the trip wires the night before. Although we were all pleased to receive the compliments we were still rather fatigued and not too excited about the CO's presence. Whether he detected our mood or felt slighted by our lack of enthusiastic responses I do not know, but as quickly as he snapped our photo, he told us abruptly to stop sitting around and get on with the job. Late in the afternoon the task was finally completed, with approximately one hundred and thirteen thousand kilograms of rice being secured.

As a newcomer to patrolling with the infantry, I was becoming increasingly nervous about the abundance of enemy camps located and destroyed. The novelty of destroying the camps had worn off. Although I was pleased the enemy had chosen to retreat as we approached, I felt we were bound to encounter and fight a sizeable enemy force eventually. Many grunts were of the opinion that the size and number of camps located by the battalion indicated they were positioned and established to stage troops for the attack on Lo Gom.

On the fifth day of the operation twenty graves were discovered in a small clearing not far from the riverbank, many appeared to have been there for some time but one was fresh. All fresh graves had to be opened. I was not looking forward to this particular task so I started to dig rather enthusiastically as a ploy to cover my next move. Having dug more than my fair share, I handed the spade to the nearest grunt to complete the exhumation. A relatively fresh body was discovered and examined to identify clothing and whether the cause of death was from a recent battle or bombardment. Resting at the base of a tree it dawned on me that Easter had just passed. Exhuming bodies so close to Good Friday struck me as a very bad omen.

The battalion was flown to a defensive position on the western bank of the Song Rai River. A new bridge was being built where Route 23 crossed the river and headed towards the town of Xuyen Moc. Artillery had been positioned in the area along with construction engineers and they required infantry protection. An opportunity to enjoy a refreshing and cleansing swim in the Song Rai with several hundred grunts was seized immediately. Naked bodies frolicked freely in the river or lounged around on the riverbank drying off in the sun reminiscent of a scene from the film 'Huckleberry Finn'.

We reformed as a troop, resting and hearing about each other's experiences to date. Sappers attached to Bravo Company had been involved in a rather large contact with the enemy on Day 1. Prior to cleaning our weapons a 'yippee shoot' was authorised. We lined up along the bank of the river and when given the go ahead, fired off round after round into the opposite bank. Kevin Smith was delighted at the opportunity to fire for the first time his recently acquired M16, the weapon he had received in exchange for the M60 several days earlier.

With the scaling down of the battalion's operational role, half the troop was no longer required and would return to Nui Dat. The names of those returning were read out and I was delighted to hear my name called. I'd be returning to my role as a plant operator. Loafing around pondering what machine I was likely to be assigned, I was amused to hear Barry the hair cream thief, vehemently objecting to me returning to Nui Dat. He went on about my experiences in Borneo and how invaluable I would be to the grunts. I was almost blushing but also fairly pissed off. The audacity of Barry's behaviour achieved the desired result. Captain Moon acquiesced to his suggestion. Barry wasted no time getting his gear packed and avoided me like the plague.

Sapper Blue Willet and I were attached to 11 Platoon, Delta Company. Camped in flat open country, denuded of almost all vegetation it was a very exposed piece of real estate. The only object I could see above ground level was the privacy screen around the latrine pit, and a string of defensive concertina barbed wire deployed around the perimeter. The only redeeming feature was the river close by could be used for swimming.

The platoon was to locate a suitable overnight ambush position. Blue and I carried sufficient explosives between us to demolish any unexploded ordnance we might find. Once we reached the hills and discovered a well-used track, the platoon deployed into an ambush position on the high side of the track. We were positioned back in depth, very much out of the way. Our only instructions were to keep quiet, stay still and keep an eye on the back door. Blue agreed to take the first shift while I sat back relaxing. There would be no brew-ups or hot food tonight. It was not long before the heavens opened up and rain began pouring down.

Within the quiet environment of the ambush the patter of falling rain was the only sound. Sleep was going to be very elusive; a short nap was the best I could hope for. To deal with the boredom I amused myself by thinking of food, food glorious food. Eating had always been an appealing way to pass time away. Sufficient moonlight enabled me to view the contents of a tin I was fiddling with. Pieces of Vienna sausage were jammed inside, they looked absolutely pathetic; not unlike circumcised baby willies. Despite my reputation for being a fang and willing to eat almost anything placed in front of me, I could not bring myself to eat cold wet sausage while sitting in the rain. However, as a challenge I emptied the contents and tried to return them back into the tin. One slippery critter after the other went in, until only three sausages remained. As I attempted to put them in one or two sausages would pop up. It was not possible to push the slippery pieces of sausage into the crowded tin. Eventually, I conceded defeat. I buried the tin and its foul contents, cleaned my hands on the wet grass and relieved Blue.

At dawn, movement within the platoon's ambush site instantly stopped. An eerie silence descended over our position. Like the ambush, the stand-to was uneventful and we made our way safely back to our riverside camp. The rest of the day was an opportunity to dry off and clean our equipment, sleep and enjoy a culinary delight concocted from the contents of several ration packs; boiled rice with melted dark chocolate and condensed milk tasted delicious! Next morning 11 Platoon's Sergeant Bob Buick informed Blue and I that we were to join 2 Platoon Alpha Company immediately. Delta Company was staying behind to protect the bridge, while the rest of the battalion moved to Xuyen Moc, the next Town along Route 23.

The platoon moved east reaching our destination on the southern outskirts of Xuyen Moc, without incident. Blue and I were directed towards the area occupied by 1 Troop sappers. A battalion size camp was to be established, with coils of concertina barbed wire deployed around the perimeter. As we chatted amongst ourselves, we received instructions to pair up and erect our shelters and were advised to dig shell scrapes in case of an enemy mortar attack on our position.

Axel Krawtschuk and I set up our shelter next to a very large log. On closer inspection we discovered that the log was not only hollow, but also we could both crawl inside if the need arose, eliminating the need for us to dig a shell scrape. We laid out our entire kit and equipment along it to dry: the contents of our packs were in desperate need of a little fresh air and rearranging.

Our main role as sappers was to conduct a daily search along the road leading to the US Army water point on the edge of Xuyen Moc, while the battalion provided security for 17 Construction Squadron engineers working along the road and developing an airstrip on the eastern side of Xuyen Moc. Two sappers would ride up front on an armoured personnel carrier. Not the safest position to ride in but it did offer the best view of the road as we looked for any signs of digging or anything else that looked suspicious. It was also close enough to the driver to have him stop when required. The rest of the section rode more towards the rear.

Once we reached the water point we could relax. The grunts were responsible for security of the water point and a half platoon guard was maintained overnight. The crew of the carriers staying at the water point for the remainder of the day set about boiling the billy. Carriers always had an abundance of water and cooking utensils with them. Eager for a reasonable feed before returning to our base, we pooled our rations: potato, meat, rice, curry powder and anything else that could be found in our packs. Using a large borrowed pot we began brewing a good stew.

The concoction was simmering away, filling the interior of the carrier with a rather pleasant aroma. We were sitting inside chatting and enjoying a mug of hot tea when our conversation was interrupted. One of the Yanks from the water point appeared at the ramp of the carrier seeking medical help. A bloodied hand was thrust forward; the flesh at the base of his palm near the thumb was peeled back like a banana skin. Blood was gushing out and dripping all around the entrance. From my position near the driver's seat, I saw more than I could cope with. I rushed out the carrier to spew but on my way I kicked over the pot. My mates were not too thrilled to see their breakfast spread across the carrier's floor.

I believe my aversion to blood came about when I was holidaying on a family friend's farm just outside Adelaide as a teenager. The three boys in the family regularly played tricks on me. When the boy's uncle decided to slaughter an old cow, we were all required to help. The carcass was slit open and the viscera removed and I was asked to take it away in a wheelbarrow to dump it. Having completed that rather unpleasant job I returned to the shed where the butchering was to take place. Unexpectedly, I was set upon by the others including the uncle, and bundled inside the carcass. While inside this wet, hot and darkened cavern, the others sat on top of the carcass preventing my escape. Eventually, I was released as they stood about laughing. I started swinging punches at everyone within reach before storming off. After that ordeal I found it near impossible to touch raw meat or eat meat. I was on the verge of becoming a vegetarian, but hunger made the smell of a Sunday roast impossible to resist.

Hearing the sound of mortars landing very close to our position Axel and I quickly scrambled into our hollow log. Sapper Kevin Smith woke from an afternoon nap and saw a ragged hole in his flimsy shelter. Then he noticed a piece of shrapnel about half the size of a matchbox embedded in the backpack he had been using as a pillow. He had missed certain death by a whisker.

After six days patrolling the road to the water point each morning and two uneventful day patrols with the grunts, our routine of restful days ended. Having read my two books and not wishing to carry them around any longer, I offered them to anyone who wanted them. Nobody was interested so I dug a hole and buried both books.

Reassigned to 7 Platoon Charlie Company with Sapper Rod Young as my new partner I was soon patrolling terrain that was the hardest I had encountered. The patrol headed into swamp country with mud up around my chest, any notion of keeping my gear clean and dry was quickly dismissed. I needed all my wits about me, just to keep my head out of the mud. Once out of the swamp I was relieved when the patrol continued on firmer ground. It was not long before the forward scout sighted an enemy camp and was certain he had seen an enemy soldier disappearing into one of the many weapon pits. Rod and I had to have a look for him.

With bayonet in hand I cautiously approached the narrow opening, feeling and looking for any suspicious signs before lowering myself head first into the darkened space. I had no torch or pistol for protection. Not that I minded too much; a torch would only show my position and a pistol fired in a confined space would knock my eardrums about. More importantly, I needed my hands free to feel my way forward. I could see a tunnel entrance at the bottom of the pit. Feeling with my free hand and tapping the immediate area with the bayonet, looking and listening for any signs of booby traps, I ventured into the dark tunnel, my body mass occluding what little daylight was there. In total darkness I moved forward, almost immediately I was clammy all over and my breathing started to falter, my hand was on something. I had no idea what it was. Initially I thought it was a snake, but it did not move. What could it be? It was round, soft and loose to touch and felt rather long. Fear was rapidly kicking in. I prodded it gently with my bayonet; there was no reaction. I could hear my breathing getting louder. Alone and shit scared I lay quietly listening to my heart pounding. I needed to get out of this claustrophobic place. Steeling myself for an unpleasant reaction, I grabbed the 'snake' firmly and retreated. At the tunnel entrance I could see it was nothing more than a long bag of rice that had been carried around the body of an enemy soldier. Grunt Corporal Laurie Drinkwater took my photo as I climbed out and rested on the enemy weapon pit.

Continuing the patrol we came to a single log spanning the

gap over a small river. The two scouts crossed. I started to cross with Rod close behind me. Suddenly one of our machine gunners along the riverbank opened up, I jumped towards the far bank, Rod, turned and ran back. A short exchange of fire across the river followed. When it ended a voice was calling for reports. Hearing, 'Holdfast what can you see?' I made a quick assessment of my very tenuous position: I was perched on a riverbank, about a metre up from the water, my boots pressed hard into the bank were all that prevented me from slipping into the river and possibly drowning under the weight of my pack. My response of, 'Nothing and I'm not bloody looking,' was not too helpful. Making my way back across the log bridge to join the others grunts jokingly said to me, 'Our hero' and 'Were you afraid of being shot or drowning?' After twenty-six days pursuing an elusive enemy four Diggers had been killed in action and six wounded. Two enemy soldiers had been killed and one captured. I was grateful to land safely back at Nui Dat.

5
The Minefield

2 May 1967

Returning to my tent after another satisfying day operating a bulldozer, Barry rushed up to me all excited.

'The minefield has claimed its first casualty,' he said.

'Who was it?' I asked.

'A Yank,' Barry replied.

Then he told me that I, along with several other plant operators, would be going out to the Horseshoe in the morning. Initially, I did not believe him, as I was one of several troop plant operators left behind to continue working on base development. But sure enough, just after dinner, all 1 Troop sappers not about to go home were ordered to have their kit packed and be at the unit's chopper pad by 0700 hours the next day. We were going to the Horseshoe Fire Support Base; an extinct volcanic feature situated about eleven kilometres from the coast and close by the town of Dat Do. It had recently been developed as a fire support base, with exceptional fields of vision over the town and ground to the east.

The minefield being constructed was laid between two substantial barbed wire fences approximately 100 metres apart and two metres high. The Task Force Commander, Brigadier Stuart Graham, was of the opinion that the barrier minefield would restrict movement of the local enemy forces and much needed supplies through the area known as the Long Green.

When we arrived at the minefield Lieutenant Joe Cazey, who had replaced Lieutenant Browne, asked if anyone had previous experience arming M16 land mines. No one had. Lieutenant Cazey and Staff Sergeant Biddlecombe returned with a Land Rover. We were off for our first mine laying experience. We drove along the fence a short distance then stopped at a bend in the fence line. A brief description was given of the M16 anti-personnel mine also known as the 'jumping jack' as it was designed to detonate after being launched about a metre out off the ground. The mine was about the size of a regular jam tin and weighed about three and a half kilograms. It was filled with TNT. Most mines would be sitting on an M26 hand grenade fitted with an anti-lift switch primed with an instantaneous fuse. After watching a demonstration, we each armed one mine. Mine arming training was now completed. Teamed up with my mate Butch Carman wearing smelly flak jackets that were still wet with perspiration from the previous arming team, we started arming mines.

Tuesday, 9 May 1967

The daily mine laying rate had not reached an acceptable total of 500 mines per day. We had only been laying the minefield for about seven to eight days and were still settling in to the role. Most of us thought laying a total of 400 mines a day was reasonable. In an attempt to achieve 500 mines laid we were ordered to work in our specific section; each section was assigned a task. Four two-man teams and a section leader would arm five four-mine clusters a total of 80 mines. Members of a second section would arm the third lane. A total of 120 mines would be armed. On completion, there would be a change over and each section assigned another task. My section would be arming first. My partner was Sapper Ashley Culkin and we were to arm the first strip of the minefield. About an hour and a half later we completed our quota of 20 mines. We moved over to the safe lane marker, removed our flak jackets and headed to an area where we had left our weapons and packs. All six arming teams assembled and relaxed, drinking water and smoking. I noticed Sapper Glen Bartholomew looked hot and agitated and was standing off a little from the group. He had left his gear elsewhere, so had no water with him. I asked if he would like a drink. Glen was a rather shy bloke who always appeared apprehensive and he reluctantly agreed to accept my bottle, but not before further assurance that I had plenty to spare. My second bottle on my belt had a drinking mug attached to it and was not so easy to remove from the pouch, it came out with the mug attached. When not wearing my web belt I always experienced a degree of difficulty removing or replacing the water bottles. Still further encouragement was needed before Glen accepted the bottle and drank heartily from it.

As we relaxed, Staff Sergeant Biddlecombe approached our position and asked what we were doing. Corporal Tony Evans replied that we had completed our task and had moved out in anticipation of receiving our next assignment; complying with the orders we had received at the morning's assembly from Captain Moon. To our amazement, Biddlecombe told us to go back and continue arming mines until he told us otherwise. We started to stash our water bottles; blokes flicked away their partially smoked cigarettes and headed back towards where they had left their flak jackets. Owing to the difficulty I experienced returning my two bottles to their pouch on my belt I was last to move off. As I was about to rejoin Ashley, Biddlecombe returned from wherever he had been and gave me a serve for being tardy about getting back to work, something or someone had obviously annoyed him, as he appeared rather agitated. My explanation about the second water bottle was dismissed. Heading back along the safe lane, I could see a flak jacket. Hopefully, it was the same one I had previously been wearing. The thought of putting on a wet jacket that someone else had been wearing only a few minutes before was rather repulsive. In addition to perspiration, many of the blokes had a plethora of tropical complaints: tinea and acne being the most common. One fellow had a most severe case of acne; pus and blood were frequently visible on his back.

I completed zipping up the jacket and adjusting it stood looking at the activity around me. Staff Sergeant Biddlecombe approached and ripped in to me again. Three times in three minute he had felt a need to comment on my perceived tardiness in returning to the task of arming. I was pissed off with his attitude and as he passed I said, 'Yes Sir, three bags full, Sir. Life as a fucking Staff Sergeant must be hard to take if all you have to do is walk up and down throwing your fucking rank around.' Then as a parting shot I yelled out, 'I did not come to Vietnam to lay mines. I came to push dirt around as a plant operator.'

I started walking towards Ashley, who was in position waiting for me. Whoompa! I was catapulted into the air with enormous force, then crashed down on my back. A cloud of debris slowly rained over me. I could hear the gentle rhythmic sound of soil landing around me despite the noise of the explosion still ringing in my ears. I closed my eyes against the gritty, sandy soil as it covered me. I felt no pain. I looked at my hands. Some fingers were missing; others were hanging loosely. My arms were red with blood gushing from my many wounds. I attempted to sit up, but I couldn't feel my legs.

'Call Dustoff'

I could hear someone moaning. I didn't know who it was. Someone else was calling for the safety pins to be replaced in the mines.

'We can't replace them.'

'Why not?'

"Jethro has them in his pocket.'

Sergeant Brett Nolan was ripping open shell dressings. He knelt beside, shielding me fro the sun. He looked at me silently for a moment then started sticking shell dressings into my guts. I felt his hands press down hard onto my stomach. He tore open more dressings. They looked terribly small in his bloodied hands. I still felt no pain, but blood was running into my eyes. It was warm and sticky. Lieutenant Joe Cazey and Nolen were telling me about the lovely nurses who would look after me once the Dustoff chopper got me to hospital. The thought of pretty nurses distracted me for a while as I lay in the minefield, not wanting to think about my life blood soaking into the ground around me. I could hear other voices nearby attending to someone else. I shut my eyes and the thought that I was dying flashed into my mind. I was not ready to die, I kept my eyes open watching all I could going on around me. I asked Brett if the family jewels were still in one piece.

'Yes Jethro,' he replied.

'Are you sure about that Brett?' I asked.

'Yes,' he said again.

'Well give my dick a jerk so I can feel it,' I asked.

Brett said he would but I didn't feel anything.

A medic from the infantry platoon that was providing protection at the minefield arrived on the scene. As he was preparing an intravenous drip line he urgently needed to get into me, I could see him tearing at the packaging with his teeth. He cut my right arm on the inside of my elbow and inserted the drip.

'What happened, did I step on a mine?' I asked Brett.

He did not reply. I was thirsty and asked for a drink. My guts were sticking out through a gaping wound that Brett had been stuffing shell dressings into; there was a look of hesitation on the medic's face. He nodded towards Joe Cazey who held a bottle and trickled a little water into my mouth. I heard the sound of choppers. 'Hold on Jethro, Dustoff is here.' Brett was speaking to me. 'You'll soon be in an air-conditioned hospital, surrounded by pretty nurses.' I lay quietly and tried to endure the pain that was wracking my shattered body. I was lifted on to a stretcher and loaded into the chopper. A second stretcher was placed above me. With a very grim-faced crewmember looking over me, we were airborne and on our way to hospital. Although I was not aware of it at the time, we landed at the Korean Army post at Cat Lo to collect additional blood products as I had consumed all that the chopper carried. This extra supply contributed to me arriving alive at the hospital.

The RAAF Dustoff helicopter landed and as I was being lifted out my right arm got stuck behind some torn fabric of the cabin. Pushed back into the chopper, my arm was freed and repositioned by my side. On the second go I was placed on a hospital trolley and rushed away from the chopper. A blonde blue-eyed US Army nurse started asking me what I was allergic to, had I had this illness or that illness, a load of questions I was not interested in or able to answer. I was watching a big black American guy behind her. He was carrying a very large pair of scissors. Stepping up close to me, he cut away the foul smelling shrapnel riddled flak jacket I had put on moments before the explosion. My bloody and dirty green army shorts were cut away too. I heard the choppers leaving as I lay quietly waiting to have my wounds treated. I was certain one leg was missing, blown off by the exploding landmine and the hand grenade it was sitting on. I was moved and immediately surrounded by people wearing masks and caps. I didn't know if they were doctors or nurses. Then my eyes closed…

Someone was nearby and I could sense his or her presence. My eyes would not focus. All I could see were blurred images. *Who was near me?* I couldn't tell. *Was it a mate or a stranger?* I called out but I didn't hear any sound. *Where was I?* My head felt like it was floating. *Was I swimming?* I was unable to keep my eyes open. Official army records show that I arrived at the hospital at approximately 1100 hours. Alpha Company 6 Battalion had made the radio call at 1020 hours. Anaesthetic was administered at 1130 hours and continued until 1930 hours.

6
Evacuation Hospital Vung Tau

In front of me was a dim glow of light. My eyes focused slowly, a cluster of coloured bulbs hung from the ceiling. *Is it Christmas? Am I at a party?* There was no sound. The silence was eerie. Looking to my left I saw someone sitting up in the next bed.

'G'Day,' I said. I heard no reply. Again I said, 'G'Day.' Still there was no reply. *Well up yours.* I tried to find a more comfortable position in my bed. My movement caught the attention of a bloke sitting at a desk nearby. He quickly came over and told me that I was in the Post Op ward of the US Army 36'th Evacuation Hospital, Vung Tau, South Vietnam. He was a US Army corpsman (medic) and assured me that I was in very capable hands.

'Have I lost my legs?' I asked.

'The doctors will be here shortly,' he replied. Before I could say anything else he asked me if I was left or right handed.

'Right handed,' I replied.

'Well, you had a little luck,' he said.

I was not feeling too bloody lucky!

'You have only lost a small portion of a finger on your right hand, but three on your left hand. Should you need to pee, just let it go as you have a tube inserted,' he said.

A tube to pee through! No way. Brett Nolen had assured me that my wedding tackle was intact. What a low life lying bastard he was. Exhausted, I lay back contemplating how I would one day sort out Sergeant Bloody Nolen. My reaction caught the corpsmen by surprise; he couldn't understand why I was so angry.

'How would you like to go through life without the family jewels, with only a piece of rubber hose to pee through?' I muttered.

'What do you mean, only a tube to pee through? You have a catheter inserted to empty your bladder to make peeing easier for you,' he told me.

A little wiser and calmer I asked about the coloured lights. They were used as nightlights over the nurses' station. As a seriously ill patient, I was positioned as close as possible to them. I was also told that the bloke next to me, who had not responded to my earlier greeting, had recently had his jaw wired making it impossible for him to talk. Time passed quietly and then increased activity by the nurses and corpsman on duty held my attention. I would learn this activity indicated a change of shift was imminent. Two nurses sitting at the desk wrote hurriedly into patients' files as a new team of nurses gradually filtered into the ward. They were dressed in the same green US Army fatigues and army boots as the male members of staff. They all looked quite cute in their uniforms. Lying there I started to wonder how good they would look in street clothes or naked. My helpful corpsman bid me farewell as he left the ward and I lay back in anticipation of a doctor coming along to explain my injuries. Pain was increasing in intensity throughout my heavily bandaged body. I feared it would increase as I became more conscious. Several nurses introduced themselves but as they used their rank, I was not overly impressed with their introduction – most names failed to register with me.

It was not long before the ward was a hive of activity: breakfast was served, beds were changed and patients were bathed. I was not offered breakfast and I was hungry. I asked Lieutenant Anne Philiben, a tall girl with short, red hair, who had just introduced herself to me, if I was going to get a feed. 'Not until the doctor has seen you.' was her reply. Lieutenant Philiben then asked me what my name was. The official hospital record showed me as John but visitors who had called in to see me while I was still in the operating theatre had called me Jethro. I explained Jethro was my nickname.

The Birth of Jethro:

Sabah North Borneo, 1965 I was with 24 Construction Squadron, Royal Australian Engineers (RAE), working on building a road through dense jungle. We'd gathered around the 'boiling billy' to enjoy a hot box lunch. Hot food after a morning of hard work was a real treat that had not happened often since I had arrived about two months previously. Corporal Tom Upson opened one of two hot boxes and discovered it was completely empty. The second hot box had three full containers of spuds and other vegetables. Shortie Buick, the troop driver, was sent back to base camp to collect our missing food. As we waited for lunch we sat around talking and enjoying our brew of sweet hot tea. Out of idle curiosity I lifted the lid on one of the three containers. It was full of spuds and instinctively I helped myself to one, then another, and another until I heard my dirty fingernails make a scratching noise on the bottom of the container. I'd eaten the lot! In the interest of self-preservation I moved away from the hot box and sat well away from my mates.

Shortie Buick arrived back soon after with a hot box full of beef stew, and we all formed up to receive our much desired lunch. The surprised look on Tom's face said it all as he discovered the potato container was now empty.

'Thompson! You bloody guts,' he yelled at me. As the remainder of the party discovered they would not be getting any spuds with their stew, I feared a lynching was about to take place, with *my* head in the noose. Charlie McKay an older and very affable character looked into the empty container and said, 'Not even Jethro could eat that much,' referring to the character from the TV series 'The Beverly Hillbillies'. Laughter was spontaneous and others expressed further unflattering similarities between Jethro and me. I was excluded from sharing in the rest of the meal and tasked to perform most of the more arduous jobs for the remainder of the day, such as carrying heavy bags of ammonium nitrate mixed with diesel that were used to blow trees out of the ground. Many of the blokes started calling me Jethro. By the end of the day I was forgiven. The name 'Jethro' however, stuck like crap to a blanket.

I asked Lieutenant Philiben who had called in while I was in the operating theatre. She did not know their names and described one bloke as being a big, genial type who spoke with an English accent and another, as a small hyperactive, scruffy looking bloke who had been hanging around the ward for quite some time. No staff member on duty could recall their names. At least the descriptions gave me something to think about as I waited for the doctor to arrive. I watched as an American Army officer strode smartly through the ward. Nurses smiled warmly towards him. He was Doctor Ben Harmon, one of the hospital's orthopaedic specialists. After looking at some paperwork at the nurses' station, he came over and introduced himself to me. He proceeded to tell me how I most probably knew that my left leg was gone. 'You only had shreds of flesh and bone hanging but there was enough flesh to form a reasonable stump,' he said. My right leg had deep lacerations along the back of it from my arse to my foot. The wound in my abdomen had been repaired, exploratory surgery found no internal damage.

What a grotesque sight I must have been. Doctor Harmon explained how the flesh from the back of my left thigh was trimmed and folded forward and upwards towards my hip. Unfortunately, this flap was a little short and did not completely cover the area satisfactorily but it was adequate. I was assured that re-growth of skin would occur in time, completely healing over the uncovered area. We then moved on to the state of my hands: a portion of my right index finger was missing, but my wrist was severely lacerated. On my left hand, only the thumb and index finger remained but the finger was in a bad way. The back of my hand had a large open wound and two pins had been inserted. One pin could be seen sticking through the top knuckle and out below the last knuckle. The second pin was not visible.

After reading my chart positioned at the end of my bed, Doctor Harmon walked over to the nurses' station; I heard him asking what medication I had been given for pain. The nurses said I had not asked for any. My hearing did not appear to be affected by the explosion and I couldn't believe what I had heard. I had been lying there gritting my teeth in pain believing medication would be given to me as a matter of course. Stupidly, I believed I would be seen as a weakling if I complained about pain. After all, I was in a ward full of wounded American soldiers. Aussie pride was at stake. When Doctor Harmon came back and asked how was the pain, I could not tell him fast enough. Morphine was injected into me immediately and as the pain started to ebb I was soon asleep.

When awake I looked closely at the yellow coloured stains appearing on my heavily bandaged hands. Thankfully, the gruesome look of an exposed wound was concealed from my visitors and me. Consciousness did not last long though as I slipped in and out of a deep drug-induced sleep. Visitors called into the hospital and checked on my progress. For many it became a practice maintained for the next six weeks, bringing me great pleasure and support. Support, that not even the most perceptive of these characters could ever begin to comprehend. I learnt later that at least one mate, Sapper Ken Gregory, could not bear to view my moribund body, dry retching at the end of my bed before bolting out of the ward. I never saw him again.

'Jethro, Jethro,' the nurse was calling me. 'Wake up! Call out to Dennis.' My mate Dennis Brooks was in the bed next to me.

'Hey Brooks! What's going on over there?' I got no reply and shortly afterwards was told to go back to sleep. In the morning, Brooks was not there. He had been transferred to 24 Evacuation Hospital, at Long Binh, up north near Bien Hoa city in Bien Province. The Roman Catholic priest with his three colleagues representing all religious denominations had assembled at the hospital to pray for all the wounded from the minefield. As my dog tags had been removed and misplaced prior to going into surgery, the padres' had no way of knowing my faith. Regaining consciousness in their presence, I was asked what my religion was. Answering Catholic, an enthusiastic, 'Told you so' came from the Catholic padre. A lapsed Catholic, I needed their combined efforts to pull me through on this occasion and thanked them all for their prayers.

Three days later I returned to the operating theatre for additional surgery. Much more surgery would be required before I was stable enough to fly home. Additional anaesthetics and painkillers added to my inability to remain conscious for any real time. I looked forward to surgery, as it was the only way of experiencing the joy of peaceful sleep. Waking from one such sleep, a nurse attending a patient next to me greeted me warmly. I was able to identify Lieutenant Lee from her uniform name patch and rank insignia. Once she completed her treatment of the adjacent patient, Lieutenant Lee moved closer to my bed.

'I am so pleased to see you are awake. We have all been so concerned for you,' she said. Before I could think of how to respond she went on to say, 'My husband and I prayed for you in church this morning.' *Husband, church, what was going on? Where was I?* My mind was playing tricks on me again.

'What were you doing in church this morning?' I asked.

'We always go to church on Sunday,' was the reply.

'But it's not Sunday!' I said.

'It's the fourteenth of May, Mothers' Day', Lieutenant Lee told me. *What a great day for my mother!* I remembered sending her some flowers a few days earlier.

'You have been out to it for quite some time since arriving here and had a lot of surgery,' Lieutenant Lee said.

'What else have they done to me?' I asked, remembering my talk with Captain Harmon.

'When you are well enough the doctors will explain everything to you,' she replied. I lay back not experiencing any real pain, and soon fell asleep again.

Doctor Nahrwold called in to examine my abdominal wound and noted my temperature was fluctuating, at times reaching a dangerously high 103° Fahrenheit. My wounds appeared clean and free of infection. More tests and investigation was needed. Sleep, the sanctuary of all who suffer emotional and physical pain kept me calm and comfortable. How I looked forward to sleeping my time away. Dreaming of life ahead of me; a life that now would not follow the path I had planned for myself on so many occasions. One vivid dream occurred after my Squadron Commander, Major Florence, had called in to visit me.

Major Florence had been a hard taskmaster who demanded an honest day's work from his men but he had the respect of most, if not all the troops he commanded. He was regularly seen strutting around work sites as his men worked to develop the Task Force Base at Nui Dat. I was happy to have him visit me. We talked freely and he asked if there were any mates I would particularly like to see. If possible, he would arrange for them to visit me before I left for home. I asked what had happened out at the minefield.

'Was it my fault? Did I step on the mine?' I was curious about the cause of the explosion and who else, apart from Dennis Brooks and I, had been wounded. I mentioned how a day or two earlier I had nearly stood on a mine when we were attaching trip wires along the outer edge of the minefield. It had frightened the crap out of the blokes with me. Major Florence told me not to worry about it for the moment and suggested we talk about it later.

When he left I fell asleep, dreaming of my mates and good times we had enjoyed on many occasions. In my dream I had actually made it back to our base at Nui Dat. Meeting and greeting many mates returning from their days' work, vigorously I thrust out my hand to shake the hand of my mate Butch Carman. Crash! Bang! A blow to my head! I woke suddenly to see I had knocked the intravenous stand to the floor and it had hit me on the head as it went down. Staff rushed to my bedside. I had actually thrust out my hand as I slept, bringing down the drip line feeding into my right arm.

Days of pain, surgery and a constant stream of most welcome visitors dragged by ever so slowly. Post op ward was a dull looking Quonset hut: an all-purpose, lightweight building that could be shipped anywhere and assembled on a concrete slab without skilled labour. The only windows I could see had air-conditioning units placed in them. With no view for amusement, the best I could do between visitors and treatment was to count whatever I could see from my bed: doctors, nurses, corpsmen, patients, and a Viet Cong prisoner with a guard nearby. The guard was a US Army military policeman and looked well out of place. The prisoner was in no shape to escape or do any harm. I discovered the guard's role was to protect the prisoner from further harm inflicted by other patients.

One futile pursuit I attempted was to count the many stitches keeping me together. Bright orange plastic coated retaining clamps held my guts together, green stitches were all over my arms and leg. Bandages covered me from belly button to foot. Abandoning my counting as a lost cause, I lay quietly daydreaming. My future was not looking too good. Janice Webb, the senior Australian Red Cross lady approached. When she had called previously, I was either off undergoing surgery or sleeping. I listened as Janice explained the role of the Red Cross hospital visitor. One very important role was to write letters home for wounded or sick Diggers and in my case, read my mail to me. My heavily bandaged hands made it impossible for me to hold anything.

I was very embarrassed one day when Janice was reading my mail to me. Paul, a friend from school, wrote regularly keeping me informed of local news and his successful love life. The detailed information of his sexual conquests was a source of entertainment and I had often read his letters to equally frustrated mates. In the privacy of a boy's only environment and fuelled by freely flowing booze, a giggle and a few ribald comments would soon have conversations well spiced up. As Janice started reading out aloud, I was initially flabbergasted, then totally embarrassed with nowhere to hide. All future mail from Paul would be definitely approached with caution.

7
Beer Supply

Many mates posted to 17 Construction Squadron based in Vung Tau not far from the hospital regularly visited me. Not that I was the most popular bloke around, but I was well placed for the guys to perve on the nurses. Sapper Ken Oakes called in for a visit and as we talked about the fellows in 1 Troop. Smithy, a good-looking black American corpsman came along, to change my catheter. He explained to Ken and me what he was about to do in case Ken wanted to make himself scarce. To my surprise, Ken was quite happy to stay and watch. As the old catheter was removed, I felt no discomfort. We were both surprised however, at the length of the tube. Smithy explained how far it had to travel to be lodged securely into the bladder.

Sergeant Jim Fraser and a few other blokes from 17 Construction were visiting when Doctor Nahrwold called by to check on the wound in my belly that Brett Nolen had stuffed shell dressings into while trying to prevent my guts from falling out. As the doctor concluded his examination, Jim asked,

'How long before Jethro can have a beer?'

'He can have a beer now if he wants one,' was the reply.

Later that afternoon Jim and Ron Dixon arrived with two cold cans of beer. Ron held one to my lips as I drank the can dry. Ron suggested I might like to save the second can until after dinner. I agreed and the can was handed to a nurse who placed it in the ward fridge and promised to help me drink it after dinner.

'I'm told Jethro is well enough to have a beer,' I heard Sapper Imants 'Arab' Avotins say as he entered the ward carrying a carton of beer. Arab, who had been with me through recruit training, corps training and in Borneo, had become one of the units more colourful characters. His ability and reputation as an extremely competent sapper with an insatiable desire to consume large quantities of alcohol attracted a lot of attention. The carton of beer was typical of Arab, who would have had every intention of joining me for a beer or two. Appreciating the difficulty I had drinking, he reluctantly surrendered the carton to the same nurse who had placed my original can in the fridge. Several other visitors arrived over the next few days with a carton of Australian beer under one arm. It was not long before my beer supplies occupied all available storage space. I was hardly drinking any, but the supply continued to grow. Eventually, additional cartons were placed under my bed. The regular beer supply made me very popular with other patients, who when permitted were invited to have an Aussie beer with their evening meal.

US Army Medical Corps top brass made an inspection of the hospital one afternoon. A very attractive nurse who appeared to be in charge made her way to the nurses' station. One of the inspecting officers opened the fridge and noticing it was full of beer said, 'There's a goddamn Aussie in here.' All eyes were on me. *I was in the shit this time.* The party moved over to my bedside, which had another carton under it. My fear was unfounded as the gorgeous nurse said hello and appeared eager to know a little about my background and progress. Prior to her departure and having obviously been given a report about my beer supply, the blonde wished me well and told me how generous she thought my friends were supplying beer to the whole ward.

Within days of being granted permission to enjoy a beer, Doctor Harmon advised me that my hand had to be amputated. I held out my left hand with the mangled thumb and index finger.

'Well, it's not much good to me as it is,' I said.

'Sorry Jethro, it's your right hand,' he replied.

'No, that's wrong, I'm right handed,' I said. Despite the heavy bandaging, my right hand looked intact. Doctor Harmon explained how surgery to my wrist had not been successful. The hand was slowly dying and had to be amputated.

The thought of my mother becoming hysterical when she heard of another amputation now occupied my mind. I would need to gradually introduce her to my amputations. Throughout my life, whenever I had observed my mother's emotional outbursts I would become extremely uncomfortable and seek an excuse to distance myself from her. I viewed them as unnecessarily excessive and embarrassing in most cases. Visions of her tearing into the bearer of bad news flashed through my mind. Many years later I was to meet and befriend the unfortunate man who had to endure my mothers' European, emotional outburst as he endeavoured to inform my father, as next of kin, of my fate. Captain Rex Bolitho would never forget his visit to the Thompson's family home at Volga St, Glenroy.

Waking up from the surgery I was eager to look at my arm following the amputation. The stump was not as heavily bandaged as my hand had been and did not look too good as it was not fully closed over. Doctor Harmon explained how the wound would be left exposed for about a week, allowing it to drain. Closure of the wound would require another visit to the operating theatre.

19 May 1967
The day after my hand was amputated Charlie Lynn called in to

visit. My small scruffy, hyperactive first visitor had been working on a bulldozer in the nearby sand dunes when he heard I was one of four casualties from the minefield. He had made his way to the hospital to gather any news he could to pass on to friends and colleagues in 17 Construction Squadron. Today, he was excited and bursting with good news he wanted to share with me, but first he wanted to know how I was feeling after the amputation of my hand.

'Jethro, you are not going to believe this but I have been selected to go to Officer Cadet School, Portsea,' he told me. He was right. I did have trouble believing my mate could one day become an officer. He was too much of a rat bag. Charlie was to return home immediately. He started taking photos of me sitting up in bed. Lieutenant Lee was nearby and Charlie invited her to have her photo taken with me. As Charlie was leaving, he said he would ring my parents from Essendon airport on his way home. Time permitting he would visit them as Glenroy was not far from the airport. Correspondence had begun between Dad and Charlie immediately after my wounding. Charlie rang home and told Dad that my right hand had to be amputated; however, I was coping well.

This well intentioned, passing on of information was to start a minor crisis between the Army and Red Cross. The Army had decided not to inform Dad of my additional amputation, as it was still highly probable I would not survive owing to the severity of my wounds. Dad had recently accepted a telegram from the Army that had no mention of my hand being amputated. Fearing that Charlie had made a mistake he rang a number that the Army had provided should he have any questions about my welfare. The duty officer was unable to comment on my condition. Dad felt the Army, unaware of Charlie's phone call, was withholding information. Determined to get clarification on my physical state, he rang a journalist he knew on the Melbourne *Truth* and explained the situation to him. The following evening the duty officer from the Broadmeadows Army camp arrived and officially advised my parents that it was necessary to amputate my right hand. The Army wrongfully assumed that the Red Cross had mentioned my amputation to Dad by letter.

Physiotherapy commenced on my thumb. At the time I could see very little value in moving my thumb backwards and forwards. This thumb would become my 'Golden Finger'. There is hardly a movement or task that does not require the use of your thumb. As I performed my thumb exercises, the physiotherapist talked to me about making and fitting artificial limbs. This information helped me substantially in my rehabilitation. I started to improve and was encouraged to get out of bed and sit in a wheelchair.

To get out of bed by myself was physically impossible. Assistance was required and lots of it. Sergeant Patnode and two corpsmen had to gently position my leg over the side of the bed and hold me upright before assisting me to stand. Having my foot actually touch the floor was my first positive step forward. Gingerly, I stood and looked briefly around me until dizziness quickly had me sitting back on the bed. Sergeant Patnode said it would soon pass and we would try again in a minute or two. We did and I made it to the wheelchair. As we were about to head outside I freaked out, so much of my body was either missing or heavily bandaged, people were going to stare at me. I knew I would be curious if I saw a bloke who was half missing. I was about to refuse to go outside when the door opened and Sapper John Betterman, an old mate from 24 Construction Squadron, and Janice Webb walked in. The company of two Australian friends that I liked and respected helped me conceal my reservations about how I looked. I ventured outside the ward.

Corpsman Gino produced a camera; John Betterman snapped away capturing the special moment with my very special friends. I never imagined that a ride in a wheelchair could produce so much pleasure and satisfaction for all concerned. I was taken into the ablution block and had my hair washed. I saw for the first time stitches just above my left eye. Not having lost an eye did make me feel incredibly lucky. Never in my life had fresh cold water felt so good as it cascaded over my head and shoulders. This delight was repeated for the next three days. My confidence about my future was improving and I started to develop a more positive outlook.

Two Vietnamese males were brought into the ward as I lay back resting. Both were covered in bandages and one had hospital traction equipment supporting one leg. A corpsman told me that they were riding a motorbike that had collided with an Australian Army Land Rover. As the Land Rover had caused the accident, the Australian Government was responsible for all financial cost incurred in their recovery. All non-English speaking patients are given an easy to pronounce name for simplicity of record keeping while in the hospital. As an Australian, I was asked to provide two suitable names for the Vietnamese. I christened them Gomer and Pyle. The Americans wanted to know the significance of these Australian names. After stringing them along for a minute or two, I reminded them of their very own *Gomer Pyle* USMC, the American TV show.

The hospital was well aware of the Australian policy that each man would take the anti-malarial pill Paludrine daily. As I was safely tucked up in a hospital bed, swallowing a cocktail of medications two or three times a day, I refused to accept the additional pill when a nurse brought the medication to me. No amount of friendly persuasion was going to change my position, or so I thought. The senior nurse on the ward Captain Gert Baker an African-American, aware of my refusal, walked over to my bedside. From the first moment I encountered her on the ward I felt intimidated by her presence. A black officer was foreign to me. Gert was an officer, black, female and very much in charge. When asked why I'd refused to take my Paludrine pill, I blurted out something about my independence and freedom of choice. Gert responded telling me that it was my democratic right to refuse to do anything I was not happy about. Feeling rather pleased with myself I started to smile. Too late, I realised that Gert had in fact pinched my nose with one hand and dropped the pill into my mouth with the other. Saying she agreed with my explanation but I would obey all her instructions while I was in her care, my defiant stand against authority was over as abruptly as it began.

Two weeks after being admitted to the hospital I was feeling reasonably well, improving each day, it looked like I would be flying home soon. My bed had been moved further along the ward towards the door and further away from the nurses' station. The move was a very positive step, reflecting a tangible improvement in my condition. A warrant officer from the Australian Field Ambulance unit, told me that patients considered well enough to travel were flown by RAAF Hercules aircraft fitted out to perform medical evacuation every second Monday. It would normally be a two-hour flight to the RAAF base at Butterworth Malaya then after a further medical check, on to Australia the next day. The thought of going home stimulated my thoughts about my future. Janice told me she had received my personal belongings from Nui Dat. I remembered my last night in Sydney and that I had not got around to washing away the tell tale signs of my last amorous encounter. I asked Janice if my summer uniform was included. She did not know, as she had not looked at the contents. Rather sheepishly, I asked if she would have a look and if it was dirty have it cleaned before it went home. I continued to improve and my spirits were soaring. Occasional trips around the hospital grounds broke the boredom. Patients continued to be admitted to the ward. Five US Navy helicopter pilots suffering from electrical burns sustained as they attempted to erect a wireless antenna swelled the ward population. The antenna had fallen across high voltage power lines. Peter Dixon, one of the pilots with serious burns to his feet, was out of bed and in a wheelchair within days. He spent many hours each day talking to me and assisting me to eat. Even after being relocated to another ward, he continued to visit and bring me packets of Sultana Bran breakfast cereal that I liked.

An Australian airman was brought in with his head heavily bandaged. He was placed next to me and I was curious to find out what had happened to him. It was difficult to keep a straight face as I listened to him tell me. Towards the end of a night of heavy drinking, he accepted a challenge from an equally pissed mate to be the first to stick his head up between the rotating blades of a ceiling fan once it had been turned off. He assured me it was a game regularly played amongst his RAAF mates. Well, he got up first but did not get down quickly enough. The fan blade struck him in the forehead. The wound was not too serious and after a few days he was discharged. On the day of my departure from Vietnam, he was with the ground crew loading the aircraft and showed me the scar on his head.

The movie *Doctor Zhivago* was showing in the hospital theatre and I expressed a desire to attend, Corpsman Gino volunteered to escort me to the theatre that evening. As I lay on a gurney in the back row, I relaxed and enjoyed the movie; removed from my own real life crisis. Back in the ward in the early hours of the morning my temperature soared and my bed was saturated by perspiration. Cold towels were applied to my forehead and body as nursing staff endeavoured to determine the cause. My temperature continued to climb. I was dangerously ill. Ice packs replaced the wet towels. The cold of the ice was overwhelming. I pleaded with the nurses and corpsmen to stop but they ignored me. Never had I felt so cold in my entire life. At one point, shivering with cold, I overheard a doctor say that it was a waste of time and effort keeping me on ice, as shivering is a defence mechanism of the body against cold. A short reprieve from the ice packs followed. On the next occasion when I'd had enough of the ice packs, I pretended to shiver. My little sham did not work, although I was commended for trying.

My temperature frequently spiked over an already dangerously high 104° Fahrenheit (40° Celsius). Doctors were unable to explain why I had suddenly become so sick. Excruciating pain had become my norm, my stomach so distended that I looked like a woman about to give birth. With no relief from pain, I was becoming scared and depressed at this dramatic reversal in my progress. I became abusive to the nursing staff, doctors and anyone else who refused my demand for morphine. With all the drugs available in a hospital, I could not understand why I had to bear such horrendous pain. I had previously received pain relief. Doctor Nahrwold endeavoured to explain the medical need to withhold treatment at this stage but explanations were not what I needed — I needed morphine.

In response to my constant demand for morphine, Gert Baker climbed up on the bed beside me and cuddled me, as a mother would cuddle a suffering child. Soothing and reassuring me that the doctors knew what they were doing and it was all in my best interest. This moment of tender intimacy worked. Not only was it reassuring, it gave me a feeling of being loved. A dose of tender, loving care was one effective way to deal with a recalcitrant patient. Later that day Doctor Nahrwold and Doctor Harmon wheeled me off to X-ray. After drinking the foulest tasting concoction, I was turned every imaginable way - being stood on my head was the only exception. Following a conversation with the radiologist, the two grim faced doctors wheeled me back to the ward.

I was prepped for surgery and taken to the operating theatre. The Catholic priest was waiting and asked if I would like to make a confession. I said yes. Heading for surgery, I thought it smart to play safe. Considering my normal environment and abundant temptations, I had genuinely endeavoured to comply with the Ten Commandments although I had difficulty with those that referred to sins of the flesh. *How could something so natural and pleasurable be a sin?* I had abandoned all hope of abstaining long ago. On the understanding that the priest would assist me with the appropriate prayers and not impose too harsh a penance, we proceeded. After mumbling my way through a string of prayers, the priest stayed with me while I waited to be placed on the operating table. Staff in surgical gowns regularly came and checked on me. Just how sick I was had not dawned on me. When we saw corpsmen carrying a large wooden crate the priest said, 'I think this is what they have been waiting for.'

Doctor MacLean examined the contents of the crate. Then he explained that the crate contained the latest, most modern piece of hospital equipment in the country: a water mattress that could warm or cool a patient according to medical requirements. It was capable of reading body temperature and other vital signs. After surgery, I had drainage tubes in my stomach inserted through my nose, and via a fresh hole in my right side a new catheter and a probe stuck up my bum. My gall bladder and a large section of my small intestine had been removed.

Regaining consciousness back on the ward I heard Lieutenant Philiben say, 'I won't be surprised if one day my uniform falls off leaving me standing here naked.'

'I hope I'm around when it does,' I said. Several nurses, including Lieutenant Philiben rushed to my bedside. *I was going to be reprimanded for talking to an officer in such a manner,* I thought. How wrong I was, they were all delighted to hear me speak and amused by my comment. Many held the view that I would perish from my wounds and some never expected me to recover from my recent surgery. Their confidence in my ability to survive had moved up a notch.

Doctor Nahrwold appeared delighted to inform me that all other organs were intact and had brought along a book with him. Sitting on my bed he endeavoured to explain, with the aid of pictures and diagrams what had been done to me. He described the function of the parts removed and reassured me that I would suffer only a little inconvenience by their loss. Morphine was again prescribed with the warning that only a limited number of shots would be available. I should therefore only call for them when absolutely necessary. Bowel surgery guaranteed that I was not going to eat or drink for quite some time.

A seriously burnt patient was in the bed opposite me. Nurses and doctors were constantly in attendance. Silver nitrate was being applied to the burns. I was told later that nurses had to be extra careful when applying this medication as any spillage or misplaced nitrate would react with their uniform material. Prolonged exposure would see a nurse's uniform deteriorate from ever enlarging holes, hence Lieutenant Philiben's comment previously.

Talking with the nurses later, I was told the burns patient was a Montagnard soldier who had survived a Chinook helicopter crash while working with the US Special Forces. He was shockingly burned; all four limbs had been amputated. The poor bloke never survived and this was considered by many to be a blessing.

Depression was becoming my constant companion as I lay helplessly in bed. I could only sleep after a shot of morphine. Thirst would wake me but no relief was offered. By now, I was developing an enormous dislike for the staff. I believed they were treating me badly, denying me food and water. I sought to be relocated to a ward that had more sympathetic and understanding staff. With misdirected determination, I made a futile attempt at departing the ward. I got my foot to the floor but that was the limit of my physical ability. Failing miserably, there was nothing left for me to do but to sulk, beaten and broken.

Depths of Despair

It is hard to imagine a more defining moment than a near-death experience. No amount of training, can prepare you for the realisation that you have come so close to death. My emotions were off on a roller coaster ride. My weight rapidly plummeted as fever and hunger ravished my body. Previously, visitors had commented on my appearance and lack of noticeable weight loss, obviously disguising just how ill I really was. Correspondence from home served only to enhance my depression, initiating frequent periods of crying. The over-worked staff could do nothing right as far as I was concerned.

Inevitably, my daily quota of morphine was exhausted. Despite my pleading for more, the hospital's position on the administration of medication was rock solid. It was not going to be changed to please me. The risk of addiction was considered a far greater risk to my welfare than a reduction in the level of pain. The frequency of intense pain combined with my constant downward spiral into depression, unleashed the most reprehensible behaviour towards everyone around me. My delight at surviving the mine blast and gratitude to doctors, nurses and corpsmen had been replaced with anger towards all who had been working hard to keep me alive. I verbally savaged anyone who came near me. Nurses treated my wounds but no longer engaged me in conversations. Leaving no doubt I had fouled my nest, Janice Webb, whom I adored, was the only person who could persuade me to calm down.

Not even the Catholic padre was able to comfort me. I felt God had let me down, delivering me into such an appalling state. 'The Lord loves you,' the padre would say. I would challenge this view arguing that God had a funny way of showing it. 'The Lord works in mysterious ways,' he replied. 'Our faith is being tested when we suffer and don't understand the reason for it.' I asked why so much pain and suffering had to be dumped on me all at once. The padre had no answer for me. My faith, although fragile, was providing me with some buoyancy as I struggled to resist slipping further into the black hole of depression.

8
More Australian Wounded

28 May 1967

A patrol from the 1st Australian Reinforcement Unit was ambushed as it moved through rubber trees conducting a clearing patrol near the Task Force base perimeter. In the short firefight, two Diggers were wounded. I was able to talk with the two new patients and hear how they were wounded. Neither had been in Vietnam long. As members of the reinforcement unit, they were to gain experience in patrolling and adjusting to the oppressive weather conditions, while waiting to be posted to an infantry battalion. Ray was shot through the bridge of his nose. The bullet passed through from left to right, grazing his cheek just below his right eye. Another shot fired hastily by Ray's mate a few metres behind him struck him in the middle of his back. Fortunately for Ray, a bandolier of machine gun ammunition he was carrying was hit diminishing the velocity of the bullet preventing it from passing through his body. The combined impact and explosion, did blow a very large hole in his back though. The second Digger wounded, Darryl, was shot close to his right hip. A Dustoff chopper evacuated both Diggers to the 36 Evacuation Hospital.

Now both Diggers would be going home. Ray was a likeable bloke and, despite the large wound in his back, was soon up and about the ward. Darryl would have to remain in bed for a very long time. At first, I felt sorry for this tall, red headed bloke from Yarraville in Victoria. However, if the hospital staff had thought my behaviour appalling, Darryl was about to make me look more like a choirboy than I ever had as a young schoolboy dressed in my altar boy garments.

The first major disturbance by Darryl was when one of the surgeons showed us the damaged round removed from Ray's bandolier that had exploded on his back. Darryl insisted that it was the bullet that had wounded him and demanded he be given the bullet. No explanation was going to convince him that he was wrong. The round had blown out about halfway along its casing, blowing a hole in Ray's back big enough to place a fist in. As the bullet was still in place, Ray was satisfied that it had come from one of two bandoliers he had been carrying and accepted it as a souvenir of his first and last combat experience.

Darryl continued to cause difficulties for the staff and embarrassment for Ray and me. Although I was still demanding morphine for my pain, I was starting to reconsider our bad behaviour. The Americans would be thinking we were a bunch of whingers. The time had come to start eating a little humble pie. When Doctor Nahrwold called in to check on my progress, I apologised for my bad behaviour and assured him that I did not mean any of my derogatory remarks and sought his forgiveness. He assured me that he understood and that my behaviour was typical and expected from a person in my situation. The shame I felt was too great to fully accept his explanation. From here on, I was going to behave. With a few minor blemishes, I did and more importantly won back the friendship of many, if not all the ward staff.

Darryl's father arrived at the hospital. Janice introduced him to Ray and me. I was not sure if this visit was because of Darryl's wounds or his behaviour. I asked Janice why my father had not been brought to Vietnam. After all, I was seriously ill and my behaviour had not been that good. Just before my departure from Vietnam, Janice told me that they had expected I would succumb to my many wounds before a visit from my next of kin could be arranged.

The days continued to slowly pass. Peter Dixon, the American Navy helicopter pilot, would visit and demonstrate his ability to balance his wheelchair on the two large rear wheels, making everyone nervous, fearing he would tip himself over. My beer supply continued to bring cheer to patients. Again, I started to actively seek ways to break the boredom of long days and even longer nights. One attempt involved sniffing and snorting to hold back the dark fluid draining from my body via the tube inserted through my nose. Each sniff or snort would move the fluid backwards or forwards. I would try to amass an amount of fluid and prevent it from slipping over the side of the bed into the bottle at the end of the tube. When I was discovered playing games with my drainage flow, I was gently reprimanded. Interfering with this natural drainage could be harmful to me. Eventually, the tube was removed indicating a degree of improvement. I was now permitted to eat and drink. A cold drink was absolute bliss but inexplicably I had lost the ability to swallow. Food sat stubbornly in my mouth regardless of how hard I tried to swallow. The doctors were eager for me to eat, as it would stimulate bowel movement that would test my repaired intestine. Despite a variety of choices and attractive nurses willing to feed me I continued to gag on the first mouthful. I was encouraged to drink soup and fruit juice regularly.

Most of my wounds were left uncovered and considered to be healing nicely. Visitors continued to drop in. Blokes just arriving in the country called in and brought me up-to-date with news from home. On Sundays, mates from the squadron who were lucky enough to have a trip to Vung Tau would call in before hitting the local bars. Less frequent visitors would make small talk about unit activities and promise to look me up when they got back to Australia Despite their familiarity, visitors continued to be amazed by the size of the orange coloured retaining clamps that now formed two rows across my abdomen.

With no more surgery being planned, I lay comfortably in my bed and started to think about life after Vietnam. As a schoolboy, when I visited Melbourne city I would look closely at the newspaper kiosk in Swanston Street that displayed a sign saying 'Operated by Limbless Soldiers'. I would strain my neck as I passed by to see a limbless soldier but all I ever saw were old men working behind the counter. The Myer department store was also a place I recalled seeing men with limbs missing. Limbless men were employed to operate elevators and as floorwalkers, providing information to customers. My prospects of a suitable working career doing something I liked were not looking too good. Becoming a limbless paper seller seemed like a very real possibility.

Letters from home had included suggestions that Dad, my brother-in-law Keith, and I get involved in a service station. As much as I liked cars and driving, the smell of fuel was not one I wanted to be around all day. What I did know, life was going to be an uphill struggle. Somehow, I'd get to the top. I had no knowledge of repatriation benefits. Doctor Harmon had asked me about financial compensation and benefits available to wounded veterans. I was only aware of a war widow's pension, that was paid in the event of a husband's death. With continued improvement, my bed had been moved even closer to the door. Major Florence called in and informed me that I would be going home on Monday. He again offered to have a few mates flown down to see me before my departure. As his previous offer had not come to fruition most likely owing to circumstances beyond his control, I did not nominate anyone specific. I was happy to see anyone who made the effort.

My mates in 17 Construction Squadron organised a going home party in my honour. Late on Sunday afternoon blokes started to assemble outside the ward. My mate Ron Beveridge was rostered as the unit's duty driver and had been requested to deliver a cold carton of beer every half hour or so. My bed was wheeled outside along with Darryl's. Ray was able to walk out. Les Day, an old mate from my time in Borneo, turned up with his guitar and sang *Mule Skinners' Blues* and many other popular songs. Mooca Moorcroft, complete with harmonica and spoons, also fronted up. One favourite with the crowd was the *'O My Doodle Bird'* that was sung frequently throughout the night. Corporal Dave Wood accepted responsibility to ensure I did not drink too much. He held the can while I sucked beer through a straw.

A bloke from England, who came to Vietnam after joining the US Marines, had become friends with a few of our blokes down at the Beachcomber Bar, and he also came along. I was told he was a hairdresser before joining the USMC. A number of blokes took the opportunity to have a haircut, courtesy of borrowed scissors. Lieutenant Brown, who was keeping an eye on her patients, was also persuaded to have a haircut, as the boys sang *'Mrs Brown, you have a lovely daughter'*. After the hospital lights had been turned down, the party broke up and my mates made their way home to the sounds of the army mantra *'Up the Old Red Rooster'*.

My last night in Vietnam was almost over. With a mixture of shame, sadness and elation scrambling my emotions, I tried to sleep. I had consumed a reasonable amount of beer but sleep eluded me. I had brought shame on the Army, as well as myself, by behaving so badly. These fine people had only my best interest at heart and had done so much to keep me alive. I relived much of my forty days. Faces and names flashed through my mind's eye. Many I would not see again before I was collected and loaded onto the aircraft taking me home. Without any idea how I would complete the task, I resolved to write a letter to the hospital staff, it would be a priority. Eventually, my elation at finally going home, combined with the effects of the beer, had me happily singing about leaving in the morning.

9
Heading Home

19 June 1967
An Australian doctor from 8 Field Ambulance, and a RAAF nursing sister who would be caring for the patients on the flight to Butterworth called in. Following a rather rudimentary examination of my wounds, I was cleared to fly. Darryl however, was not going without bunging on one more turn. When the medics from the Field Ambulance called to transfer the three of us to the Hercules aircraft, Darryl refused to be transferred to a stretcher. He wanted a conventional hospital bed. To my surprise, his demand was complied with. Despite all that had been done for him, he could not leave the ward with at least a modicum of expressed appreciation. At this point I started to think that maybe I'd been unfair in my attitude towards him. *Maybe his wounds were far greater than I imagined?* Over the course of the next six months his behaviour eroded any sympathy I might have had for him.

Brigadier Colin Gurner, from Army Headquarters Canberra, was in Vietnam conducting an inspection of medical facilities, specifically the way wounded soldiers were transported home. Australian press had recently published stories describing the conditions under which wounded Diggers were being transported home compared with the luxury flights available to politicians. At the airfield, Janice Webb introduced me to the brigadier. While we waited to be loaded, cameras were produced. Janice fussed over her wounded Diggers one more time making sure we looked our best. Brigadier Gurner wanted pictures to accompany his report. The moment I had been looking forward to had finally arrived. My stretcher was placed and secured into position on the bottom of a two-tier structure running almost the length of the specially fitted out RAAF Hercules. My abdominal wounds prevented the use of standard restraints. After being closely examined by one of the nurses on board, I was secured with sheets tied around various parts of my body.

As I lay on the narrow stretcher envying Darryl's spacious bed, I looked for somewhere to position my hand comfortably. It was awkward owing to the pin sticking out both ends of my finger. Noticing a strap hanging loosely from the stretcher above me, I placed my hand through the strap. It provided support for my whole arm, ensuring that the pin did not snag on my bedding. When everyone was loaded, including a number of walking wounded and Diggers heading home, the ramp was raised and the engines started. Suddenly, my hand was pulled and squeezed hard against the underneath of the stretcher above me. I started hollering as loudly as I could and thrashing my right stump around to gain some attention over the noise of the engines. My plight was noticed and my hand released. The patient above me, unaware that I was resting my hand on his strap, had simply pulled it tighter.

Once we were airborne, those who could were permitted to move around the aircraft. Brigadier Gurner came and sat beside me. Conversation was difficult, owing to the noise of the engines. A crew member handed a lunch box to the brigadier. He asked if I would like a turkey sandwich. Although doubtful of my ability to swallow, I said, 'Yes Sir,' as I was feeling hungry. He held out a sandwich then swiftly returned it to the lunch box. Smiling, the brigadier repositioned himself; I guess he had momentarily forgotten that I could not feed myself. Sitting on the edge of the bench seat he placed the sandwich close to my mouth. Biting timidly into it and relishing the freshness of the bread, I started to chew slowly. To my surprise, I swallowed without any sign of gagging. Another three or four bites and I waited for the next sandwich. As the brigadier and I completed our lunch, I was rather amused by the thought of being hand-fed by a brigadier. My mates would be impressed.

After a little over two hours flying we landed at Butterworth. Without fuss, all patients were transferred to waiting ambulances and driven the short distance to 4 RAAF Hospital. Patients were quickly settled into big open wards with a million-dollar view overlooking the Malacca Straits and the island of Penang. Medical checks were performed once again and dressings changed. The Digger responsible for tightening his restraining strap on the stretcher above mine was placed next to me. 'Kevin Stephens from Drouin, Victoria,' he said. He was a National Serviceman, a machine gunner with 7 Battalion, and had been shot through both legs while on patrol. He was encased in plaster from toes to groin. As we talked Kevin asked, if I knew a bloke called Bruce Bevan.

'Yes he's in my troop,' I said.

Kevin told me Bruce was also on the flight heading home after injuring his arm; so was the squadron's second in charge (2IC) Captain Graham Hellyer, who had suffered severe spinal injuries in a helicopter crash.

After an early morning 'bird bath', all patients were reloaded onto the Hercules to continue our journey home. I settled down comfortably with the intention of sleeping as much as possible. I could not say with any certainty that patients had been surreptitiously administered medication before boarding but sleep did appear to come relatively easily. The need to pee woke me and as I peed, I noticed a wooden box labelled with Dennis Brooks' name. I asked the nurse what was in the box. When she told me it contained the personal belongings of a bloke killed recently, I understood immediately that Dennis had died from his wounds. Memories of Dennis who had hootchied up with me and Butch on the Horseshoe invaded my thoughts.

Sometime into the flight, one of the four engines developed a mechanical problem and was shut down. Crew members began asking passengers what they had in their luggage, as it may have to be jettisoned. Whether this was a real concern or just a way of gaining everyone's full attention was unclear but they certainly had our focus. Kevin Stephens had a number of items still in their original packaging bought for him by the Red Cross girl the previous day and understandably, was not too keen to have any of his gear jettisoned unless it was absolutely necessary. Likewise, I also had a new portable stereo record player and a large bottle of Johnny Walker Black Label whiskey. I suggested that the whiskey was worth more than I was nowadays, so they could jettison me if it became necessary. Although I was only joking, I discovered some time later that a file note was made suggesting I had suicidal tendencies.

Despite the excitement caused by losing an engine, I went back to sleep but not for very long. Gently, I was shaken awake and advised we were about to land. I lay back believing that the long flight was about to end without incident. When the tailgate was lowered, I was stunned to see the same people who had waved us off earlier in the day. We had returned to Butterworth! I was back in the bed that I had occupied the previous night. The engine needed to be replaced and an extended stopover of three or four days could be expected. The news was well received by most of the passengers because it gave them more time roaming and shopping in Penang. The hospital environment was one of the best you could find. Cool, large airy rooms opened out onto wide shady verandas. After our morning birdbath and treatment of wounds our beds were wheeled out onto the veranda for a picture postcard view across the water to Penang.

Our tranquil surroundings were interrupted by Darryl's behaviour when a young Asian nurse attending him apparently hurt him in the process. He struck and abused the nurse. Witnessing this vile act, I threatened to leave my bed and hit him. Kevin Stephens, who also witnessed the blow and heard my threat, started laughing. He jokingly encouraging me to get up and have a go, knowing full well the futility of my threat.

An RAAF male nurse, instructed to remove the clamps from my stomach, stood with a conventional pair of surgical side cutters in his hand. He shrugged his shoulders and said a more substantial tool would be required, but doubted if any were available. He returned later that day with side cutters he had found in the boot of his car. After sterilizing them, he attempted to cut the first wire clamp. As he applied pressure to the cutters, his free hand pressed into my abdomen. I let out a scream that would have woken the dead! The nurse backed off bewildered by my reaction and apologised for hurting me. After a short break, he repositioned himself and with a double-handed grip, he succeeded in removing all the clamps.

Twice a day nurses irrigated the wound in my left stump. The hole created by the lack of flesh was still large enough to accommodate a golf ball. Ray, who had observed the American nurses treat the wound, happily described how it had previously been done. His advice appeared to be appreciated. Three days later, we were airborne and heading for RAAF Base Richmond. Prior to landing we were advised about restrictions on duty free alcohol and tobacco. Commonwealth Customs officers would conduct a search of personnel possessions before we could leave the aircraft. One enterprising passenger knowing he was over quota approached my stretcher and asked if I would mind if he concealed his excess under my blanket. He suggested it would simulate my left leg. I was impressed by his imagination. After we landed a Customs officer moved through the aircraft, glancing briefly in my direction. Immediately after he passed I was removed from the aircraft. Cold rain was belting down, a forest of umbrellas kept most passengers reasonably dry.

While being held in the staging area, I could hear Darryl carrying on, complaining about the rough handling by the ground crew. Again, I threatened him with violence. If only I could get up and at him! We'd all had enough of Darryl by now. Severe flooding between Richmond and Ingleburn made it impossible for the Army Land Rover ambulances to get through to 2 Camp Hospital Ingleburn. We would have to wait for the flooding to ease. *What was one more obstruction to our journey home?* The next day Kevin Stephens and I were loaded into an ambulance for the journey to Ingleburn. On arrival at the hospital the ambulance doors were opened and a voice asked, 'Which one is Sapper Thompson?' I indicated it was me. An elderly looking bloke in civilian clothing climbed into the ambulance and squatted between the two stretchers. While looking at the wound in my right side, he called for a kidney dish and scalpel. He pierced the wound. Puss squirted from my body like a ruptured water main. The kidney dish was inadequate to contain the muck squirting from my side. As I was wheeled into the hospital, the civilian was identified as a visiting specialist who had been summoned urgently in response to a report on my condition before leaving Richmond. The drainage wound had apparently healed over prematurely on the outside, causing a backup of fluid in my abdominal cavity. It was not a great start to arriving home.

Kevin and I were in adjacent beds. Initially, Darryl was on my other side but thankfully, the matron had him moved further along the ward. Bad blood between us must have been common knowledge. Privacy screens were placed around our beds, as we were about to receive a full medical examination. Looking through a gap in the screen towards Kevin, I said, 'Did you see who she was going to put next to me?' Before Kevin could respond, Matron stepped around the screen and said, "She" is the cat's mother. I'm the Matron and you'd better not forget it in future.'

Bloody hell what's up her nose? I thought, trying hard to keep a straight face. Kevin was behind her silently mimicking her admonishing me. Imposing her rank on me was apparently more important than showing a little understanding and compassion. We were not going to enjoy our stay here.

Ingleburn in June is bitterly cold in total contrast to the tropical climate we had just left. Desperately in need of a pee and without the privacy of a screen owing to the urgency, I endured the embarrassment as a nurse held the urinal bottle in place.

'Since when can water run uphill?' Kevin asked. Not understanding his remark the nurse looked at him then at my exposed genitals. Suffering from the cold, all was pointing towards the ceiling. The nurse started to blush as I started to pee. The stream under full pressure arched beautifully over the end of my bed to puddle on the floor.

Dad happened to be in Sydney on business. The Army collected him from his motel and brought him to the hospital that evening. He told me that Mum was flying to Sydney tomorrow. I suggested it was a waste of money as I would be in Melbourne in a day or two. I was also mindful of her emotional displays that embarrassed me tremendously. Dad told me that I should know there was no stopping my mother once her mind was made up. Knowing that I could be just as stubborn, I went to sleep thinking about how to handle the developing confrontation.

The next morning we had our usual birdbath and after breakfast all beds were made. Kevin and I could not believe what we saw happening next. A senior sister stood at one end of the ward conducting an inspection: the beds had to line up, all the Red Cross emblems on the counterpanes had to form a continuous line the length of the ward, all wheels had to face the front and God help any patient who moved around in bed disturbing the alignment until after the formal morning inspection.

I mentioned to a nursing sister the problem I had with my mother and said that if she did visit the hospital, I would not accept the visit. A little while later a doctor came along to discuss the background to my maternal relationship and what had caused the estrangement. I tried to explain how my mother's behaviour embarrassed me. He failed to understand or appreciate my position, walking away saying he thought I was an ungrateful bastard. He was so wrong! I was not ready to confront my mother with my disabilities. Visiting hour arrived and a sister asked if I would accept my mother's visit. Once again, I refused. Noting my mother's emotional state, a nursing sister permitted her to view me through the observation window in the duty nurse's office, unbeknown to me.

Thirst woke me but I was unable to reach my water jug. I looked around for some help. All patients near me were sleeping. Reaching over to my bedside table, I was able to secure my empty urinal bottle by inserting my thumb through the handle. Swinging it gently against my bedside table I tried to attract some attention. Clang-clang-clang went the swinging urinal with the noise reverberating through the darkened ward. However, no assistance came forth. Once again, but a little harder I clanged. A voice somewhere in the darkness said, 'What's all the clanging about?' Calling out that I needed some help, a patient appeared and asked what the problem was. Once I told him, he went off looking for someone to help me. The duty nurse rushed to my bedside and apologised for neglecting my call. She had heard the clanging and assumed it was Darryl being a pest again and thought he could wait until she had finished whatever she was doing at the time.

Kevin Stephens, Graham Hellyer, Darryl, Ray and I were examined and cleared to fly on to Melbourne. The flight attendants had gone on strike grounding most commercial flights so the RAAF were quick to help, providing a Hercules aircraft to fly all patients south to Laverton Air Base. After four days at Ingleburn, we returned to Richmond.

10
Repatriation General Hospital Heidelberg

26 June 1967
Civilian ambulances were waiting to take us to hospital. Captain Hellyer was going to the Austin Hospital for specialist spinal treatment. The rest of us were going to the Repatriation General Hospital at Heidelberg. After a long, slow drive through peak hour traffic on a cold, wet, miserable Melbourne afternoon we arrived. The tedious admissions process was finally completed. We waited to be wheeled to our wards with a nurse keeping a close eye on the four of us. She told me about a patient recently returned from Vietnam who had also lost a leg. He had survived the battle of Long Tan in August last year only to lose a leg in a mine explosion three months later. Fitted with an artificial leg, he had been out dancing with his wife, the nurse cheerfully told me. At the end of a very long and arduous day, I was not really interested in hearing about anyone's dancing ability.

Kevin and I were admitted to Ward West 2, the orthopaedic ward and placed in opposite beds in Bay 3. After seven days travelling the first part of our journey along the road to recovery was over. The four beds in Bay 3 looked as if they had been in service for a long time. Originally painted a creamy yellow much of the paint had chipped off leaving dark patches of rusty brown metal; unlike the modern beds in the 36 Evacuation Hospital. Across the top of the beds, traction equipment was fitted. Kevin would be in traction, as were the other two patients in the bay. Observation checks of our blood pressure, temperature and pulse were carried out. Satisfied all was in order, family members who were waiting to visit were ushered to our bedside. I braced myself for my mother's arrival:

'My Johnny! Oh my boy! What have they done to you?' my mother wailed, as she rushed down the passageway before throwing herself across my bed repeating her cry, 'My Johnny, my Johnny.' Luckily for me a bed cradle placed over the lower part of my bed to keep the bedclothes off my wounds provided some additional protection as Mum waved her arms wildly about. Although my mother's distress was genuine, I could not help feel that even on this occasion her display was exaggerated. Maybe, I just didn't understand what it meant to see your only son critically wounded.

Nightly visiting hours were between six and eight o'clock with the exception of Wednesday when only afternoon visiting was permitted. Visitors gathered in the foyer between the East and West Wards waiting for the doors to open. At five minutes to eight, the senior nurse on duty would start ringing a small bell up and down the ward to indicate visiting time was over. Many visitors would look into our bay through the large windows as they made their way along the corridor. Some would actually stare straight at me. *Being stared at by strangers was something I was going to have to get used to.* I doubted that I was going to like it but I would never be able to conceal my amputations. At this stage of my recovery however, I was not ready to cope with strangers' curiosity. The nightly parade of visitors gawking at me as they passed became an irritation. I would ask my visitors to draw the privacy curtains on their arrival, an action that regularly incurred the wrath of the senior sister on duty.

My weight on admission had been estimated at no more than six stone (38 kg) approximately half my weight in Vietnam. I was not much more than skin and bone. My mutilated left hand and missing right hand made it almost impossible to assist myself. I was totally dependent on the nursing staff to eat, drink, toilet and bathe. It was embarrassing and I felt the loss of dignity that was intensified by my dependence. Languishing indefinitely in hospital did not appeal to me. My immediate aim was to achieve a modicum of independence. A recurring dream of me forlornly walking deserted city streets eating fish and chips and sleeping in bus shelters or on a park bench had troubled me since my early days in hospital. The dream was so vivid it was frightening and accelerated my loss of self-confidence. My mind was preoccupied with devising ways and means to fend for myself, as I struggled to stay positive. Fearing the unknown, I regularly lapsed into shitty behaviour. The staff remained supportive and understanding, but I feared their tolerance was waning.

Deputy Matron Burns called by to introduce herself, a jolly looking middle-aged lady with a robust figure and a pleasant smile. I would soon learn the smile could fool the most recalcitrant patient. On her first visit she objected to my bare chest. Staff were informed that I must be covered up at all times. The staff had earlier abandoned all attempts to dress me in hospital pyjamas. My high leg amputation made it impossible to even secure a hospital bikini. Lying naked under the bedclothes was considered the best option and a modesty towel would cover me whenever I was examined or receiving treatment. Pyjama tops not only bunched up and caused uncomfortable ridges, but they restricted my limited ability to use my arms even further. Using my arms like paws, I could hold a cold drink or turn the pages of a book. Refusing emphatically to wear a top sparked off the first of many confrontations with Matron. I knew my position was understood but staff had to follow instructions. The only reason given for the insistence to cover up was that my bare chest could offend female visitors. *Stuff the visitors, they don't have to look.* My mother learned of my objection and fearful I would get into strife with the Army, brought in a couple of tee shirts and suggested that I should cover up at least during visiting hours. Appreciating her concern and not wishing to cause her any more anguish, I agreed.

An ambulance took me to the Repatriation Artificial Limb and Appliance Centre in South Melbourne to meet Doctor Klein, a specialist in limb fitting and design. Resting on a stretcher in the doctor's office I met the team of 'limb makers' who would produce and fit my artificial limbs. The centre foreman, Ivor Appleton, was introduced. He was wearing an artificial arm, having lost his right hand during the Second World War with the Navy. I watched him closely as he inspected my stumps and assisted with casting my right stump. One way or another he managed to hold wet plaster strips and apply them to my stump. I was so impressed! A temporary arm would be produced within days, enabling me to practice and gain some familiarity with the use of a split hook.

3 July 1967

It was my twenty-second birthday. Matron Hanrahan paid me a visit and wished me a 'Happy Birthday'. Matron was an army nurse in the Second World War. Her service ribbons were proudly displayed on her uniform. She was a cheerful woman and wished me a speedy recovery. In the afternoon I was assisted into a wheelchair. Nurses needed help from Victor, one of the orderlies on the ward, to lift me from my bed and place me in the chair. I was given a brief tour through the ward as a birthday treat before visiting hours. Sister Chris Morton introduced me to many of the patients as I was wheeled in and out of each bay. I noticed that there were six beds in each bay, similar to the beds I occupied in Vietnam. The last room, known as the sunroom was home to about ten long-term patients waiting to be relocated into private accommodation.

While I waited for the flow of visitors to stream past my window, I reflected on my first week in Heidelberg. So far I had been x-rayed, poked, probed, pushed or pulled in every imaginable way. I had swallowed a colourful cocktail of capsules, pills and potions, had countless needles in my bum and been shaved from nipples to knee. I was sure it had all been necessary but I was tiring of the intrusion and constant assault on my dignity. I'd had to fast for twelve hours or longer prior to going to the operating theatre on two occasions. Surgery modified what remained of my left leg and one of two pins in my hand had been removed.

Extensive exposure to anaesthetics over a relatively short time resulted in a collapsed lung, adding to my woes. At least nine operations, some lasting for many hours over the last seven weeks had put too much strain on my system. The pain in my chest was becoming more unbearable with each breath. Unable to conceal my pain from Mum, her characteristic overreaction aggravated me immensely and exacerbated my stress. In future, I would tell my sisters when surgery was scheduled and hope that they would discourage Mum from visiting for a day or two. Visiting the hospital each day since my return was relatively easy for Mum. If Dad or my sisters were not available to drive her, she would catch a bus to the hospital entrance in Bell Street.

Blinking to focus after a late morning nap, I saw an image of a lovely young lady with shoulder length blonde hair standing by my bedside. Believing the vision was a dream I shut my eyes again, wishing to recapture and continue the dream where I had left off. She was Rosemary Fleming, an occupational therapist who'd been assigned to assist me in the use of my artificial arm. The temporary arm was only a plaster cast of my lower right arm with a split hook that opened in two parts attached with a basic harness similar to a shoulder holster to hold the prosthesis in place. To open the hook

I shrugged my left shoulder forward, a cable anchored to a ring in the harness pulled the hook apart. Thick rubber bands fitted to the hook closed it once I relaxed my shoulder. Wearing a modified training prosthesis, Rosemary explained how together we were going to develop ways to regain some of my lost independence. I was an eager and willing patient if, for no other reason, than to prolong the lovely Rosemary's visit. Rosemary explained how my body shape would change as I improved and regained some weight and muscle tone. A permanent arm would be made at a later date when doctors considered my medical condition sufficiently stable.

Eager to impress, I worked hard and practiced at every opportunity, and enthusiastically looked forward to Rosemary's visits. Within a week I was able to type a letter to my friends in Vietnam and more importantly, the doctors and nursing staff at 36 Evacuation Hospital. Sitting up in bed with a small typewriter on my bedside table, I held a short wooden dowel tipped with a rubber cap in my hook. I searched the typewriter keyboard for the correct letters, regularly asking Kevin for assistance with the spelling.

Doctor Rush, the ward doctor assisting orthopaedic surgeon Mr Hodge, came along one morning to remove the pin that had been inserted through my finger to hold it together. Assuring me the removal would not hurt, he grasped the end of the pin sticking out just behind my fingernail with a pair of surgical pliers and gently eased the pin out. He released my finger. It hung forlornly like a piece of limp macaroni. Insufficient bone had regenerated between the first and second knuckle. My mangled hand was measured and an aluminium splint created to support the finger.

Despite the attractiveness of the nurses, being fed and bathed by them had no appeal. Many nurses cleaning my teeth would either press too hard and too deep causing me to gag, others would apply hardly any pressure at all providing only a cursory brushing. Shaving with a safety razor was also a little hazardous. Almost every nurse inflicted a nick or two. Rosemary and I conceded after many hours of practise that the temporary artificial arm contributed very little towards performing these daily tasks. Holding a knife was the only exception. Having regained my appetite I was eager to eat almost everything placed in front of me. However, relying on the nursing staff to feed me challenged my patience.

Prior to mealtime a dinner tray would be placed on my bedside table. Once the food arrived from the hospital kitchen in mobile food warmers it was served directly to the patients by senior nursing staff. Occasionally, I would be asked my preference. The norm however, was to accept what I was given. Being in Bay 3 my meal was served soon after arrival on the ward. It was always warm if not hot. While the other three patients were eating, my meal went cold. Rarely was a nurse available to feed me until all the patients had been served. Older nurses gave me their full attention as they gently and carefully fed me. Annoyingly, young garrulous nurses frequently engaged in conversation with other patients, enthusiastically gesticulating with the fork as I chased the impaled food. Food would pass close to my mouth but not close enough. Frustrated and annoyed by my futile attempt to capture the food or have the nurses pay more attention to my needs I struck out at the dinner tray in frustration, pushing it off the table and scattering food over the floor on several occasions.

After a couple of weeks to recover from the collapsed lung, I had another visit to the operating theatre to have skin removed from my right thigh and grafted to the open wound on my left stump. From my previous experience in 36 Evacuation Hospital I knew that the actual graft would be free of pain. However, the area that provided the skin would be extremely painful. The severity of the pain was greater than I remembered the first time. Four days later as I was getting over the pain I was told that the dressing on my thigh would be removed in the morning. I feared the nurses would use the 'grab and yank' method, so I prepared to remove the dressing myself. Throughout the night I used my thumb like a chisel to gently ease the dressing away from my thigh. I feigned sleep whenever a nurse shone a torch towards me as they checked on me. Carefully, I worked my way through the adhesion caused by congealing blood. Gritting my teeth, I silently endured the pain as the dressing separated from my sore tender skin. By morning the dressing was resting freely around my ankle. As the nurses bathed me I saw my thigh. It was bright red and angry looking. My leg looked like it had been ring barked; if I was a tree I would soon be dead.

The number of amputees on the ward surprised me. Most had one leg off, however there were patients with no legs. They relied on wheelchairs for movement and appeared to be Second World War Diggers, although at least two looked to be First World War fellows. I felt an affinity developing and started making eye contact with them. Another two amputees from Vietnam were on the ward and regularly called in for a chat. Tony Twaits was a regular soldier, solidly built and reasonably tall with an unruly mop of red hair. He was wounded in action with the 5 Battalion's Long Range Reconnaissance Platoon. Fitted with a temporary prosthesis he attended the amputee clinic daily. He was hopeful of an opportunity to retrain in army administration and soldier on. David Young was a slightly built bloke with a thin comical looking face and a mischievous sense of humour. David had been conscripted and posted to Vietnam with 7 Battalion. Three weeks after arriving in Vietnam, David's platoon was hit with friendly artillery fire. Shrapnel struck David shattering his left leg. The wound was so severe his leg was amputated above the knee.

11
Miss Gray-Wilson and Mr Hodge

Miss Gray-Wilson, the senior physiotherapist, who had been treating me almost daily had arranged for me to have a saline bath. A large stainless steel bathtub originally designed for patients with severe burns was located in the physiotherapy centre, which was as far from Ward West 2 as you could possibly travel and still be within the hospital grounds. The opportunity to soak in a bath was going to be luxury. With the exception of my visits to the shower block at 36 Evacuation Hospital in Vietnam, I had been washed in bed since being wounded nearly three months previously.

I was collected from the ward by Miss Gray-Wilson. She wheeled me head first on a hospital trolley along the duckboards towards the physiotherapy centre. On the way I learned that only the dead were wheeled feet first. We were moving at a reasonable pace. It was imperative we arrived before her team of physiotherapists dispersed throughout the hospital. All hands were needed to lift and support me in the bath. Miss Gray-Wilson was almost running and I was very impressed with her fitness, which was not bad for a lady in her fifties. Six young physiotherapists were waiting and greeted me with cheerful remarks. Miss Gray-Wilson, satisfied the bath water temperature was acceptable, instructed her young colleagues on how she wished to proceed. Up and over I went, the water was absolutely delightful, warm and salty. Totally submerged in warm water and surrounded by young ladies I lay back and let my imagination run wild.

I fantasised that I was a wounded Roman warrior, laying back and sipping wine surrounded by delightful maidens feeding me grapes. I soaked up the warmth of the steamy bathhouse. Warm water and daydreaming was a bad combination and it was not long before I felt my dick reacting to my fanciful thoughts. Momentarily I was delighted with the result, then I remembered where I was and mindful that a wet white bikini was not going to conceal my ever increasing arousal. Blushing with embarrassment I started kicking the water furiously, disturbing the smooth flat surface of the bath water in an attempt to conceal my untimely erection. Miss Gray-Wilson's reaction to my sudden display of restlessness was to pull the bathplug. As the girls lifted me from the bath and dried me, I was unable to look at them without blushing a little more. Once covered with a blanket, I relaxed a little. As I was wheeled back to the ward, I recalled that over the last three months nurses had attended to my every need, day and night. Suggestive comments about their physical and sexual attributes by patients and visitors were regularly expressed. Surprisingly, I had felt no desire or interest towards the nurses, other than appreciation for their presence and willingness to treat me. The lack of sexual interest had been on my mind for some time; being impotent would be the last straw. Telling Kevin about the experience in the bath he said with a grin, 'Well, it's good to know that part of you is still working.'

Head nurse on the ward was Harry Jenkins, a former World War Two army medic, who had nursed at RGH Heidelberg for over twenty years. He was single and dedicated to caring for his patients. Harry returned to the ward each Friday after two days off, with a block of Cadbury's chocolate for Kevin and me. Later in the morning Harry would head up the entourage that accompanied Mr Hodge, an orthopaedic surgeon, on his weekly ward rounds. Mr Hodge, also a war veteran, had practised almost exclusively at RGH Heidelberg and possessed the most appalling bedside manner. Regularly, he would light up a fresh cigarette as he examined my wounds. The ever-increasing ash came perilously close to falling onto my exposed wounds on many occasions as he talked freely to those around him. My eyes were always locked onto the ash - miraculously it never fell.

Mr Hodge was slightly built with piercing dark eyes and a gaunt face that did not smile too often. Despite his harsh appearance and brusque manner, I liked the man and he had my total confidence. One morning however, I did have serious doubts about the man's mental stability. He was examining my left stump a few days after he had operated, pressing around the wound with a knife taken from my dinner tray. When he finished his examination he threw the knife onto the floor saying, 'You won't want to use that knife, will you?' I lay back speechless.

Kevin and I were constipated. We were told iron tablets had that effect on most patients. So we decided not to take them. Each morning I was required to take a load of pills. I persuaded the nurses to give me my iron tablets last, then I manoeuvred the pills under my tongue while the nurse reached for my glass of water. I pretended to swallow then spat the tablets out once the nurse had left. Kevin was able to flick his pills away. Betty, a cheerful middle-aged lady and one of many domestics who kept the ward spotlessly clean, daily dragged her vacuum cleaner into our bay. We could not resist smiling as we heard our pills rattle their way up the vacuum pipe. Betty was well aware of what Kevin and I had been doing and regularly threatened to report us, but she never did. In return for her silence we had to endure countless tales about her teenage son who was constantly in trouble. We would also laugh enthusiastically each time she mentioned that she had a very *healthy* cleaner.

Mr Hodge was keen for me to spend less time in bed and encouraged me to have weekend leave when I felt up to it. Still very dependant on nurses for bathing and toileting, going home would not be achievable for a little while longer, but the thought of going home was something I looked forward to. Feeding myself had become less of a problem with the use of a 'Splayd' fork held in a palm strap attached to my hand, and a knife with my hook. When Mr Hodge heard about my progress with feeding myself he arranged to come see for himself one lunchtime.

Mr Hodge, Harry, Miss Gray-Wilson and Rosemary gathered around my bed. Lunch was spaghetti and meatballs. I felt the urge to toss the lot on the floor. However, with an impressive audience assembled to observe my most recent achievement, I calmed myself down and accepted the challenge. As more and more spaghetti covered my face and chest, I had to concede defeat. Appreciating my effort Mr Hodge asked what would I like to eat if I had the choice?

'Fish and chips wrapped in newspaper,' I answered.

The following Monday Mr Hodge called in and had a quick look at my stumps. As he was about to leave he turned towards me and said, 'Enjoy the fish and chips.' To my delight and surprise Rosemary appeared in the doorway with a parcel wrapped in the morning newspaper and placed it on my bedside table. The smell of hot fish and chips urged me onwards as I struggled to find a way into the parcel. I tore into the newspaper with my teeth only to discover a second white paper wrapping. Another bite into this paper and the delicious smell of fish and chips splashed with vinegar wafted around Bay 3 attracting a number of curious onlookers. Kevin and my other companions enviously looked on, as I set about enjoying my meal. Rosemary later explained how Mr Hodge had arranged for my lunch to be purchased from a nearby shop and had them covered in the additional newspaper wrapping, as it was now illegal to use newspaper for food wrapping. I was astonished that a man who notoriously projected such an insensitive attitude could be so thoughtful.

12
Surprises

Assistant Matron Burns called into the ward around midnight and noticed that my bed was obstructing the entrance to our bay. She attempted to push it back into its correct position. The noise woke all four patients up. Roy, the duty nurse, suddenly appeared and helped Burns push my bed. As my bed was pushed backwards, Kevin's bed started to move forward. They stopped to look at the situation and discovered both beds were tied together. Angrily, Burns untied the beds and demanded to know who was responsible. I could not have pushed my bed forward even if I could manage to get out of bed and the other three patients were in traction. It was a mystery. Over breakfast, Kevin confessed he had been removing the cords from his pyjamas each morning and saving them. In traction he had no need for pyjama pants. He had accumulated quite a number of cords and had amused himself by plaiting them together. The previous night he had been unable to sleep and had fashioned the cords into a lasso. While I slept, he lassoed the end of my bed and pulled it out far enough to obstruct the doorway. Tying the cord to his bed, he then went to sleep –

mystery solved!

Breakfast this particular morning was a little rushed. Domestic staff were cleaning, sweeping, mopping and dusting more diligently then ever before. The nursing staff also appeared to be exceptionally neat and tidy. They were constantly fussing around our beds, fluffing pillows, emptying pee bottles and straightening bedclothes. The usual cheerfulness that was normally generated by the staff as they went about their duties was noticeably absent. Curiosity was growing in our bay as we all sensed the developing tension. Head nurse Harry Jenkins looked flustered and we could hear him issuing instructions to the staff with a tone of urgency. He appeared in the doorway and informed us that a very important visitor would be arriving shortly. We must not call for bottles or bedpans unless it was absolutely necessary until the visitor had left. He looked at me and said harshly, 'Please try and eat lunch without making too much of a mess.'

Lunch arrived early, Kevin had a liking for tomato sauce on all his meals, and when he asked for the sauce bottle Ralph, a male nurse, came along and applied a small dollop of sauce on his dinner. 'More than that,' Kevin said. Ignoring the request, Ralph turned to move away. Kevin snatched the bottle from Ralph and liberally applied the sauce as Ralph attempted to retrieve the bottle. In the struggle that followed tomato sauce was squirted up the adjacent wall and window. Then the top of the bottle came off and the remaining sauce splashed all over Kevin's bed. When the struggle was over Kevin's bed was a mess, it looked like someone had slashed their wrists. Nurses rushed to change his sheets and the domestic staff hurriedly washed down windows, walls and floor. When all appeared to be back to normal, Ralph reached for Kevin's small radio sitting on his bedside locker. Kevin said, 'Don't touch that,' but Ralph foolishly persisted, claiming the radio had to be turned off. Kevin attempted to grab Ralph's hand but only managed to grab hold of Ralph's thumb. That was enough. Kevin bent it backward demanding Ralph leave his radio alone. Ralph refused, Kevin responded by applying more pressure. Suddenly Ralph let go and rushed from the ward. A very red faced Harry stuck his head in the bay and said, 'We'll talk about this later.' Afterwards we were told that Ralph's thumb was broken. I had no sympathy for Ralph as he had treated me rather badly on many occasions. On one occasion he washed me in icy cold water as a joke, some joke on a cold, Melbourne winter morning.

Our important visitor's imminent arrival was heralded when almost every staff member on duty was summoned to the ward entrance. They lined up in order of seniority. In anticipation and suspense we all lay quietly. Matron Hanrahan, resplendent in full uniform and escorted by Harry, entered our bay. Harry introduced Senator McKellar, the then Minister for Repatriation. The VIP party moved to each bed. The Minister vigorously shook hands with the other three, but when he came over to me, he patted me gently on the head.

Each bed had a radio headset for use by the patient. It was difficult for me to reach because it was hung over the top end of the bed. Reading was possible but with some difficulty. Propped up in bed with a number of pillows I could slowly turn the page with my thumb as my right stump held the book steady on my table. Newspapers were more difficult - pages regularly fell to the floor. Movies were shown each Monday evening at the hospital's St John's Theatre and amateur groups performed on Wednesday evening. I had not been able to attend either the movies or the theatre yet.

After breakfast I was feeling good and comfortable with myself, smiling happily as nurses attended to my dressings and administered my medication. Eating had become more enjoyable with the use of the palm strap. It was another step forward. Savouring the warm fuzzy feeling associated with success I was lying back listening to patients and staff talking about going to the movies that evening. I envied the patients who were up and about. Some of the younger patients were actively pursuing nurses to accompany them to the theatre and hopefully enjoy a little kissing and cuddling on the way back to the ward.

While Nurse Elaine was rubbing my back with a soothing cream she asked if I was going to the movies. As I was still very much bed bound, I thought it was totally out of the question and said so.

'If you were permitted to go, would you like to go?' Elaine asked.

A change of routine and an opportunity to meet other patients from Vietnam appealed to me. 'Yes, I'd love to go if it was possible,' I answered. Later in the day Elaine informed me that I could go to the movies on a trolley if someone was available to escort me. *Well, that was the end of that idea.* To my delight, Nurse Elaine said she would call for me after dinner and take me to the movies. When Elaine left the ward Des, a patient recovering from knee surgery, started carrying on about how I had undermined him. He had chatted Elaine up earlier in the day about going to the movies, but she had declined so she could accompany me. Speechless, I lay back in my bed not believing my luck. A pretty and popular nurse had chosen to take me to the movies! After dinner, Elaine arrived to collect me dressed in a short skirt and matching blouse. Her hair was neatly brushed and she had that wholesome girl-next-door look. A bloke would definitely ask her out based on looks alone. A hospital trolley was placed beside my bed and I scurried across unaided. I was so full of enthusiasm to be going to the movies.

We talked as we travelled along the duckboard pathway that linked the old single storey wards and ancillary buildings across 50 acres of hospital grounds. I was wheeled inside the theatre and placed behind the last row of seats. Looking around I saw a number of nurses accompanying patients dressed in hospital gowns and many members of staff. While I was talking with some other patients I noticed Elaine was missing. I became a little agitated fearing that she had simply parked me at the theatre and gone off to mix with her friends or other patients sitting in the stalls. I could not see her anywhere in the theatre. As the lights started to dim, she appeared by my side with a chair and sat close to me.

After my outing with Elaine, my emotions soared and plummeted. At times I felt confident that all would be well, I just had to give myself time. On other days, unpleasant dreams about life after hospital and uncertainty about my abilities sent me crashing down into a bottomless pit of misery. The slightest issue could trigger a bout of aggression. Nurses told me that I was gaining a reputation for being obstinate and rude. I knew that was not the real me. I respected and admired the fine people who had been helping me recover from my wounds.

I realised regaining sufficient independence to live freely in the community was going to require more than achieving success over my physical disabilities. Conquering my emotional fluctuations about accepting a lifestyle that was very different to what I had previously known was going to be my real challenge. Through the long lonely night hours I asked myself the same questions, night after night. *How will I be accepted once I leave hospital? Will girls want to associate with me? Will I ever marry and have a family? If I ever do marry, how will I hold and play with my children?* No, I just couldn't see any of it happening for me. For weeks I had listened to tales about some of the nurses getting a little fresh with patients, teasingly enjoying a little slap and tickle. One nurse, I was told, daringly hopped into bed briefly with a patient. *Half their luck.* I envied those fellows.

13
Determination over Arrogance

Steady progress towards gaining my independence encouraged me to be a little more adventurous. As each day passed I sat out of bed a little longer. I even developed a way to hold the urinal bottle in position when required, lessening my dependence on the nursing staff. This achievement however, triggered a nasty verbal encounter with one of the registrars on the ward. Reaching a little too far for the urinal bottle as the need to pee was becoming urgent, I knocked it off my bedside table. As it clattered along the floor, Doctor Chew happened to call in to examine me.

'Doctor Chew, could you pass my bottle please?' I asked. Doctor Chew looked around arrogantly. To his disappointment, no other staff member was present so HE had to reach down to pick up the bottle.

'You should say "please" when you ask for something John,'
'I did say "please",' I replied.
'I didn't hear you,' said Doctor Chew.
Kevin who had been listening from his bed said, 'John did say

"please" Doctor Chew.'

'Well, I did not hear him, so he can say it again.' Doctor Chew held the bottle out towards me. Although I was about to wet myself, I'd had enough of his arrogance.

'You can stick the bottle up your arse for all I care,' I yelled.

Startled by my outburst, he dropped the bottle and left. Not to be defeated, I hurled myself out of bed hitting the floor hard but unhurt. I retrieved the bottle and rested it against my thigh and peed.

Feeling relieved and victorious, I placed the near full bottle out of harm's way. Sitting on the floor naked, I considered my next move. *How would I get myself back into bed?* I might as well have been at the foothills of Mount Everest. Hopelessness was now replacing my earlier euphoria and I began to regret the stupidity of my impulsive and reckless behaviour. Shuffling along the floor on my bare bum, I made my way to a space between my bedside cabinet and the wall. Returning to my bed unaided became my objective. Without hands, it was going to be difficult. *If only I could stand!* Slightly opening the lower drawer of my bedside cabinet, I placed my left arm along the top edge of the drawer and pressed against the wall with my right stump. I attempted to force myself up off the floor. I couldn't support my weight. After numerous painful attempts, my efforts started to look rather futile.

Observing my lack of progress Kevin said, 'Shall I call for help?' I did not answer determined to succeed. I pushed down on my left arm and pressed my stump even harder against the wall ignoring the pain. Pushing down on my foot lifted me sufficiently to place my left arm on top of the cabinet. Success was now within reach! A little more strain on my arms and I reached a standing position. Exhausted, I stood savouring the moment. I was standing for the first time unaided. This was a major achievement in my recovery. The anxious look on Kevin's face was now replaced by a beaming smile.

'Nothing is going to stop you now,' he said. Nurses had rushed to assist me but I was determined to complete my task unaided. Shuffling my foot slowly along the floor with my back pressed against the wall, I positioned myself to fall onto my bed. I pushed off the wall and collapsed across the bed. One final effort was needed to drag myself completely onto the bed. My first mountain had been conquered. I was elated but totally stuffed. As I lay back exhausted, my jubilation was shattered when blood was discovered on my bedding. I had scraped off much of the skin grafted to my left stump.

Mum becomes a courier

I had asked Mum if she would bring in a six-pack of beer next time she visited.

'Are you allowed to have a beer in hospital?' she asked.

'Probably not,' I said.

I doubted that Mum would actually bring the beer, so I didn't mention it to my three mates. Next evening Mum arrived carrying a heavy overnight bag. Nervously looking around and swearing at me in Maltese, a six-pack was removed from the bag. Sitting close to my bed, Mum removed the cans from the plastic collar. Two cans were placed under my bed sheet. Then she handed two to Sergeant Jim Press who was in the bed next to me with a broken leg and two to Kevin. The fourth patient in our room declined to join us in a drink. He was a lieutenant in the Citizens Military Forces and also had a broken leg. He had earlier asked that we call him 'Sir' especially when he had visitors. Kevin and I, not too concerned about disciplinary repercussions, had told him to go and get stuffed. Apart from that he wasn't too bad to get along with. Jim was first to open his can and we heard the hissing noise as the gas escaped. Kevin looked towards the nurses' station and I looked towards the doctors' and sisters' lounge. The coast was clear. Opening the remaining cans with a little more caution we drank to each other's health.

Feeling a little apprehensive, Mum decided to head home

early but not before opening the second can for me. Kevin asked how we were going to dispose of the empties. I had expected Mum to stick around a little longer so I had not given any thought to the empties. Now we had a problem. My three colleagues in traction could not help, and despite my recent venture out of bed, a repeat performance was out of the question. As we discussed our problem, David Young, the Nasho who had been wounded when his platoon was hit with friendly artillery fire went passed in a wheelchair. He was seeing his girlfriend to the door. As he returned, I called him into our bay and asked if he would mind collecting the four empty cans and place them under the cradle on my bed. To our surprise he said that he thought he had heard the sound of cans opening. Surprisingly, he could not smell the beer as he passed by. We agreed that the normal hospital odour had masked the beer smell. With six empty beer cans in my bed I wondered how I was going to manage when the duty sister came along with my nightly medication. Jim suggested that we all fart when Sister arrived to further mask the smell of the cans and our beer breath.

I fell asleep soon after taking my medication. Waking up early the next morning with six empty beer cans in my bed, I kept an eye out for a friendly nurse to help me. George, the ward cleaner, came into view.

'Good morning George,' I said.

'Ah, gooda morning Johnny,' he replied in his heavy Greek accent.

I indicated to him to come closer. When he was beside my bed I asked if he could help me out and lifted my leg to reveal the empties under the sheet.

'Youa naughty boy Johnny, you gonna get me in the trouble if Matron finda this,' he said.

'Yes George, me too get in trouble,' I said. He left the bay and returned a few minutes later with a half full dry garbage bag and quietly placed the cans into it.

Over breakfast we commented on how well we had slept, agreeing that the beer had helped. Distribution and disposal had to be sorted out before we called on Mum again. When David called in to see how we had managed the previous night, we had our answer. David would be invited to join our little drinking club and he could dispose of the cans.

Mum was now more relaxed about our beer drinking and would bring in a dozen cans on request. Our method of distribution and disposal was working well. David would roll up in his wheelchair and collect the beer from Mum who would sit quietly by my bedside. Three cans each were quickly passed to Jim and Kevin. David stuck his cans in the pocket of his dressing gown and mine were safely tucked under my bedclothes. To ensure Mum only brought beer in on nights of least activity, we would place an order by phone with her. I would ask a nurse to ring home to see if Mum was coming to visit that evening. If she was, could she bring some Dim Sims with her. It was hard to keep a straight face when one nurse told me how much she liked Dim Sims, obviously hopeful of getting one that night from me.

On sunny winter days beds were regularly wheeled out onto the balcony. The view from the second floor, while not particularly attractive was a pleasant change from four plain walls. I enjoyed the warm feeling of sunshine on my body and face. The fresh air was most welcome. The all-pervading hospital smell was noticeably absent. As my bed was returned to my floor space in the bay, nurses undid a bandage from around my leg. Until now I had not noticed that it was also secured around the bed frame. When I asked a nurse why I was bandaged to the bed, she blurted something out and hurriedly left the bay. Harry Jenkins later explained that it was a precaution against falling off the balcony. Puzzled by the remark, I lay silently pondering the explanation when I heard Jim say, 'They don't want you jumping over the balcony.' Then Kevin reminded me of my remark to the RAAF crewman as we returned to Butterworth. Someone had taken me seriously and concluded that I was suicidal. Nothing could be further from my mind though.

Life was difficult and it would become more difficult as I got further along recovery road. Apart from a brief moment as I lay in the minefield, I couldn't recall ever giving in and giving dying a second thought. I knew that if I pulled the shutters down and switched off, it would all be over; there was no coming back! I might not have been the brightest star on the tree but I knew even if I had to stand on the sidelines and look on that life was interesting and I was willing to salvage whatever I could from the wreckage. Languishing indefinitely in hospital gives a person time to think and weigh up the options. Doctors may have had possession of my body as they skilfully repaired bone and tissue but my mind still belonged to me. How I would ultimately live my life was a decision only I could make. Not only had I defied the odds, I had enjoyed a number of small achievements. From small wins, big victories would come.

Buoyed by my recent achievements, I was feeling good with myself. I asked if I could visit the bathroom instead of having to use the totally humiliating and uncomfortable bedpan. My request was denied. I was still considered too weak according to the nursing staff. My buttocks had unhealed wounds and hardly any padding on them. Having to sit on my arse all day did not help the wounds heal. An inflatable rubber bedpan was now available to me most mornings. Kevin, still in traction, was eager to try it after I told him how much better it was than the stainless steel version, which we had christened the silver saddle. Unfortunately, only one rubber pan was available to the ward. Patients aware of its existence were requesting it as early at five thirty in the morning. Kevin called for it at five o'clock.

It must seem unbelievable that sitting on a toilet could be considered a major achievement by anyone other than a mother potty training a young child. But the first moment I was behind a closed door with privacy and a degree of comfort was as memorable as my first army parachute jump. Some assistance was still required because I couldn't manage the paperwork owing to the splint on my hand. However, just to sit alone, relax and savour the moment. What a delight!

I had an urgent need to visit the bathroom late one afternoon. Joe, an orderly, wheeled me down to the far end bathroom and placed me in a cubicle. As he closed the door he said he would be back in ten minutes. While waiting for him to return, I started to feel cold, sitting on the throne naked. My dressing gown was on the other side of the door on my wheelchair. I sat patiently, hearing toilets and the urinal being flushed regularly I realised that visiting hours had started. I was getting colder, so cold my teeth were starting to chatter. I called for help but no one responded. I called again and again, louder and louder, but still got no response. I heard the bathroom door open, footsteps then the urinal flush.

I yelled, 'Help, help.'

A voice said, 'Have you got a problem?'

'Yes, can you go get me some help?' I asked.

'Okay, won't be long,' the voice said. What seemed like a very long time passed then I heard the voice again. 'I can't find anyone to help.'

'That's just great,' I said, more to myself than the person on the other side of the door. 'Could you go to the kitchen around the corner and ask them for help?' I asked. Before I could ask for my dressing gown to be passed over the door, I heard the bathroom door open and close. Eventually, Victor the second orderly on duty and a student nurse rescued me.

Once I was back in my bed Victor wanted to know how I got to the toilet by myself.

'By myself my arse! Your offsider Joe took me down there and forgot me.'

Victor then told me he was the only orderly on duty. Joe had finished at six o'clock, that evening. The five-minute warning bell was ringing, visiting time was almost over. I must have been on the loo for well over an hour.

'Well, what a useless bastard he is,' I muttered. The prick had parked me on the loo, realised it was knockoff time and left, without telling anyone where I was. Lovely!

14
Squadron Casualties

Kevin returned from surgery with his left leg encased in fresh plaster from hip to toe and in traction. Once the plaster had fully dried and hardened Miss Gray-Wilson cut an oval shaped section out of the cast with a vibrating saw. The window exposed his mangled calf muscle that constantly oozed smelly sticky liquid. The viscosity of the liquid dripped so slowly that it resembled a stalactite formation. From my bed the odour was repulsive and the view distracting. I had to avert my eyes to avoid dry retching. Kevin was seriously embarrassed by the smell of the discharge. Toilet deodorisers were positioned around his bed but they had little effect. Pressure cans of air freshener were made available and Kevin sprayed regularly. After about three days, I set myself a challenge: to eat a meal without averting my eyes from Kevin's direction because the putrid smell occasionally put me off my food. Even though the discharge was cleaned away regularly nothing could be done about the smell. After several attempts I succeeded.

Many of Kevin's visitors were familiar with unpleasant sights and odours associated with farm work, but Kevin still discouraged them from going to the right side of his bed. Most complied, but not all. A bunch of his mates called in for a visit and one ignored Kevin's warning. After a very brief glance into Kevin's wound he fainted. He lay flat out on the floor until revived by nursing staff. A face-saving explanation was that it was not the wound that was disturbing – it was the association of the wound on a friend.

As I gained strength, I was given greater access to a wheelchair. Using my right foot to creep forward, I made it over to Kevin's bedside. Curiosity was getting the better of me; I wanted to see for myself why his leg attracted so much attention. Going towards Kevin's bed I held my breath, the odour was so much more noticeable. I steeled myself for one quick look. Dad had recently had a look and described the wound as being a hole that went right through his leg. One brief glance was all I could manage before backing away. Miss Gray-Wilson walked in as we were talking about Kevin's leg and explained that because it had only been three months since the enemy bullet had smashed the bone in Kevin's leg, it would need much more time immobilised to heal. Damaged flesh and tissue however, also needed treatment, which was why the window had been cut in the plaster. When we heard that maggots were being used to clean away the sloughing tissue around the wound I almost fainted.

Unable to sleep one night, I was passing the time away talking with Roy the duty nurse. He asked if I knew Terry Renshaw, a sapper in 1 Field Squadron. I certainly did, he was a Nasho from Wangaratta, Northern Victoria. Roy said he had recently attended Terry's funeral, as he was a friend of Terry's older brother. Immediately, I believed Terry had perished as a result of my behaviour. *Oh God, what had I done?* The eldest of my three sisters, Freda, called in to visit the next afternoon and I told her about Terry. She was aware of the funeral and said that Terry was not involved with my accident. Two other mine explosions had occurred, killing a number of sappers. Freda could not remember the names of the sappers involved. She did know that Ray Deed and Dennis Brooks were involved with my accident and had died from their injuries. *Two sappers were dead as a consequence of my actions.*

Miss Marie Nolan, the senior Red Cross representative at the hospital, offered to find out who the other sappers were. The next day Marie returned to my bedside and read out the following: exploding mines had killed Ray Deed, Dennis Brooks and Terry Renshaw from 1 Troop. Gregory Brady and John O'Hara from 2 Troop had died in another mine explosion. Corporal Tony Evans, Sappers Ashley Culkin and Eric Holst were wounded along with me. Sappers Lother Sempel and Bruce Bevan were wounded when Terry was killed. Glen Bartholomew had died from a gunshot wound at the Horseshoe nine days after we had shared a bottle of water. Six sappers from the squadron had been killed within three weeks. My friends who had regularly visited me at the 36 Evacuation Hospital had never once let a word slip about these casualties. Whoever had instructed them to withhold such shocking news from me must have fully understood my fragile state at the time. My admiration for my mates soared.

The mental anguish racing around my head was going to beat me into submission and failure if I could not deal with the reality of these tragedies. Feeling despondent was not going to help my friends or me, but what could I do? I would have to atone for my action! Would I be able to retain the respect my friends had shown me or would they grow to resent me?

The bell announcing the end of visiting time was a very welcome sound. Sleeping pills soon had me off in dreamland escaping the harsh realities of life. With hardly any education, my employment prospects were looking gloomy. My army training was not going to assist me to earn a living and I had not taken advantage of army education courses. A limited social life without romantic prospects was looking even more certain than ever. It was time I started to seriously consider my future, regardless of how painful I found the subject.

I had left Brunswick Boy's School with my Junior Certificate in December 1961 having only passed by the skin of my teeth. I had done well in most non-academic subjects, with the exception of English; all other subjects had been a total failure. Knowing my report card was guaranteed to earn me at least a tongue lashing from the old man, I had decided to destroy it. One of my classmates was mowing the school's front lawn. As I walked past him, I dropped my report card in front of the mower and he ran over it. Unfortunately, not only did the cylinder mower cut my report card into nice wavy strips, the headmaster was looking out of his window and had seen what I had done. After picking up all the pieces, I had to stick them back together. When I left the headmasters' office he warned me that he would be ringing home that evening to ensure that my parents received the report card.

In the Army I had to put in a lot of extra hours burning the midnight oil to get through my training. Practical exams were often not too difficult - although I never excelled in any particular field. My relatively shy personality ensured I was never comfortable when attention was focussed on me, whether it was in the field or the classroom. In addition to shyness, although I could swim, run, and play most ball sports reasonably well, I always felt awkward. To conceal my shyness and awkwardness I projected a humorous disposition. This behaviour ensured that I remained a follower rather than a leader in any team situation. But now, with a desire to overcome adversity and succeed in my rehabilitation, it was essential I put in the time and effort to take the lead.

15
Friendly Visitors

A middle-aged couple quietly stood at the entrance to Bay 3 and looked at the names on the beds before stepping towards me. I wondered who they could be. Mr and Mrs Brooks introduced themselves - Dennis Brooks' parents. *Oh, no, they've come to rip into me for killing their son.* With nowhere to hide I sat motionless waiting to hear what they would say. Mrs Brooks was a frail, sad looking lady burdened with immense grief. Mr Brooks looked a little sturdier but there was deep sadness behind his stoic appearance. I waited for them to talk, sitting quietly, suppressing the urge to scream out how sorry I was. When they spoke, there was no rage. In sad voices they wanted to know as much as I could tell them about Dennis. I told them how Dennis, Butch Carman and I had hootchied up together on the Horseshoe the week before the accident. I spoke of how we had been in adjacent beds for a while in hospital before he was transferred.

'I don't believe he was in any pain,' I said. 'I never heard him ask for medication. He was sleeping the last time I saw him.' It was all I could tell them before they left.

Regular visitors to the ward had become familiar and friendly towards Kevin and me. Other patients had been telling their visitors that we were wounded Diggers from Vietnam. Gifts of fruit and chocolate were frequently handed to us and very much appreciated. On one occasion, a little old lady brought in a shirt, which she thought I could wear without much difficulty. It was very thoughtful but definitely not a shirt of my choosing and it remained hanging on the back of my bed. Whenever the lady came by I told her how I looked forward to wearing the shirt when I was able to leave hospital.

Well-meaning visitors, many of them total strangers, handed me copies of *Reach for the Sky* with words of encouragement. I couldn't bring myself to tell them that not only had I read the book in Vietnam. I also had a growing number of copies in my bedside cabinet! I was starting to appreciate how people were genuinely interested in helping me. I looked forward to visitors. It had become like an endless surprise party, not knowing who was going to turn up next.

A soldier came towards me dressed in the Army's new winter uniform with Vietnam campaign ribbons on his chest. He was walking with a slight limp. When he got to me he threw his right leg up onto my bed. Balancing on one leg he said, 'Peter is the name and this is what a wooden leg looks like.' I was stunned by my visitor's audacious display. Peter was also eager to stay in the Army and was working at the Central Army Records Office at Albert Park near Melbourne.

Each Monday evening two members of the Limbless Soldiers' Association visited their members in hospital. Tony Twaits and David Young had joined the association and I had been invited to join. When they called on me they placed a packet of cigarettes on my bedside cabinet. I thanked them and said that I didn't smoke. I was invited to keep the cigarettes anyway and give them to a mate. One of the two operated the Limbless Soldiers' kiosk in the city, the very same kiosk that I walked past as a kid, straining my neck to see a limbless soldier. Both men had a leg off below the knee but it was hardly noticeable. Only the slightest limp indicated they had a problem walking. We discussed the problem of phantom pains that occurred regularly. I could actually feel my amputated limbs and it was the strangest of sensations. I was almost tricked into believing the limbs had regrown. Most amputees also experienced nerve storms. A nerve storm is a sudden painful sensation that strikes unexpectedly at your stump. On occasions the severity and suddenness of this has actually tossed me out of my bed. I was told that doctors didn't appear to understand the difference between a phantom pain and a nerve storm.

The men from the Limbless Soldiers' Association asked if I would like a visit from a member who had lost an arm. The following week, Mr Charlie Moor arrived. All the fingers on his left hand had lost a joint or two. His right hand was missing and he wore an artificial arm with a hook. Charlie told me it was best that I didn't try picking up eggs with my hook because after twenty years he still broke them. With a cheerful smile he told me beer glasses were okay, just to be sure to have the hook set at the right angle, otherwise I'd spill most of the beer down my shirt.

To demonstrate his dexterity, Charlie struck a match and lit a cigarette. Then he held a half-inch length of cigarette ash between the two sections of his hook without crushing it. Pulling back his coat sleeve he revealed an artificial arm covered in paint spots. *Had he decorated his arm to humour his children?* He noticed me looking at his paint-covered prosthesis.

'I'm a painter and paper hanger.'

'Oh yeah,' I said not believing him.

'I am, truly,' Charlie insisted with a straight face. By now Mum and Dad had arrived and Dad immediately recognised Charlie as the one-armed man he had previously seen painting the local doctor's surgery. Inspired by this most delightful and amusing visitor, I told myself that never again would I tell jokes about one-armed paper hangers.

Each Sunday afternoon new patients arrived at the hospital, carrying a small overnight bag and looking a little apprehensive. Most were due for surgery the next morning. With a spare bed in Bay 3, I would have a new person to chat with by the end of the day. A World War Two bloke came in and settled into bed 15, next to mine. As we ate dinner we talked a little about why he was in hospital. When he heard that I had returned from Vietnam, he told me his son had also recently returned and had been in 1 Field Squadron. When I told him that I was in 1 Field Squadron, he said, 'You might know Barry,' I looked at his nameplate on the bed. I could not believe my eyes. Barry, the hair cream thief? What an incredible coincidence!

After four months, three hospitals and three flights a former tent mate's father was now my new ward mate. I hoped that the father was more amiable then his awful, self-indulgent son. My dislike of Barry had intensified when I had to stay out on Operation Portsea for another two weeks because he had whinged so much. I heard how prior to embarking for Vietnam his dad had entrenched in him the necessity to have all injuries or illnesses recorded in army records. This information might one day be critical to making a successful claim for treatment and compensation with the Repatriation Department. Barry had taken notice and had ensured that every scratch, pimple or the slightest pain was reported to the Regimental Aid Post. He must have been a pain in the arse to the medics.

General Sir Thomas Daly, the Chief of the General Staff, had been calling in on Kevin and me each Wednesday for several weeks. We knew that his father was a patient in Ward East 2. Following a formal introduction, Sir Thomas had said, 'Call me Tom.' His father was no doubt his main reason for visiting the hospital, but Kevin and I were rather pleased to have such an important and high-ranking visitor. A knight of the realm no less!

My mate Charlie Lynn was now an officer cadet at the Officer Cadet School, Portsea and visited occasionally. On this occasion, I was lying back on my bed talking with the General, when Charlie turned up. Without thinking about the fact that they were both serving soldiers, I introduced Charlie and Tom by first name only.

'Good to meet you mate,' said Charlie, as he reached across to shake hands.

'Pleased to meet you,' replied the General. 'I'll be off now John, you two will have plenty to talk about.'

'Have you known Jethro long?' Charlie asked.

The General explained how he had only recently met me while visiting his father in the hospital.

'We only know him as Jethro in the Army,' Charlie was now telling the General. 'I'd like to visit more often but the bastards are pushing us pretty hard.' Without drawing a breath Charlie expressed his opinion about a number of his instructors at Portsea. We heard how several were showing an extraordinary interest in Charlie. The General listened as Charlie carried on.

'Yes, they appear to be pissed off about me being a former Nasho, with Vietnam service, and not only do I have an army driving license, I'm endorsed to drive almost every vehicle in the Army.'

'Oh, so you are still in the Army?' asked the General.

'Yes, I came home early from Vietnam after being selected to attend the Officer Training School Portsea,' Charlie proudly said. 'What about you? Done any time in the services?'

'Yes, I'm in the Army too,' the General said with a sparkle in his eyes.

'Well, you know what it's like. There is always someone trying to shaft you.' Before I could get a word in to warn Charlie who he was talking to, he was off again.

'What Corp are you in? Do you have any rank?'

With a thumping heart and a sweaty brow I was waiting to

hear the General's response. He nonchalantly announced he was the Army Chief of General Staff. Charlie's face transformed from a cheerful cheeky smile to a look of: 'Oh Shit.' He was speechless.

The General bid us farewell and gave Charlie a look that said, 'I'll you see again!' After a slight pause allowing for the General to move out of earshot, Charlie looked at me and burst out laughing, then set to abusing me in the best Digger language he could muster. What a remarkable afternoon - entertained by the highest-ranking soldier in the Australian Army and an officer cadet. You couldn't get much lower than a cadet.

16
The Sunshine Club and Weekend Leave

August 1967

With no visiting hours on Wednesday nights, I was surprised when a lady came in and offered coffee.

'Milk coffee?' she asked. 'You were asleep last month when we arrived so we didn't disturb you.' She introduced herself as Mrs England from the Sunshine Club.

The club was a small group of ladies who had either served in one of the services during World War Two or were mothers of former servicemen. Some of the ladies brought along their family members when they were available. The Sunshine Club had been visiting the hospital, specifically Ward West 2, on the first Wednesday of the month for many years. Milk coffee sounded really good but I would need it served in my special cup. Mrs England returned a few minutes later with my cup but it was too hot for me to hold. She helped me drink my coffee and I listened to her talk about the ladies in the club. What a patriotic bunch they were! I expressed my gratitude for their consideration and assured Mrs England I would be looking forward to the club's visit next month.

Concluding his Friday examination of my wounds, Mr Hodge again encouraged me to have a day at home over the weekend. He warned me to take it easy and not to drink too much while away from the hospital. On Saturday morning my younger sister Sue and her boyfriend Angie drove me home. As Angie was helping me get from the car to the wheelchair, Mum rushed out and excitedly started issuing warnings to be careful. We slowly headed towards the front door and I heard a variety of phrases spoken in Maltese giving thanks and praising the Lord and the Virgin Mary. Although I don't speak the language I am able to recognise it when it is spoken.

The smell of home cooking wafted from the kitchen. Mum had prepared some of my favourite foods: baked macaroni, large stuffed zucchinis and a traditional Maltese *Pudina*, a delicious bread and cocoa pudding. Eagerly, I sampled some of the dishes. Mum was illiterate in both English and Maltese and so unable to read a recipe. She depended entirely on memory and years of practice when cooking. Despite her lack of education I don't ever recall her cooking being a failure. On this special occasion, Mum was disappointed with how little I ate. Still unable to go to the toilet unaided, I was desperate to avoid the need to go while at home. I was working on the theory that if you don't put it in – it won't come out.

That night, I looked at my naked body for the first time in a full-length mirror. I was startled by my appearance. It looked like shrapnel had entered my left side tearing into the front of my left thigh ripping off my leg. Where my left leg once was, was now a small firm round bundle of flesh. My family jewels were hanging lower than my stump, the scar line testament to how close I had been to becoming a eunuch. Twisting a little and looking over my shoulder I could see the back of my right leg, it had many scars from my bum to my foot and huge chunks of flesh were missing. Shrapnel had also scarred the back of my left hand and arm. Across my abdomen two enormous scars stood out like railway tracks.

Where the restraining clamps had once held me together were four very distinct rows of holes. I looked like I'd been shot with a machine gun. My belly button was now misshapen and scar tissue indicated where shrapnel had entered my abdomen. My arms reminded me of a clock face with one arm shorter than the other. Black shrapnel still imbedded in my body from head to toe made me look like I'd been sprinkled all over with black pepper. Now I could understand why Kevin often called me leopard bum. What I saw was rather frightening. Doctors had explained earlier that the pieces of shrapnel lodged in my body and limbs were too numerous to surgically remove however, some pieces would work their way out over time.

My sleep that night was constantly interrupted by really vivid dreams. Reoccurring images of me sleeping on a park bench kept waking me. In another dream I was about 40 years old and still living at home, dressed in brown corduroy trousers and a maroon and grey panelled cardigan, sitting watching TV with Mum and Dad. Lack of sleep left me listless and drowsy the next day. Wheelchair access around home was limited and restrictions on my ability to access the toilet and bathroom were exasperating. I was eager to return to the familiarity and comfort of hospital, my sanctuary. Knowing Mum would be disappointed if I returned too early, I arranged with Angie to collect me around mid-afternoon. Over lunch it was impossible to stop Mum loading up my plate with scrumptious food. The temptation to abandon caution was great but I stuck to my original plan, and ate sparingly.

As we finished lunch Blue Lisle, who had taken me out for a beer when I was home on pre-embarkation leave, called in for a chat. His son John was now a paraplegic as a consequence of a car accident. Over a cold beer, Blue started telling me how much better off I was than his son. He had no money, no job and worse of all, the loss of all sexual function. Blue constantly referred to the benefits of being a 'TPI' and how lucky I was to have the Repat (the Commonwealth Repatriation Department) look after me. I certainly felt lucky to be alive, but otherwise I was looking at a bleak future full of uncertainties. Listening to Blue making comparisons between his son John and myself became quite annoying. Not because of the comparisons but I was having difficulty following what he was saying.

I asked Blue, 'What's a TPI?'

'The best rate of pension you can receive, and a load of other benefits,' he replied.

Still none the wiser I asked, 'What does TPI stand for?'

'Totally and Permanently Incapacitated, It's a pension paid to Diggers who are so badly disabled they can no longer go to work.'

I had a desire to return to work one day and said so.

'Don't be too hasty to reject anything the Repat offers you lad,' Blue added. 'The Army would still be paying you; your bank account must be looking good. Not like my John, poor bugger,' he said.

Until now I had not thought about money. My army pay was accumulating in my pay book. A sergeant from the Army Cadre office at the hospital had visited me soon after admission and advised me to only withdraw a small amount to cover immediate needs. Before Blue could carry on with the conversation I excused myself and escaped to the bedroom. When I joined the Army in 1964 I allocated 10 quid (20 dollars) a fortnight to my mother to assist with household expenses. Not that I had any altruistic view of my responsibilities to the family. Mum had always taken a substantial portion of whatever money I had earned delivering morning papers before school and later when I started work. While on leave prior to going to Vietnam, money did not appear to be a problem at home. I had asked Mum to open a bank account for me and deposit the 20 dollars each fortnight. Mum agreed and gave me the impression she was delighted I intended to save sufficient money to buy a new car on my return.

I now asked Mum for my bank account, keen to see the

amount saved. I anticipated an amount of at least $280 and intended depositing most of my accrued army pay, in preference to leaving it in my pay book. Mum was unable to find my deposit book and said she would bring it in to me. She never did. No bank account had been opened. Mum had chosen to keep using my money for her own use. Annoyed with my mother's deception I cancelled the allocation and arranged with Sue Grey, the Red Cross representative on the ward, to open an account and deposit my money each payday.

For days all I could think about was my conversation with Blue. *Why should I trouble myself wondering about what I will do once I leave hospital?* According to Blue, money would not be a problem. Dreaming about a life free of money worries was enjoyable until I had more visions of myself sitting at home watching TV with Mum and Dad. Money might solve some of my problems, such as buying a new car and nice clothes, but I knew there was more to life. *Would I be able to dress myself? Would I ever walk or drive? Would I ever know again the sensual feeling of a girl?* The frequency of my disturbing dreams was starting to bother me.

17
Beginning to Have Fun

Mr Jenken, the hospital's social director and manager of St John's Theatre, regularly organised trips for patients to the football and the races. I had agreed to go to the football but after a terribly restless sleep I was not so willing. Disabled people were a regular sight around a hospital and I was adjusting to being looked at as I moved around the grounds. At the Melbourne Cricket Ground (MCG) where there would be thousands of spectators, it would be a very different experience. *Was I ready to face being in the midst of such a large crowd? Would people stare at me? Would they point and talk about me?* I would be on unfamiliar ground with nowhere to hide.

Nurse Fay, a stunningly attractive girl, only recently assigned to the ward, came along with a wheelchair and slowly I moved from my bed. Fay noticed my lack of enthusiasm and asked if I was all right. I told her how I was feeling. With a meaningful tone in her voice, she said the day would come when I had to go out, I could not hide here forever. Her words were challenging. With a gut full of apprehension I headed down to the front entrance. David Young was on crutches and talking to a number of casually dressed nurses, who were also heading to the football. A furniture van with a rear ramp parked nearby was our transport. When all the wheelchairs were secured in position, we set off. At the MCG we were directed to an area reserved for our group. David handed me his crutches, then gripping the handles of my wheelchair he started hopping along behind me. He appeared to have no difficulty propelling me forward. We zigzagged our way through the crowd, until we reached our seating.

Watching the game between Melbourne and Footscray reminded me rather painfully of more things in life I had lost. Never again would I be able to run, jump or kick a football. If I was to ever marry and have children, I would never be able to play footy or any other game in the backyard with them. As the superbly fit and agile players tackled each other in pursuit of the ball, it all started to become too much for me to watch. Determined not to become depressed, I told myself that I was never in the same league as these players anyway and so I had not lost anything. Playing with children was not an issue at the moment either. Right now, I should enjoy myself. One of the nurses had a cold beer and a hot meat pie for David and me, which I really enjoyed. We returned to the hospital after watching Melbourne score a close win over Footscray. I had scored a pie and a beer and had the pleasure of some delightful company. Dinner and an early night were all I needed to finish off a challenging day.

September brought about a slight improvement in the weather. My general health continued to improve and I enjoyed many outings. I had been to the football, horse racing and to the drive-in movies and our secret beer drinking continued undetected. The only low point occurred while sitting in the bathtub having my hair washed. The orderly helping me bathe pushed my head under the water to rinse off the soapsuds. An excruciating pain down the side of my face had me scrambling out of the bath screaming in agony. Stunned by my reaction, the orderly raced out of the bathroom as I thrashed about on the floor. He returned with a nursing sister and they helped me into a wheelchair and returned me to my bed. An urgent appointment with Mr Sykes an ear, nose, and throat specialist (ENT) was scheduled for the next day. A perforated eardrum that would require surgery was diagnosed.

Occasionally, I had the use of a wheelchair, but could not push myself along too well without hands. I had to depend on someone willing to take me for a ride. Ray, whom I had seen very little of since we arrived at the end of June, called in to visit. His back had healed and he was to be discharged from hospital any day. He suggested we go and visit Darryl. He was happy to push me, so off we went. Entering Ward West 1 a tall slim nurse asked if we were there to visit Gunner Bentley. Out of curiosity, we said yes and were shown to his bed. Greg Bentley was also a Vietnam casualty who had suffered shocking abdominal injuries. He was sitting up in bed and appeared happy to have visitors. He told us he was wounded by friendly artillery fire while on patrol as an artillery radio operator. He had been with Delta Company 6 RAR earlier in the year and was wounded in the incident that claimed the life of Company Sergeant Major Jack Kirby, who had been awarded the Distinguished Conduct Medal (DCM) for his bravery at the Battle of Long Tan. The nurse who had shown us the way returned and requested we move on, as she had to assist Greg with his colostomy bag. Before leaving we asked where we would find Darryl.

As we were about to enter Darryl's room, a sister challenged our presence in the ward. She really had her knickers in a twist.

'What are you doing here,' she snapped.

'We've come to see Darryl,' Ray said.

'Well, it's not visiting hours yet so get back to wherever you came from,' she yelled at us. We turned quickly and made our way back towards the door. As we were passing Greg's bay the nurse we had spoken to earlier said, 'Come back tomorrow. She won't be on.' The next morning we called in on Darryl. It was obvious

Darryl was still a misery guts so we said goodbye as quickly as we had arrived.

Staff and patients jealously protected ward or department wheelchairs, as they were scarce as hen's teeth most times you needed one. I asked Harry Jenkins the ward head nurse, if it was possible to secure a chair for my personal use within the hospital. Days later, after believing he had forgotten me, he turned up with a dilapidated green wheelchair. It was old, bulky and lacking any ward identification. I was a little disappointed with the chair but pleased Harry had remembered. I took myself for a ride, crawling rather slowly forward. However, because the small wheels were at the back if I used my leg to push myself backwards, I achieved a reasonable pace and was able to steer the chair by wiggling my bum on the seat. Looking over my shoulder was the only difficulty. After a few trial runs along the corridor I was satisfied. I parked the chair by my bed and sat in it whenever I could, hoping to establish ownership. I also thought its crappy appearance would be sufficient deterrence to staff and patients alike from wanting to use it.

When permitted, I would head off exploring the hospital grounds. Initially, I felt a little silly roaming around backwards in a wheelchair, dressed in a pair of shorts, slipper and hospital dressing gown. My unique style of movement attracted many strange looks from staff and visitors. Appreciating my freedom, I disregarded the inquisitive glances and raced uphill and downhill, zoomed along the duckboards backwards, silently and effortlessly, passing pedestrians and others in wheelchairs. The duckboards were a covered walkway about eight feet (2.2metres) wide and linked all buildings like a maze crisscrossing the hospital grounds. One area not covered by the duckboards was the doctors' and nurses' quarters located towards the front of the hospital grounds. I made my way along a pathway towards the accommodation area. A sign saying 'Swimming Pool' appealed to me. Unable to locate a pathway heading in the right direction, a cross-country ride seemed the only option. With great difficulty, I pushed myself up a steep grassy bank. The pool was now only a short ride across the lawn. The area was deserted but I had no difficulty imagining young nurses frolicking in scanty bikinis. I would definitely return when the weather improved.

Kevin was now allowed out of bed and also had the use of a wheelchair. It had a front footrest that folded upwards to support his plaster-encased leg. Together we roamed the grounds ensuring that we were always at the Red Cross Centre in time for morning or afternoon tea. Miss Nolan and her staff made Kevin and I most welcome, as they did all patients.

Receiving weekly Holy Communion soon became a casualty of our newfound freedom. When we arrived in June we agreed to receive communion once a week. Each Tuesday Father Ryan, the hospital Catholic priest, would turn up at our bedside before breakfast and serve communion. As my health improved I felt less inclined to receive his ministry. Now, after putting in big days roaming the hospital, sleeping uninterrupted until breakfast had become a priority.

One afternoon I returned from the limb factory fitted with a new artificial arm, Nurse Margaret excitedly rushed towards me opening her arms to give me a friendly hug. Unfortunately for Margaret, my nice shiny new hook opened as I held it towards her. It straddled her right tit and unintentionally closed. Margaret pulled back before I thought to open the hook. As her uniform pulled away, the hook slipped forward pinching her nipple. Margaret raced off to the bathroom rubbing her chest. The mishap became the talk of the ward with many patients offering to kiss Margaret's tit better; I believe all offers were rejected.

September was a good month. I was getting about meeting people and feeling good with myself. Regularly, I went into the next bay to visit the blokes there. They too had a beer supply established. Only problem was they liked drinking the large size Fosters cans. To hold them I had to wear my artificial arm. Believing the coast was clear late Sunday afternoon I was happily drinking a can when Sister Johnson, a committed Mormon walked into the bay. Unable to conceal my beer, she headed over to take it off me spouting the evils of the demon drink as she approached me. I was not about to let her take it. As she reached for my can I shrugged my left arm forwards, and in doing so, unintentionally opened the hook and released the can. It fell to the floor. Well shaken, beer came spurting out and the can spun wildly across the floor, to the amusement of all six patients looking on. Sister was now on her hands and knees reaching for the can under a bed. I tumbled out of my chair and reached for it too but it was a little too far from me. I headed under the bed after my precious beer.

There we were the two of us, scrambling under the bed seriously determined to capture the elusive can. I wanted to drink what was left – Sister wanted to empty it down the sink. The can ran out of energy and came to a stop. Empty of its content, I was no longer interested and returned to my wheelchair. Sister was more than a little angry with me. She began shaking a finger at me for creating a mess. I accepted the tongue lashing with the most contrite look I could feign. Not only was she a good-looking sort and a fine nurse, at least three other blokes were concealing beer cans under their bedding.

18
Mobility can be Dangerous

At least six younger patients from the ward now had access to wheelchairs and regularly assembled to roam the hospital grounds via the duckboards in our little convoy. Meetings at the hospital gymnasium had become popular, and it was located close to the Red Cross Centre, which was a reliable venue for refreshments. With my artificial arm I was able to hold a bar with small weights attached and exercise my arms. There were plenty of spills and crashes as we played a variety of ball games in our chairs.

As a group we could not resist the temptation to race each other along the duckboards. Travelling backwards on the downhill section I discovered that I could take corners tighter and faster by pressing onto the middle railing of the handrail structure that boarded the walkway. With no hands on the propulsion wheel of the chair, I didn't have to worry about injuring my hands, unlike the others. Their caution allowed me the opportunity to pass on the inside as they slowed down to take the corner. Once in front I hogged the middle of the pathway and obstructed their progress. My steering ability had developed superbly. With just a twitch of my bum, I was able to effect a change of direction. My braking ability however, was a little untidy, pressing my foot down as hard as I could to stop safely, or alternatively, steering into a wall in an emergency.

Returning to the main multi-storey building from the duck-boards we used one of two self-opening doors either side of the main foyer. A pressure plate in the floor operated the doors. I had developed a method of opening them without having to stop and wait. First I crossed over the pressure plate from one side turned away from the door did a U turn and raced on through. One afternoon Kevin was looking out the window and saw me crossing the road as I approached the walkway. Knowing I always took the right hand side down the walkway. He raced to the automatic doors and reached up with his walking stick, turning off the power. As I raced down and crossed over the pressure mat, I did my snazzy turn and raced towards the doorway. To my surprise, it did not open and with no time to press my foot down hard to stop, I slammed into the closed door. My head was thrown back on impact. Fortunately, it did not strike the door. I felt as if a truck had hit me. I was stunned and in total disbelief that I could have misjudged my entrance so badly. Once I got my breath back, I sheepishly looked around but no one appeared to have noticed my blunder. *How could I have missed the pressure plate?* Attempting to regain my composure before anyone came along I noticed movement on the other side of the door. I could just make out Kevin, who was reaching up towards the power point. Instantly I understood what the bastard had done to sabotage my normally impressive entry. While I was abusing him in some of the foulest language I could muster for the serious harm he could have caused me, he could not stop laughing. He only wanted to know if I'd damaged my wheelchair and bemoaned the fact he had not had his camera with him.

When I was first allowed out of bed Miss Grey-Wilson had

brought along a four-wheeled padded trolley for me to lie face down on and paddle myself around. The idea was to strengthen my abdominal muscles. For amusement I would hitch it behind Kevin's wheelchair and he would tow me around the ward. Ostensibly, Kevin was working on strengthening his arms by pulling the extra weight. Whenever the passageway was clear, he would race out into the foyer with me in tow and turn sharply back into the ward. The exhilaration produced by the whiplash effect gave me a real buzz. On the last occasion we used the trolley, Kevin raced out into the foyer and did two complete circles before straightening up, impressing our small audience. The speed generated was surprisingly fast as I whipped around on my trolley. I saw the stairway looming in front of me and I chickened out, opting to fall off and let the empty trolley race towards the steps. I lay motionless on the foyer floor listening to the noise as the trolley crashed and banged its way to the floor below. Admonished severely by the sister in charge that night was punishment enough I thought, but she took our toy and went home. My trolley was never seen again.

Behind the wheel

Finding the keys to Dad's Falcon car was too much temptation for me one weekend when I was visiting home. I had no trouble convincing my brother-in-law Keith that it would be good to see if I could manage to drive. Keith helped me down the back steps and into the car. Then he drove to the deserted housing estate nearby. It was all nicely laid out with sealed streets and pathways, but no houses. Trying a number of positions around the steering wheel, I opted to hold on with my thumb and palm while pressing my right stump against the wheel. My right hand had been amputated just above the wrist, so I had plenty of forearm left to apply pressure with.

I drove in and out of every street available. Turning at slow speed was a little difficult but not beyond me. Initially, Dad was supportive of me driving. After all, I had Keith with me and I guessed he admired my spirit. Excessive confidence however, put an abrupt end to my driving when I attempted to take a corner too fast. As the steering wheel turned freely I failed to compensate by reducing my grip accordingly and lost control. Keith reacted quickly and grabbed the wheel avoiding further injury to me, or the car that had bounced unceremoniously over the kerb. Dad had seen my little blunder as he was looking over the back fence and put an end to my driving.

19
Army Medical Board and IQ Test

The Army sent a car to take me to Southern Command Personnel Depot at Watsonia. I had an appointment with Doctor Boutcher, a civilian employed by the Army. Once he completed his medical examination he saw fit to reprimand me for not wearing my artificial arm. I tried to explain that it was still very uncomfortable. Without the slightest indication that he appreciated my difficulty, he rather brusquely told me that much in life would be uncomfortable. We talked about my future. I had spent many sleepless nights pondering what lay ahead and what I would like to do. It all looked rather bleak but I was confident that I would master my artificial limbs sufficiently to gain some independence. Education, or the lack of it, would be my biggest obstacle to holding down a job, any job imaginable, within my physical capabilities. Doctor Boutcher told me the Army would not have a job for me but would keep me on the payroll while undergoing rehabilitation. Adding more dollars to my bank account had an instant appeal. A cheque from the Repatriation Department had started arriving each fortnight boosting my savings. Watching the total grow was encouraging and each time the balance reached another thousand, I bought a box of chocolates for Sue my friendly Red Cross lady who attended to the shopping and banking needs of the patients on Ward West 2. Okay, I was not exactly the last of the big spenders but Sue appreciated my little gift.

Returning to hospital after my visit to the Personnel Depot I was in no shape nor enthusiastic about going down to the Psychology Centre after lunch. I went reluctantly, more out of curiosity than a desire to comply. I had no idea what a psychology test was about. Mr Rosenberg introduced himself as a psychologist and with him was a young, neatly dressed bloke, who was a psychology student. I was told the student would be observing the test. I answered questions about ink splashes and listed jobs that would appeal to me in order of preference assuming that I could have any job I wanted. *If only life was that easy*! Tests with blocks and puzzles challenging my ability to pick up and place objects in their correct position within a certain time also tested my frustration levels. When asked to name three Australian Prime Ministers, I thought, *too easy*. Barton, I remembered from school was the first, Holt was the current one and Menzies had been Prime Minister for almost all the time I had been in Australia. There had to be a trap. I hesitated too long. The next question was asked before I answered. Arithmetic questions definitely blew me away. Rosenberg and his student had a little chat between themselves then I was dismissed.

Mrs McLeod, the senior social worker at the hospital, had been visiting and talking with me for many weeks. One of her major concerns was my reluctance to go home on leave and when I did go home, I only stayed there for a few hours. I was unable to get across to her the difficulty I had with my mother. Mum's extreme protectiveness was smothering and stifled my attempts to fend for myself. The only real joy I derived from going home was Mum's cooking.

Mrs McLeod suggested that I have a talk with Doctor Benson,

a former World War Two RAAF pilot. He had studied medicine after the war and now was a rehabilitation specialist. I agreed and it wasn't long before Doctor Benson called in to see me. He was a tall, slim man with wavy hair and a most pleasant smile. After a long bedside talk we agreed I should no longer rely on sleeping pills. He arranged for me to go and sit in the ward kitchen and read whenever I could not sleep. Regularly, I took myself to the kitchen during the night. Little reading was done because domestic staff and junior nurses congregated there while patients slept. Over a cup of hot tea and toasted sandwiches I had many enjoyable conversations until I was ready to return to bed. Our next meeting was in Doctor Benson's office. He had the results of my recent psychology test and looked concerned. Rosenberg had concluded that I behaved childishly to conceal or avoid the reality of my disabilities. I didn't see myself acting childishly. I have always had a sense of humour; some would say, at times a twisted sense of humour. Laughter was a good way of easing tension.

This disclosure got well and truly under my skin and I asked to read the report myself but as it was contrary to policy my request was refused. Appreciating Doctor Benson's position did not prevent me from saying what I thought about the policy. Everyone on the hospital staff including any student nurse, student physiotherapist and office staff could read about John Thompson but not John himself. 'What a load of crap,' I said. I was about to storm out of his office. Doctor Benson said he understood my concerns and he felt that much of the report was wrong. He invited me to prove it. What a challenge! He may as well have asked me to climb Mount Kosciusko. *What hope did I have against the hospital?*

Rosemary Fleming, my lovely occupational therapist, had a more encouraging opinion about my abilities noted in my file. Her opinion was based on my enthusiasm and the physical results I had achieved. We agreed to continue working on a variety of ways to deal with simple everyday issues that I would encounter: such as dressing, eating and bathroom activities. Rosemary had already arranged for me to receive coaching in arithmetic from OT students at the hospital. Several times a week I would take myself down to the Occupational Therapy Centre and spend one or two hours with one of the students to improve my basic arithmetic.

20
A Mixed Fortune

Despite continuous visits and fittings at the limb factory all attempts had failed to provide me with a suitable artificial leg. My stump was too short to accommodate a suction bucket that would hold the leg in place, even with the use of an over-the-shoulder strap. Regularly, my hopes soared when a temporary leg stayed on as I walked between the parallel bars. *Walking was looking good.* However, the moment I sat down I heard a blurting sound (like a beer induced fart). The suction was lost and the leg fell off. Not only was I disappointed, the dedicated limb makers who were trying so hard, to get me up and walking were also disappointed. When we heard Doctor Hughes, who was in charge, say he believed I could not be fitted with a leg; it almost broke my last thread of hope. Most of the limb makers at the factory were amputees themselves, many having lost their limbs as prisoners of war twenty-five years earlier. You could never meet a more determined bunch of fellows and they were not ready to concede defeat.

Ivor Appleton, the Centre foreman, suggested we try a style of leg known as a Canadian Hip. Doctor Hughes did not agree believing that my stump was too long.

First my stump was too short now it was too long, when do I get a break? All I could understand was that the style of prosthesis being talked about was only suitable for an amputation that included the hip joint. I still had my hip but only a very short piece of thigh-bone was connected to it.

Arriving back at the hospital I saw a brand new fold-up wheelchair parked by my bed with a label identifying it as my personal property - courtesy of the Repatriation Department. Being confined to a wheelchair for the rest of my life was not what I had planned. The notion held no appeal despite my enthusiasm for my old wheelchair as an efficient mode of transport around the hospital.

Two more operations were scheduled, one to repair my damaged eardrum, the other to have bone grafted into my finger between the first and second joint. Both were going to seriously curtail my freedom to roam the hospital for an indefinite period. While I could, I'd spend much of the day exploring the hospital grounds. Returning from one excursion I met the nurse who assisted Ray and I when we were visiting Darryl: Jill. She was on her way to start her shift on Ward West 1. I took an instant liking to her and started chatting away about nothing in particular. As we rode the lift I asked her if she ever went to the movies. She said, 'Occasionally.'

Whether I was deluding myself or not I did not know but I was determined to try and win her over. I had nothing to lose and plenty to gain. It was about time fortune started to turn for me. For three days I strategically positioned myself along the path between the nurses' quarters and the hospital foyer. Around mid afternoon, shift change, I would meet Jill as she made her way to or from work. Convinced Jill was showing more than a little interest in me I asked her to accompany me to the next performance at the theatre. When she agreed it was a real boost to my confidence. I could not wait for Wednesday to come round.

It was only a small crowd so we had no trouble finding a seat out of the way. I was hopefully going to engage Jill in a little kissing and cuddling. Mr Jenken the theatre manager soon put an end to my plotting when he insisted the audience move to the very front and centre seats to present a more compact group for the cast. My amorous intentions evaporated when we relocated as requested. After the show we made our way along the duckboards. I mentioned that I was aware of a suitable place to stop for a little canoodling if we had time. Jill either didn't hear me or simply ignored me and never responded. As we reached the foyer Jill said if I wanted to go to the movies the following Monday, she would collect me from the ward.

Mr Hodge accompanied by Mr Keon Cohen, an eminent orthopaedic surgeon in Melbourne, examined my finger and told me that they would perform a bone graft on Monday. Bone would be taken from my wrist and placed between the first and second knuckle. After surgery I would have to stay in bed for at least a week to minimise the risk of injuring my hand. That was going to be hard to take. Back to the humiliation of bedpans and being bathed in bed. My scheming to seduce Jill had to be temporarily shelved. I was warned not to expect too much improvement in the finger but with only a finger and thumb on my mangled left hand I was desperately hopeful of gaining some additional movement. Hopefully, I'd be able to dress myself without assistance. With the aid of my artificial arm and my thumb, I could accomplish most tasks associated with dressing despite the presence of the splint on my hand but buttons remained beyond my ability

Over the weekend I underwent a variety of procedures in preparation for surgery: X-rays of my hand and lungs, blood tests and a host of medicines were injected into my bum. By Sunday morning I was well and truly off my food. Personally, I thought that was a good thing as I was not too eager to use the bedpan again. I was sticking to my theory of not putting anything in – so nothing would come out.

Late in the afternoon I wheeled myself next door to spend a little time with Mr Watson: a First World War Digger who had lost both his eyes. Despite his blindness, on his return to Australia he had attended university and become a physiotherapist. As we discussed the merits of our fancied horses in Tuesday's Melbourne Cup field, I became aware of his walking frame. I stood and rested on it for no reason other than curiosity. I discovered that I could comfortably support myself, although the wheels did pose a degree of danger. I returned to my bed and thought about modifications that would enable me to use crutches. Next time I went to the limb factory, I would mention it to Ivor Appleton.

After surgery on Monday morning all I wanted to do was sleep but nurses had to monitor my progress and I had to pee before they would leave me alone. They hovered close by until I delivered for them. I needed help to perform this very basic task. The only part of my hand visible was the thumb protruding from fresh bandages. The hand hurt and was extremely swollen, it was not going to be much good to me for a few days.

Tuesday 7 November
I wanted to read the papers to catch up with the latest Melbourne Cup news. With my hand out of action I relied on Kevin to read aloud whatever he thought was relevant. It was irritating to lose my independence again so soon after mastering ways and means to care for myself. I feared frustration would again affect my attitude. Miss Grey-Wilson called in and after looking at my hand told me that a new splint would be ready by Friday. Once it was fitted I would be free to roam. This encouraging news eased my anxiety and I fell asleep. Shouting and cheering woke me as Roy Higgins on Red Handed won the race that stops a nation.

On Wednesday night the Sunshine Club arrived and I met one of Mrs England's younger volunteers. Sandra was easy on the eye, petite with black hair and a student nurse at a nearby hospital. Keen to chat her up, I exaggerated the amount of assistance I needed to hold my cup. My ploy worked well, and I was able to monopolise Sandra's presence in the ward until Mrs England needed help in the kitchen. I saw nothing wrong in using my disabilities to my advantage, there had to be some benefit to all the pain I was going through.

Thursday night visiting hours were over and I was looking forward to a good night's sleep. Tomorrow I should be cleared to get up and about again. A nurse told me that Maureen at the enquiries desk in the foyer had just rung to say that a couple of blokes were looking for me. *They couldn't come up, but I could go down.* Once the nurse was out of sight I took off in my old reliable wheelchair. Kevin Smith and Ken Oakes, two mates from Vietnam were standing at the desk grinning like alley cats after they have swallowed the canary; only on this occasion it was a few beers. The third bloke with them was Ken's brother. Maureen was shutting down her desk and suggested we find a more isolated place before security turned up and moved the boys on.

We headed to the car park and decided to make a quick trip up the road to the Tower Hotel to buy a couple of six packs. Returning to the hospital, we sat and talked as we drank our beer. Suddenly, a security guard rapped on the car window and informed me I was in a heap of trouble. It was after midnight and I had been reported missing when the ward staff failed to find me. No sooner had I got back into my bed then I was stuck with two needles in my bum; one was the nine o'clock needle I'd missed earlier. Being with my mates and listening to their yarns about my old troop filled my head with enthusiasm and determination to get out of this place sooner rather than later.

A midweek race meeting was on and Mr Jenken had organised his furniture van to take staff and patients. David Young, Kevin Stephens and I were going. We all dressed in civilian clothes. After hours of practise in front of a mirror with my artificial arm and thumb I could manage to tie a reasonable Windsor knot. I looked rather dapper, as did Kevin and David. A small group of nurses were also having a day at the races. On arrival at the track we soon had the girls place our bets and collect a beer for us. In return, we shouted them lunch. My chosen horses were as slow as the hours passing before surgery when you are fasting but regardless of my lack of success, I had a good time.

Back at the hospital we met Father Byrne who told Kevin and me how smart we looked all dressed up. He was in a hurry but said he looked forward to seeing us later in the chapel. Confused by his remark, we asked Mr Jenken what was going on in the chapel that evening. He informed us that the newly ordained Archbishop of Melbourne was saying mass. Not particularly interested in going to chapel or meeting the Archbishop we made our way back to the ward and changed our clothes. Dinner was being served but we did not receive a meal. We were told our dinner was being saved for us until we returned from chapel. It seemed Kevin and I were going to mass whether we wanted to or not.

We headed down to the chapel and Father Byrne came over and expressed his disappointment that we had turned up in our hospital gowns.

'You made the effort to dress smartly to go to the races, but could not make the effort to dress up for the Archbishop,' he said in a most abrasive tone. Our reply that we had only just learnt of His Grace's visit did not wash. Reluctantly, we entered the chapel and found an out of the way corner to park ourselves. We were very impressed by the crowd and arrived just in time to get a position that allowed a full view of proceedings. As a child, although I may not have followed the mass (especially when it was in Latin), I enjoyed the colour and movement of the event.

Archbishop Knox entered the chapel. He looked grand in his robes of office with Father Byrne and other clergy assisting looking like the poor cousins. We waited for the service to start and joked about how we would react if we were asked to kiss his ring. The Archbishop gave a most interesting and humorous talk in which he recalled his brief experience with the Puckapunyal Army Camp, about an hour drive north of Melbourne. Holy Communion was served and the line of worshippers appeared to be endless. At the conclusion of the service Father Byrne introduced Kevin and me to the Archbishop, thankfully, we received no invitation to kiss his ring.

21
Romance

Monday 4 December 1967

After five days in Ward 5, the Ear, Nose and Throat ward, recovering from surgery to repair my perforated left eardrum, I returned to Ward West 2 and the bed I had occupied for the last five months. It was good to back in familiar surroundings. I was eager to start roaming around the hospital grounds again. Tonight I was going to the movies with Jill. We had arranged a date when she visited me in Ward 5. As we sat and watched the movie, I was figuring out where we could find a little privacy afterwards. Once the movie ended we made our way along the duckboards. It was a calm, early summer evening with just a slight breeze blowing. As I talked aimlessly to Jill I continued to assure myself that she was rather keen on me. But I did not know how keen. If I tried to get a little fresh she might reject me. *With my left arm in a cast, how was I going to make a move on Jill anyway?* Being caressed with a mangled hand in a cast doesn't sound or look too romantic and an artificial arm has no tactile qualities, it really has no place in a romantic encounter.

I remembered the Post Office's open-fronted waiting room had a bench seat along the back wall, as we approached it was in darkness. I turned towards it and Jill followed. We now had our cosy little place for a kiss and cuddle. Our first embrace was awkward and clumsy. I did not know where to put my arms. Wild amorous expectations surged through my body and it was obvious that I would require mutual desire and cooperation to pursue them. Jill's behaviour had not indicated a willingness to participate in any more than a kiss and cuddle. As I pondered my next move, a bright light lit our position. A hospital security guard doing his rounds was coming towards us. I pushed myself backwards towards the guard in an exaggerated display of annoyance, telling him what a lousy interfering prick I thought he was, while Jill dashed off towards the Nurses' Quarters. Thwarted in my ambition to seduce Jill, I went home to bed determined that I would find a more secure location in anticipation of another opportunity.

Wednesday evening the Sunshine Club ladies arrived and milk coffee was being distributed. I was more interested in chatting up Sandra again but she arrived late. On her way to the kitchen she stoped briefly by my bed and told me she'd had to work late but she promised to stop by later. When Mrs England was helping me drink my coffee she told me that Sandra had her own car and had driven herself to the hospital. When the ladies left, Sandra stayed talking to me for a little while. When we noticed the Sister in charge looking disapprovingly in our direction I offered to escort Sandra to the car park. Feeling a little more confident about chatting up girls after my earlier success with Jill, I was going to try my luck with Sandra. Unfortunately, she was tired after a hard day and eager to get home. Boldly I asked if she would like to give me her phone number, she did but asked that I didn't ring too early in the morning.

That night I had a most delightful dream about girls; lots of girls were in my life and accepting my busted body. It was so different to the dreams I'd previously had. Romantic encounters with gorgeous and delightful women were endless. Then the nocturnal orchestra of a sleeping hospital ward penetrated my dream and woke me. Unable to recapture my dream I lay awake fantasising about Jill and Sandra fighting jealously over me.

Friday 8 December 1967

I was lying on my bed thinking about how I would spend the weekend as I waited for the weekly visit from Mr Hodge. Jill was working late shifts on Saturday and Sunday but I was going to have time with her that evening. Sometime during the day however, I planned to ring Sandra. I could not help thinking that I might be pushing my luck. So far all I had achieved was a friendly little cuddle with one girl and secured the phone number of another. It had been a long time since I had known the sensual pleasure of being with a girl. I still had doubts about whether I ever would again. Only I could take the necessary steps to find out.

Doctor Boutcher had suggested that I attend *Maryport* a Department of Social Security residential rehabilitation centre at Mount Martha on the Mornington Peninsula. I had some reservations about moving to unfamiliar territory. As Mr Hodge and his entourage entered our bay, he pointed his finger at me and said, 'Don't you move,' I'd regularly incurred Mr Hodge's wrath for being absent from the ward as he made his rounds. He removed the splint from my hand and concluded his examination.

'It's looking good. We'll have it x-rayed and if all is well the splint can be discarded.'

I was unable to stop smiling at the good news. Without the splint I would be able to bathe myself again. Then I heard Mr Hodge say, '*Maryport* will be good for you but not before we fit you with a leg. I think you'd better stay here a little longer.'

I was feeling well and as much as I looked forward to the day I would be officially discharged from hospital, I knew I still had a long way to go before I could live without assistance. Doctor

Hughes at the limb factory had raised an objection to my suggestion about making me a pair of crutches. To achieve the required height two pairs of crutches would be needed; regulations only provided for one. He had to seek approval from a higher authority. My design idea looked like it would be thwarted by red tape. However, Ivor Appleton understood my idea and had started making the crutches in anticipation of approval being granted. After a successful test walk, he was confident I would have them by Christmas.

Returning from x-ray I met Jill at the cafeteria and asked her to meet me after dinner.

'Don't know if I can cope with anymore excitement this week,' she said.

I assured her I had found a very secluded place for us to spend a little time together. We agreed to meet in the main foyer after dinner. I was now convinced Jill really did share my desire to be alone with me.

Kevin and I had roamed the hospital and explored every nook and cranny that could be found, riding elevators to every floor including the basement, ignoring signs saying: 'No Unauthorised Entry' or 'Staff only'. We had been asked to leave a variety of work places. Our ambition was to gain entry to one of several Nurses' Quarters for no other reason than the challenge. No amount of persuasive charm was going to get us through the front door nor were we able to find an accessible back door. Our best find was our ability to gain entry into Ward West 3. The ward had been shut down for maintenance and refurbishing. After the tradesmen had knocked off for the day, access via the service elevator from the basement was simple. An additional bonus was that the electricity and phones were not disconnected.

I took the service elevator to the third floor. As it was a Friday I was confident that the maintenance workers would have left early. The ward was deserted but a faint smell of fresh paint lingered. The vacant sunroom looked huge without any beds. All other bays were bare, no beds or furniture, even the curtains had been removed along with all door fittings. I found the door handle to the main door was still in place. I tried the door and it opened but there was no handle on the outside. Satisfied that I had a safe place to bring Jill, I headed back down to Ward West 2. Sitting on a fresh blanket I'd helped myself to as I passed the linen closet, I made it back just in time for dinner. I told Kevin that I'd be away from my bed during visiting hours and asked if he could note if anyone turned up looking for me. After freshening up in the bathroom, I made my way back up to Ward West 3 and used the ward phone to ring the Nurses' Quarters. I asked Jill to take the elevator to the third floor and wait for me. She agreed without hesitation and said she'd be there in fifteen minutes. Looking through the window in the door I saw her arrive. She looked a little nervous alone in the foyer, dressed in a very short skirt and a summer short sleeve blouse. Her long black hair was flowing freely over her shoulders. *Nurses' uniforms really did conceal so much beauty from patients,* I thought as I admired her. Seeing no one else in the foyer I opened the door and beckoned Jill to enter.

We embraced momentarily and spoke briefly as we made our way to the sunroom. Shutting the door behind us I wedged a spoon I'd kept from dinner under the door for additional security. We moved towards the windows, guided by the faint moonlight. I removed my dressing gown and placed it over the blanket on the floor. Jill hesitated a little then sat down. With the agility of an alley cat I was out of my chair and beside her. My movement took Jill by surprise. When I felt her apprehensiveness I backed off a little. My left hand was still in the splint and my right stump had no immediate appeal as a way to seductively caress my girlfriend to sexual arousal. Gently moving closer to Jill, I caressed her back with my stump, then with my splinted hand. Now with my arms around her in a clumsy embrace, we kissed briefly. I pondered my next move. How would I proceed? With only one leg and no hands to support me, I felt well and truly stymied.

Jill did not speak but looked inquisitively towards me, as she lay on the blanket. Slowly, I leaned forward and positioned myself on top of her with my forearms along the floor supporting me. The feel and warmth of her skin against my own enhanced the pleasure as we became one. Together we lay with our own thoughts. *Did I really mean that much to her?* It was a physical act, one that I had seriously doubted I'd ever experience again. Jill had given me the most precious gift a woman can give a man. I felt enormous appreciation for what I had just received. Filled with renewed and reinforced optimism about my future, I did not want our time together to end but the distant sound of bells ringing announced that visiting hours on the wards were over. Our memorable moment had come to an end.

Together we took the service elevator down to the ground floor and made our way to the main foyer, as I began reliving the experience over in my mind. Jill was quiet and I feared she was regretting her willingness to give herself to me. As we said goodnight all notions of her having regrets were dispelled when she agreed to meet me the following Wednesday. Sleep and beautiful dreams came easily that night. Over breakfast Kevin wanted to know why I had a spare blanket on my wheelchair. Caught by surprise I replied, 'The wheelchair seat is becoming hard and uncomfortable.'

'It's not the seat that's becoming hard,' Kevin said.

22
The Juggler

Sunday afternoon Jeanette, a mate's girlfriend drove me to a lovely park on the banks of the Yarra River. Cold beer and chicken sandwiches went down a treat as we sat and talked about her boyfriend John Passant, who still had about six months to serve in Vietnam. The tranquil surrounding fuelled my thoughts about Jill. After a minute or two of silence Jeanette, noticing my far away look, asked what I was thinking.

'The Pom, (John's nickname) would be very jealous if he could see me now.'

After relaxing in the sunshine, we headed to Jeanette's family home. Jeanette's mum served a delightful afternoon tea. Before returning to the hospital, I asked if I could use their phone and called Sandra. Her mother told me she was at work and would be home in the morning.

Monday morning I raced down to the Physiotherapy Centre where I did regular exercises in preparation for the day I would finally walk on an artificial leg. I completed my routine and headed over to the Red Cross Centre. I was confident Miss Nolan would let me use her phone but she was busy when I arrived so I rolled into the billiard room. The room was empty. Out of curiosity, I took up a cue, holding it with my hook and making a bridge with my splinted hand, I practised hitting balls around the table. Many shots would have attracted loud shouts of derision from my mates as I miscued or failed to hit the balls I aimed for. Engrossed in my new challenge, I forgot about ringing Sandra. Eventually, I was potting balls, even if they were basic straight shots.

After lunch I was eager to return to the billiard room, but first my splint had to be removed. Mr Hodge was calling in when he had finished morning surgery. I had to stay by my bed space and wait. Now I had a reasonable excuse for not ringing Sandra earlier. *A little white lie would do me no harm.*

Sister Chris Morton, who was about to leave the hospital to have her baby after Christmas, called in to invite me to dinner on Friday. Chris had regularly taken David Young and me to the races over the last three months. Without hesitation I accepted the invitation and to my delight I was welcome to bring a friend. Knowing that Sandra had her own car instantly enhanced her appeal. Selfishly, I turned on whatever charm I could muster to accelerate our friendship. Sandra agreed to accompany me to dinner.

Jill returned after two days leave. Sitting out in the cafeteria garden we were alone and able to speak freely. Jill said she would not be willing to return to the sunroom with me, as its openness made her feel vulnerable to discovery. This concerned me. I would need to locate a more acceptable place to create a love nest if I wanted to experience the delights of intimacy again. As I headed up to the ward I began to feel guilty. My actions and attitude had been all about satisfying my own selfish desires.

On Friday I woke full of wonderful expectations about my date with Sandra that evening. After lunch I attended the Red Cross Christmas party for staff, patients and friends. Cast members from the stage plays, 'Fiddler on the Roof' and 'Man of La

Mancha' currently playing in Melbourne provided wonderful musical entertainment. Mingling with members of the cast, in particular the attractive female members fuelled my ego. An *Age* newspaper photographer asked if he could take my photo with two actresses. Without hesitation I agreed. *What a picture to send to my army mates.*

Although I was showering myself, I was still having trouble holding the soap and found it almost impossible to wash under my left arm. Shaving had presented fewer problems once I'd developed a grip that held the razor securely between my thumb and finger, much the same way I had been holding my special cup. Dressed in street clothes, I sat quietly in my recently issued wheelchair. Just after five o'clock I headed down to the main foyer. I kept close to a wall where I would not be so noticeable and anxiously waited for Sandra. Jill was working and there was always the possibility of meeting her in the foyer.

Sandra arrived wearing the shortest mini skirt I had ever seen. It was a real turn on, but I wasted no time heading to the car park. Once in the car I relaxed and started to appreciate her suggestive clothing. Sitting close to her as we drove through Friday evening traffic, I could not help but wonder if the outfit was intended to increase my attraction to her or to tease me senseless. Either way it was working. Pre-dinner drinks and chatter flowed freely and the delicious aroma of roast beef and vegetables wafting out from the kitchen stimulated my appetite. As dinner was served, Sandra leaned over and told me that she was a vegetarian.

Taken by surprise, I said, 'That's fine, I'll eat your meat.' Sandra did not appear too pleased with my indifferent remark. Chris became aware of Sandra's vegetarian diet and appeared a little flustered, as there really was nothing else to offer. Rather graciously, Sandra agreed to eat only the vegetables despite being baked in the same dish as the meat. Chris gave me a nice little serve for not letting her know earlier so that an alternative dish could have been prepared.

The drive home was a little tense. I had not handled the situation too tactfully. Actually, I had stuffed up big time showing a lack of sensitivity and understanding. I was feeling not too clever at this point and berated myself for fouling up, certain that I had ruined any chance of a romantic conclusion to our first date. Arriving at the hospital, Sandra parked away from the glare of the lights and did not appear eager for me to leave. However, the romantic atmosphere that I had felt as we drove to dinner was now missing. Nervously, I asked Sandra if she would like to accompany me home next Wednesday for a family Christmas party. I assured her that I would make Mum aware of her vegetarian diet. Although I expected Sandra to turn me down, she accepted. Quitting while I was in front, I sheepishly said goodnight and made my way up to the ward.

Monday 18 December

I expected to see my photo with the two actresses in the paper but Prime Minister Harold Holt's disappearance over the weekend, in the surf off Cheviot Beach at Portsea, occupied almost every page. Being upstaged by an event of national importance diminished my disappointment. My thoughts turned to Jill and our date that evening at the theatre. With little interest in the movie, we left and headed for Ward West 3. This time I took her to the ward's refurbished linen closet. This smaller room provided greater security against untimely intrusion and a cosiness that enriched our time together.

Wednesday evening I waited for Sandra in the car park well away from the main foyer. We drove home to Glenroy in an atmosphere of happy expectation. She met all my family, friends and neighbours. We squashed snugly into a chair at one end of Mum's lounge room. Sandra sat close to me – I assumed for support. While I enjoyed the pleasure derived from her closeness, her mini skirt had caught the attention of most men present. Old Blue was hovering around appearing to be interested in my progress and talking about his son John while leering lecherously. Later in the evening, Blue enhanced his reputation of being 'a dirty old man' by obstructing Sandra as she returned from the bathroom and attempted to fondle her. Sandra deftly brushed him aside having experienced similar encounters regularly while at work. When it came time to leave, it was obvious I had drunk too much. With some difficulty, I managed to get into the car, while Sandra stowed the wheelchair. As we drove past Coburg Lake opposite Pentridge Jail, I suggested we park for a while. Sandra parked in an area familiar to me from previous adventures. The euphoria brought on by my expectations was suddenly replaced by an overwhelming feeling of nausea. Unable to wind down the window quickly enough, I disgraced myself by spewing in Sandra's car. *Not a good look when you are trying to impress.*

With a hangover that felt like someone was pounding my head with a rock, I was not capable of attending the limb factory the next day. Bed was the only place I wanted to be. The nursing staff, well aware of my drunken state, left me to suffer through the day. I was pleasantly surprised when Sandra called in on her way home and thankfully was not too annoyed with me. *How understanding is this woman?*

Christmas

Sandra invited me to spend a few days with her family at their beach holiday house at Dromana. I remembered going down to Dromana a few years back; it was a small bay side holiday town towards the southern end of Mornington Peninsula. Sandra was working Christmas Day so she would not be able to head down until Boxing Day. I liked the idea of being away with Sandra for a few days but doubted we would have much time, if any to be alone.

Mr Hodge on his Friday morning rounds was not too pleased with me. He had heard about my hangover and my missed appointment at the limb factory. Following a stern warning about drinking excessively, he told me I could have unlimited leave over the Christmas period providing I kept the ward office informed of my whereabouts, and was present next Friday for his morning rounds. Then, wishing me a Merry Christmas he left. Head Nurse Harry, told me later that he had never known Mr Hodge to give anyone so much freedom as a patient. That afternoon many patients were discharged and others had been granted leave to go home for Christmas. Kevin went home to the family farm. Peter, the limbless soldier who had introduced himself as he showed me his wooden leg a few months ago, had returned to hospital and was now confined to bed following recent remedial surgery on his stump. I was pleased to be getting away from him as he had become rather irritating with his endless yarns about his part in the Battle of Long Tan.

The days were warming up and I planned to take myself off to the swimming pool. My ear had not troubled me since the operation a month earlier. Swimming had always been a favourite sport of mine and I had wondered whether or not I would still be able to swim. I visited the linen closet and collected another pair of pyjama pants and a towel. The pool area was deserted. Rolling my chair to the very edge of the pool, I paused as thoughts flashed through my mind such as: *What if I don't float the right way up?* There was nobody around to help me. I shut my eyes and tumbled in. With great relief, I floated to the surface. My buoyancy was good and I relished the freedom as I moved unrestricted around the pool. Getting out was something I had not thought about though. Climbing the short ladder was out of the question. After several attempts, I succeeded in hauling myself over the edge of the pool at the shallower end, losing my pants along the way. I dried myself and put the spare pyjama pants on. As I was retrieving my wet pyjamas two young nurses came along for a swim. I perved on them in their brief bikinis, then headed back to the ward to prepare for my evening out with Sandra.

Christmas Eve

With Chinese take-away for dinner, we arrived at Sandra's family home. The car was parked so close to the front door, I was able to hop inside, leaving my chair in the boot. We ate our dinner quietly. I felt we had a lot to talk about but we were not talking. A cold beer would have been nice but I had none, water was all that I was offered. Just as I was thinking I had made a big mistake, Sandra started talking excitedly about herself and showed me a letter from one of her girlfriends. She had mentioned me and her friend had expressed delight that Sandra was attracted to me and keen to spend time alone with me. *Is that an invitation to race her off to the nearest bedroom?* Sandra asked what time I had to be back at the hospital. With mounting expectations I mentioned the freedom Mr Hodge had granted me. Sandra cleaned the dishes before joining me on the couch. The lights were out and we sat close. Again, I felt awkward as to how I should proceed.

Sandra was sitting on my right side and I felt uncomfortable about putting my artificial arm around her in a cuddle. Without any warning she stood up and asked me to follow her. Hopping closely behind, I did. We went to her bedroom. As Sandra started to undress I needed no invitation to do likewise. Together we snuggled up in her single bed. As we had only kissed briefly before tonight, I was delighted with our speedy progress. *Was it total spontaneity or a burning desire that Sandra had to seduce me? Was I seen as a curiosity or a person to be pitied?* I soon forgot about why it was happening and enjoyed the moment. The feel of a warm female body against mine quickly had me aroused. The bed was small but lying on a mattress was so much more comfortable than a blanket on the floor. Without the splint on my hand and the comfort of the bed I was able to move freely into position and Sandra was obviously no stranger to making love.

On awakening, Sandra busied herself preparing for a long day on duty. As we made our way into Ward West 2, Sandra said she would call for me before the start of visiting hours. I washed and got into bed to catch up on some much needed sleep but Peter, in the next bed began questioning me about what we did or didn't do. His questioning was only interrupted when Matron Hanrahan entered our bay. Dressed in her ostentatious uniform her visit to the wards on Christmas day had become legendary. The mountain of flowers sent by grateful former patients and displayed proudly in her office was another example of the esteem Matron was held in. After a brief chat she continued on her journey of goodwill.

With expectations of another sleepless night followed by a drive to Dromana in the morning, I was content to sleep away the hours. My overnight bag was packed and I waited near the car park for Sandra to arrive. I had agreed to call in at Mum's for a Christmas day dinner before heading off to Dromana. We arrived just as dinner was being served. Sandra was hungry but I had already enjoyed a scrumptious dinner at the hospital earlier. Sitting at the family dinner table with a girlfriend was a sight that obviously delighted Mum, who not long ago doubted I would ever sit at her table again. When Mum asked me about going back to the hospital that night I said yes, and reminded her that I would be away until Thursday. When we left Sandra told me how she felt herself blush when I was asked about returning to the hospital. Home alone at Sandra's, we turned on the TV and sat together. For comfort I removed my prosthetic arm. We canoodled for a while before heading to bed. Snuggling up close it was not long before Sandra was asleep. I remained awake listening to her gentle breathing rhythm and remembering the many lonely nights I had endured since waking up in hospital nearly eight months ago.

We made good time as we headed south along Nepean Highway. Spotting a signpost to Mount Martha, I asked if we could take a

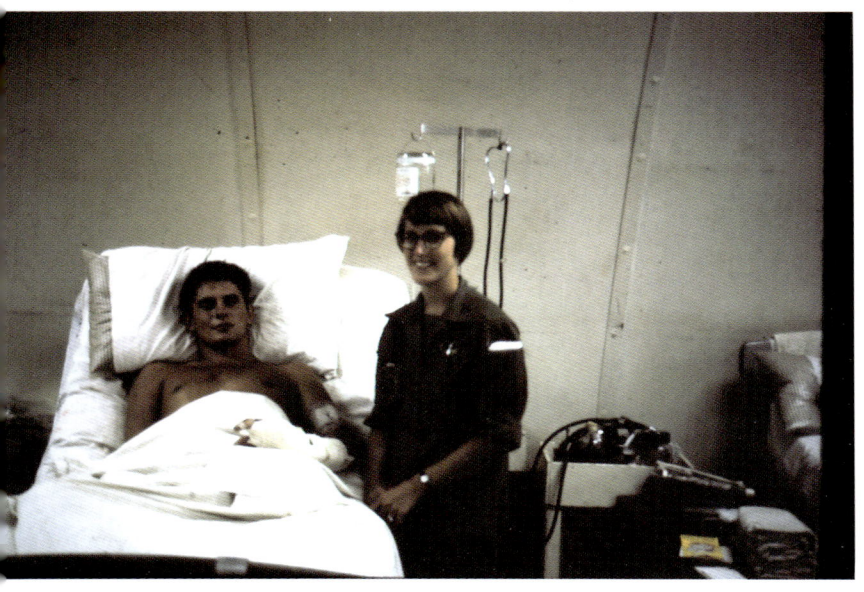

*May 1967, Jethro and Lieutenant Nancy Lee
(Photo courtesy C Lynn)*

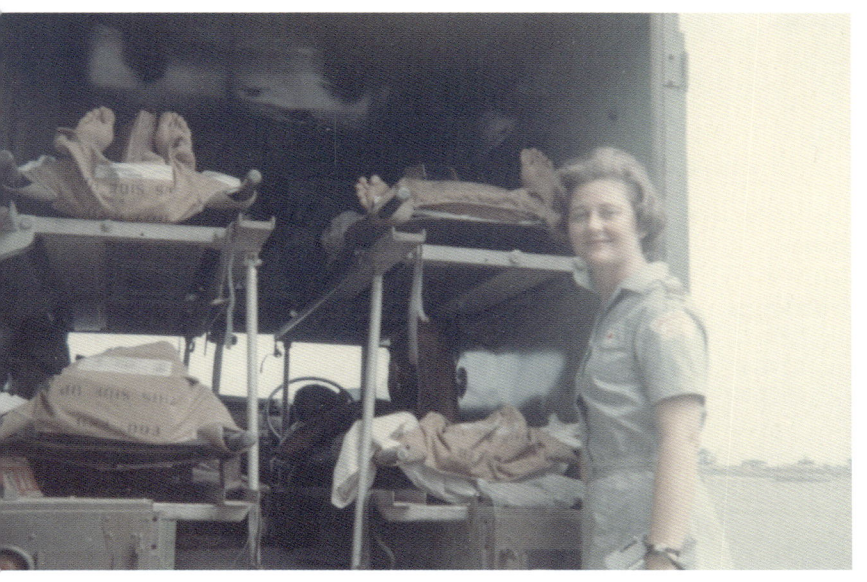

*Red Cross member Janice Webb seeing off wounded
Australian Diggers at Vung Tau Airfield 1967 (Photo
courtesy J Webb)*

Welcome Home Parade Sydney 1987, Jethro, Brett Nolen & Charlie Lynn
(Photo courtesy L Sheehan)

1968 Officer Cadet Charlie Lynn (second from right) and General Sir Thomas Daly (second from left) meet again in more formal circumstances. Did the General remember Charlie? (Photo Courtesy C Lynn)

Perle and Jethro in 1978

The Pom's wedding December 1969

After searching a tunnel on Operation Portsea with 6 Battalion, I display my find, a bag of rice. (Photo courtesy L Drinkwater)

Test-firing weapons was regularly carried out under supervision. From left to right: Staff Sergeant George Biddlecombe, Sapper Robert 'Blue' Willet, Sapper F Oakes, unidentified sapper and Corporal John Green (Photo courtesy J Green)

December 1966. Our last Saturday night in Sydney before we left for Vietnam. From left to right: Jim Long, Charlie Lynn, Jethro Thompson, Jack Campbell, Jim Fraser and Toby Tobin.

1964, With rifle over shoulder Jethro completing a twenty mile march at recruit training.

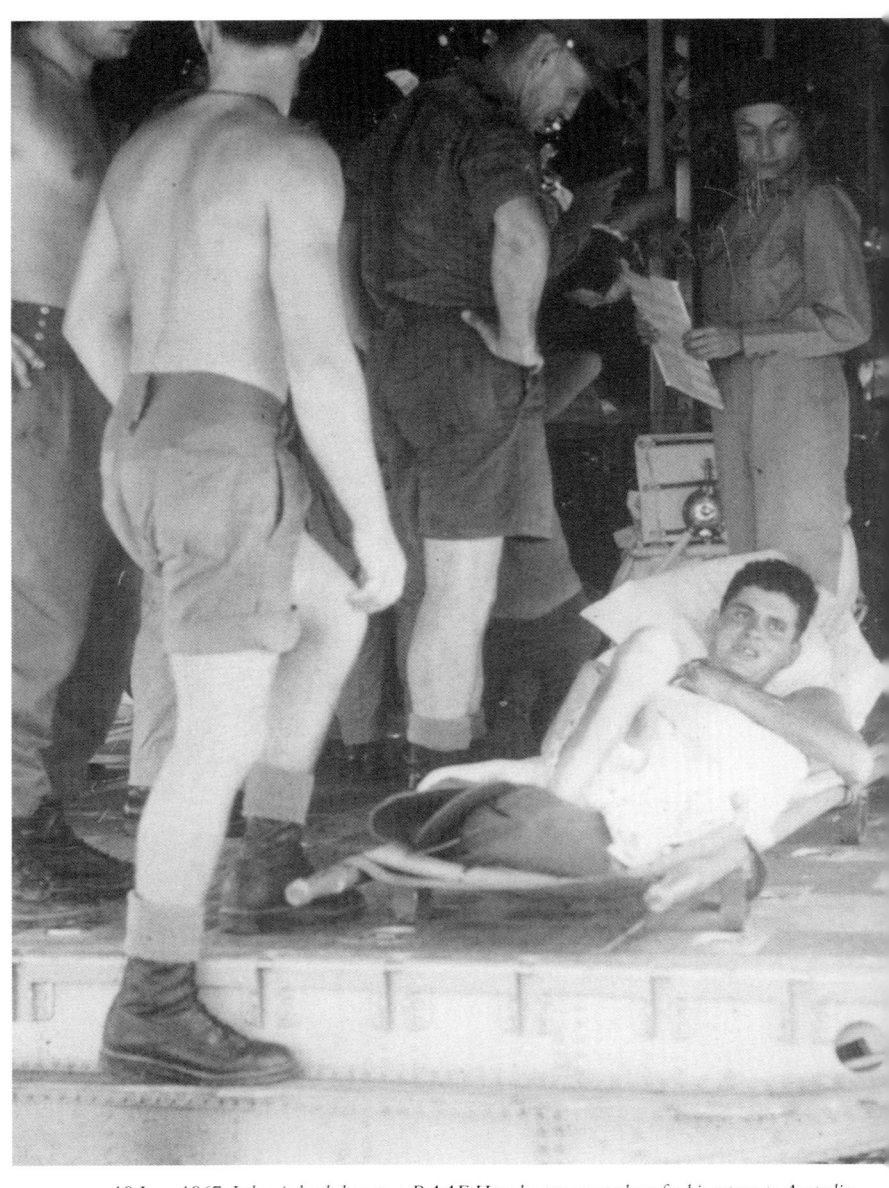

19 June 1967, Jethro is loaded on to a RAAF Hercules transport plane for his return to Australia.
(Photo courtesy Brigadier C Gurner)

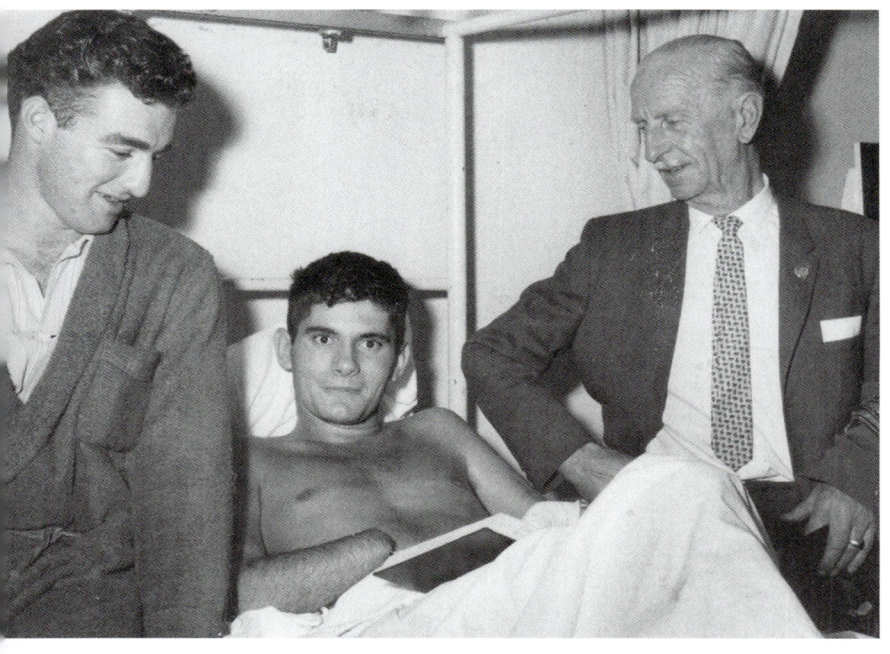

Tony Twaits, Jethro and Jack a friendly visitor.

...istmas morning 1969, Lucien & Eddy Dixon help Jethro ... the snow-covered slopes at New Canaan, Connecticut.

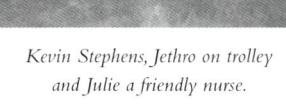

(Photo from my collection)

Kevin Stephens, Jethro on trolley and Julie a friendly nurse.

The mine field

Jethro and Sister Johnson at RGH 1967

detour and check out *Maryport*.

'No, we don't have time, we'll go there on the way back,' Sandra replied.

I sat back and enjoyed the scenery. I was going to attend *Maryport* rehabilitation centre in the New Year. Mr Hodge had agreed with Doctor Boutcher that it would be advantageous to start my rehabilitation program while waiting for a suitable leg to be produced.

No sooner had we arrived at the beach house when Sandra told me she was off to catch up with some friends. Naturally, I expected to be going with her and hurriedly finished drinking my coffee.

'No, you won't be able to manage the stairs,' she said.

I amused myself talking with her parents and young brother. He was fascinated with my artificial arm and wanted to know how it worked. I didn't tell him at first. He made many suggestions but did not get close. Sandra returned with an invitation to a party, again I expected to accompany her, but no, too many stairs again. Disappointed about my exclusion, I tried to appreciate Sandra's desire to catch up with friends she'd known for many years. I spent the evening talking and playing cards with her parents before heading off to bed. It was very late when I heard Sandra return. I expected her to come and talk with me for a while but she didn't. The lights were turned off and I heard her go to bed. Wide-awake I spent the night thinking about the previous two days.

After breakfast Sandra was off again. I sat alone and reflected on what was happening. *Had Sandra taken me to her bed in a moment of weakness or desperation? Had I fulfilled Sandra's needs while giving her an opportunity to show me some kindness, because she felt sorry for me?* It was hard to reconcile her behaviour with what she had written to her friend. By the end of the day I felt used. The thought that my disabilities were in any way responsible for my rejection was too distressing to consider. The reality however, could not be ignored.

I was trying hard to accept my disabilities and my limited abilities. I had convinced myself that Sandra was not capable of, or prepared to face the burden of having a disabled lover. *Could I really blame her, would I be willing to accept a disabled girlfriend?* So far, I'd been involved with two nurses with mixed results. *What would it be like with a girl not associated with the hospital environment?*

I had no doubt that a disabled person could take advantage of a 'wham baam, thank you m'am,' moment of sexual gratification, provided they had the money. I didn't think that was what I really wanted. Before lunch, we headed for Melbourne. It was a fast, quiet trip with no detour to Mount Martha. I saw no point in asking what had suddenly caused the gulf between us. I accepted that the memories of two delightfully passionate nights would be all I would have from our short time together. I could not imagine what Sandra was thinking but hoped she had no regrets.

Fending off large doses of melancholia, I went to Ward West 1 looking for Jill. I was told she would be on duty tomorrow afternoon. Working a late shift wouldn't allow me much time to inveigle my way back into her favour. The next day I waited for her in the main foyer. The reception was a little frosty, which was understandable as I'd not been in contact with her for nearly two weeks. There was no doubt she knew I'd been away, but hopefully not with whom. I asked her to meet me in the morning to which she agreed before hurrying off.

Hesitantly, I headed down to the hospital cafeteria to meet Jill. I would not have been surprised if she hadn't turned up, after all, I had treated her rather badly, although I had no intention of disclosing what I had been up to since we were last together. When Jill arrived, I felt her air of annoyance towards me. Staff and visitors were starting to gather in the cafeteria waiting to be served. I suggested we go for a walk and headed towards the pool. Talking constantly about how pleased I was that we had time to be together must have sounded good to her as I felt Jill's coolness thawing a little. An exaggerated account of my first swim and two recent dips had Jill smiling and telling me what a reckless fool she thought I was. *If only she knew how reckless I had been lately.* As we made our way back to the foyer I felt confident that she was still attracted to me.

New Year's Eve 1967

My sister Sue and her fiancée Angie were calling for me to take me to a party at Blue's. I felt good about not having to avoid being noticed as I waited in the main foyer. In fact, I went out of my way to be seen, wishing many nurses a Happy New Year and letting them know I was waiting for my sister. Jill was working and hopefully she would hear I was going out with my sister. At the party, memories of Sandra's departure from my life and the uncertainty about my future with Jill constantly encroached on my thoughts. Blue's son John was now living at home with his parents, after renovations to accommodate his wheelchair, he displayed an encouraging acceptance of his handicap as he mingled with guests. Comparing our disabilities, I felt that physically, I had the advantage, despite John having two good hands. I had greater physical freedom and mobility, not being totally confined to a wheelchair. Also, I was confident that if one day I was to marry I would be able to experience the joy of procreation.

23
Preparing to leave Heidelberg

January 1968

I headed off early to the limb factory. Previous lack of success had affected me significantly. I was on the verge of abandoning all hope of ever successfully wearing a leg. This morning the leg felt secure with a modified shoulder strap; it stayed on as had the previous attempts but when I sat the familiar blurting sound of the suction giving way was clear to all involved. The leg failed to stay attached to my stump. Also, my artificial arm was now chaffing rather badly due to substantial shrinkage of my stump. A new arm would have to be made for me. I returned to the hospital in a low mood. The problems with fitting a leg, the shrinking arm and still hurting from Sandra's rejection, were all taking their toll. The only glimmer of hope was that my new crutches were successful but I could only move slowly with them. I retained my trusty dilapidated wheelchair as my main mode of transport around the hospital grounds.

Unexpectedly, I was off to surgery once more to have a cyst

removed from the scar line on my left stump. It was not a particularly serious situation but I had to stay in bed for a few days. I had not mentioned the cyst or the need for surgery to Mum who happened to be visiting when a nurse came along to shave me in preparation for surgery. No reasonable explanation could satisfy her that it was only a minor procedure. After surgery I just wanted to sleep. Despite my pleading, Mum stubbornly continued to visit.

It had been a year since I went to Vietnam. Almost all my mates had made it safely home and many had visited me over the last two months. Toby the former Nasho I'd shared a hotel room with on my way to Vietnam was now posted to 22 Construction Squadron, in Western Australia called in with his wife on their way to Perth. Jack Campbell, who I'd been on the flight to Manila with, turned up looking very impressive in his summer uniform with three campaign ribbons and corporal stripes. Les Hutton, a much older bloke than most of my mates and a real rough diamond visited and wanted to know who I had been screwing. He kept saying that he knew I'd not let a chance go by. Whenever a nurse entered the bay he would ask, 'What about this one?' To avoid embarrassment I tried to encourage Les to leave. I went down to the main foyer with him thinking that would be a way to persuade him to head for home. I did not want to offend him, he was a mate and I appreciated the effort he had made getting out to the hospital. We arrived in the foyer at the most inappropriate time. It was shift-changeover for most nurses. Les was having an absolute ball, openly ogling every nurse that came our way. With unfortunate timing Jill came by and gave me a friendly pat on the shoulder and a 'nice to see you look' as she went by. Les recognised the display of affection and said, 'You're shagging that one.' Jill may not have heard but many others did and observed me turning red with embarrassment. It was defiantly time for Les to leave.

Having made up with Jill, I was eager to re-visit our love nest but not too keen to lie on a blanket spread on the floor. Something more appropriate had to be found. Prowling around Ward West 3, I had noticed that refurbishing work on the doctors' and senior nurses' lounge appeared to be completed. All the furniture had been returned and the very large leather couches looked positively more comfortable than the floor. During evening visiting hours, Jill and I made our way to the ward. We did not turn the lights on to avoid attracting unwanted attention. From the main entrance, the lounge room was the first door on the left so we had no difficulty finding it in the dark. As Jill made her way to the leather lounge guided by the moonlight, I parked my wheelchair and started to hop towards the couch. Stumbling, I lost my slipper. Endeavouring to regain my balance, I landed on something sharp puncturing my foot and all my amorous balloons.

'Ouch, shit ouch!' I said, as I struggled towards the couch. I had not noticed the large centre carpet square was not in place. Wooden anchoring strips with upturned tacks that secured the carpet however, were very much in position. As I hopped bare footed towards Jill, I had landed on them. With blood flowing freely from my foot, we hurriedly made our way out of the ward. Jill was more than a little alarmed by the neat row of holes she saw in my foot. All I could think was that I was being punished for my wicked selfish ways.

I had an unexpected return visit to Ward West 3 a few days later, after a chance meeting with Matron Hanrahan who, with one of her deputies, was carrying a fashion mannequin into the elevator. I was curious as to what they were doing so I tagged along with them. In one of the refurbished bays a bed had been made up. The starched white sheets, with immaculately made hospital corners, were as square and sharp as I'd ever seen. Pillows were stacked and fluffed up and flowers in a large vase on the bedside cabinet finished off the display. Two mannequins were dressed in nurses' uniforms. Matron told me they were getting ready for a public relations photo shoot in the morning; a professional model would pose in the bed.

'You have so many beautiful nurses around the hospital. Why use mannequins?' I asked.

'It would be too difficult to select the right girls,' was the reply. *What a load of codswallop,* I thought.

That evening I had to call on every ounce of my persuasive ability to have Jill join me in the ward and hop into the nicely made bed. Together we relished the feel of the crisp sheets and the comfort of being in a bed. Our daring and mischievous behaviour under the gaze of two mannequins, standing close by like silent sentinels, culminated in a feeling of total satisfaction. As we left the ward I could not help thinking that we had just drafted a fresh scene for Goldilocks and the Three Bears.

Unable to sleep I took a walk on my crutches, and sat alone in the foyer. I reflected on my time at Heidelberg. I had been well treated and had a load of fun. I would miss the staff and some of the patients but I knew that to stay any longer would be counter productive. I had already started to feel like part of the establishment. Going to *Maryport* would be a new challenge.

Alone with my thoughts, I didn't hear Nurse Fay approach and sit beside me. Fay was the nurse who had given me a pep talk a few months back about facing up to the outside world. We had become friendly and regularly had late night chats whenever it was quiet on the ward.

'Here you are,' I heard her say. Kevin and I had declared Fay the most attractive nurse we had met, and we had met many gorgeous looking nurses, occupational therapists and physiotherapists. With few exceptions they all had delightfully happy personalities. Fay however, had it all: long auburn hair, beautifully shaped hazel eyes and a light brown complexion with the most delicate sprinkle of freckles. Not too tall or too thin, all the curves and bumps were nicely proportioned and in the right place. Her delightful smile was capable of warming the heart of the most cantankerous patient. We sat and talked for a while, I heard about her boyfriend who was at university. They were in a stormy off-again-on-again relationship. Studies and irregular working hours at the hospital did not help their situation. We talked about my transfer to *Maryport* and how we hoped to keep in touch. Encouraged by our late night chat, I asked Fay if she would give me her phone number. When Fay said she would give it to me later, I thought she was avoiding my request.

Working the early shift next morning Fay was very busy in our bay making beds. As she finished she handed me a piece of paper. We all watched her leave, I know what I was thinking and pretty sure what the other three patients were thinking too. I read the note Fay had handed me. It was the phone numbers for the Nurses' Quarters and more surprisingly, her home address. Should I not be able to reach her at the hospital her parents would let me know her whereabouts. *Holy Dooly! I had made a hit with Fay. How lucky could a bloke get?* Ditched a month ago by a sheila I fancied more than I realised and selfishly exploiting another who I felt a little guilty about, now it seemed like I could make some progress with Fay. *Who cares about not having a wooden leg that stays on?* I was on a roll and feeling good.

To my surprise Sandra called in with a few items of clothing I had left behind at Dromana. Still harbouring some resentment and hurt over being so abruptly cast aside, I was curious to find out why she had flicked me. I felt that she was still attracted to me although she did not say so. I assumed her plans for life did not include caring for a physically disabled man. This realisation hurt deeply. I asked if we would remain friends. When she replied that her affection was not something she could turn on and off like a tap, I felt that was exactly what she had done a month ago. I decided then and there, that I wanted nothing further to do with her.

My inflated ego had taken quite a heavy blow that I had not got over. I languished around my bed space and became totally disinterested in pursuing anything that might help pass the time.

My discharge from the hospital could not come quickly enough. The realisation that emotional wounds are painfully more complex than physical wounds constantly occupied my thoughts. I would have to deal with the problem somehow. In the past, I accepted that once dumped you moved on. If you didn't, you could miss out on whatever might be round the next corner. The difficulty for me was facing up to why I had been dumped. I was physically disabled and there was nothing I could do to change that.

Jill, unable to cope with my erratic moods, had started to avoid me. I was in no position to explain what was troubling me. Occasionally we talked about how we would maintain contact when I relocated to *Maryport*. However, deep down, I doubted that our hospital romance would survive separation. Jill had given me so much, more than she would ever realise. She was a supporter, who encouraged me to believe in my own ability and helped develop my growing confidence. In return I betrayed her trust. Feeling pretty low and ashamed of myself, I appreciated Jill's absence.

While my discharge was imminent not much was happening to me. I was left alone to attend physio daily for walking practice and maintained my visits to the occupational centre for educational coaching that the delightful Rosemary had arranged for me many months previously. Whenever I had the opportunity I went and practised on the billiard tables.

Saturday 3 February 1968
Unexpectedly, I met Fay in the main foyer, her eyes red from crying. Over a cup of coffee I listened as she told me how she had been stood up the previous night. Her boyfriend hadn't phoned to say he wouldn't be calling for her. Fearing the worst, Fay had a worrying night, as she was unable to make contact by phone. She had only just reached him but they had argued. She was certain he had been out with another girl. Feeling more than a little sorry for her, I invited her to walk down to the Red Cross Centre with me; I would show her how good I was at snooker. After showing

off my limited ability with a pool cue, Fay was up at the table with cue in hand and challenged me to a game.

Within minutes I was being flogged. Fay looked like she was having fun. Her earlier disappointment appeared to be behind her. As we chased balls around the table we frequently brushed up against each other. I sensed we were igniting an emotional and physical attraction. It became obvious we were deliberately bumping into each other and I was holding on to her longer than necessary, exaggerating my need for assistance. My heart was racing with arousal. Exhausted, I sat on the spectator's bench. Fay came and sat with me as a friend, not the student nurse. I looked at her, her beauty capturing my full attention. With an ever-increasing optimism, I believed all the wonderful thoughts racing through my head would actually come to fruition. I convinced myself that her boyfriend was not worthy of any loyalty from her or me.

I asked Fay what she was doing for the rest of the evening as she pushed me back to the ward. Hearing she would be staying in her room, I asked if she would like to spend more time with me in the evening. She said yes if it was somewhere other than the ward. I suggested we meet and have coffee after dinner. Gulping my dinner down I prepared myself to go and meet her. Cautiously, I made my way to the foyer and the cafeteria. Aware that Jill was working an afternoon shift I doubted that I would be able to explain the pillow behind me and still maintain a look of innocence if we were to meet.

Fay had changed out of her jeans into a sleeveless summer dress revealing her lightly tanned arms and shoulders and her hair was hanging loosely down her back; she looked absolutely delightful. Her smile was unquestionably for my eyes only. It left me in no doubt that our friendship was developing into something special. With my blood racing and my heart pounding I reached out to Fay, touching her gently on the arm and asked her to follow me. As I pushed myself slowly backwards down the western corridor towards the nurses' lecture rooms and the service elevator, Fay followed. We did not speak as we stepped out on the third floor. We reached the doctors' lounge and entered. I wedged the door shut with a spoon. The carpet had still not been replaced. Mindful of my last visit I safely transferred to the couch. Alone for the first time, fully aware of our mutual desire to be with each other we embraced. I felt the release of a load of negative and depressing thoughts from within me. Oblivious to time we relished the pleasure we were bringing to each other. Very few words had been spoken. There had been no need to talk. While Fay snuggled close to me I began regretting that my time in hospital was almost over. Another opportunity to be together before I left on Tuesday was highly unlikely. As we separated to leave Fay said, 'John, will you call me when you settle in?' I was speechless. *Did I mean that much to Fay?* Sleep did not come easily that night. I'd enjoyed an experience so delightful that I wanted to share it with everyone around me. I knew I couldn't, not even with my mate Kevin.

Over the last six weeks I had enjoyed the pleasure of three delightful girls. They had considered me worthy enough to share great intimacy and passion with them. Two boosted my ego and enhanced my confidence to deal with the unexpected. The third reminded me how emotionally fragile I was. Collectively, they diminished my fear that I would grow old alone and unloved.

Tuesday 6 February 1968

After 224 days, I was discharged. Bed 16, Ward West 2, Repatriation General Hospital Heidelberg, had served me well. I had received the very best medical treatment and been cared for with love and affection by so many of the hospital staff. I walked out on my crutches. Not quite the departure I wanted, but at least I was standing.

24
Maryport Rehabilitation Centre

On arrival at *Maryport* I was introduced to Matron Smith who told me I was too late for lunch but could have a cup of tea and a biscuit. I was more interested in being shown to my room, so I declined the offer. Matron was telling me what was expected from me. I showed some interest and patiently waited to be taken to my room. I was to share with a bloke called Ray who had been a resident for about six months and would help me settle in. Late in the afternoon, Ray entered the room and introduced himself. As it was nearly five-thirty he suggested we make our way to the dining room. Ray pointed towards a long table at the far end,

'That's where the staff sits,' he said. Patients or Residents as they were referred to had an allocated place at a table for four and had to present themselves each mealtime unless they had been excused. I shared a table with Ray, Cyril a bloke about forty, and another bloke with only one eye.

As staff members entered the dining room I watched them closely. Two younger females followed three older ones to the long table. Cyril noticed my scrutinising look and identified the first three as nurses. The taller of the two younger girls was an occupational therapist from Western Australia, and the other a physiotherapist from Melbourne. Cyril told me that more staff would be around in the morning. After dinner I sat in the common room, which was a combined sports room with a billiard and ping-pong table. It was also the main entry to the building. Cyril introduced me to a number of male residents. One fellow came along and introduced himself as Dave Denehey and asked what unit I was with in the Army. He then told me a rogue elephant in Borneo had killed his brother. I remembered reading about a Special Air Service patrol losing a member just before I left for Borneo in 1965. As Dave looked and sounded quite normal to me, I asked why he was at the centre. I thought he might have had an anxiety problem as a consequence of his brother's death. I was wrong. He had fallen out of a car and been dragged along the roadway as his legs were caught up in the seatbelt. He assured me he was making good progress.

I sat for a while watching blokes play snooker, happily remembering my game with Fay. A public phone booth was located on the front veranda. I was told younger residents liked to sit on the couch and answer the phone. If the calls were for a staff member they would race down the hill to the Staff Quarters and summon the wanted staff member. If the call was for a resident a loud shout from the doorway was the extent of their effort. The Staff Quarters were strictly out of bounds to residents, but running a legitimate message was an exception. In the morning, I sat in my designated place and enjoyed a hearty breakfast. A table for four in a large dining room, all nicely laid out was very different to dining in the Army or more recently, eating in bed or beside it. Waitresses brought our meals; choices were few if available at all. I was more than happy to eat almost anything placed in front of me, my only concern was the small portions. As I ate, I noticed one of the nursing sisters heading my way.

Sister Walsh introduced herself and said, 'John, would you go to the office after assembly?' Cyril knowingly suggested that I was about to have the Riot Act read to me by the centre manager.

Morning assembly was rather amusing. I sat on a long table at the back of the gym with other residents who had difficulty standing unassisted. A young athletic looking lady with long black hair in a pony tail, dressed in dark blue tights stood out front with her hands on her hips. A number of the more able-bodied residents stood close to her. To the sound of the Seekers' *Morning Town Ride'* an exercise routine started. Residents with a variety of physical and intellectual disabilities tried to emulate the actions of those out front. After about 15 minutes and more Seekers' music the exercise period was over for the day. Residents dispersed in all directions. I headed for the centre manager's office.

A smartly dressed tall skinny bloke was smiling as he greeted me while I recovered from the uphill walk. I heard his name but as I was a little puffed, I didn't catch it. I was bound to call him Sir, so it didn't matter.

'Well, how was your first night?' he asked.

'Comfortable enough, Sir,' I replied. For the next half hour I was 'yes sir-ing or no sir- ing', to a load of questions that covered everything from laundry, dress, behaviour, going on leave and appointments in Melbourne. I was expected to keep myself clean and presentable at all times and most importantly, no alcohol was permitted on the premises. Nothing of value was to be left unsecured in my room. The Army would visit from nearby Balcombe camp to pay me each fortnight. If I had any problems I was to take them up with Doctor Boutcher when he visited or the Centre Manager when he was available.

'So, who did you say you were?' I asked, feeling like I had just been conned.

I headed back down the hill looking for morning tea. The crowd was leaving; morning tea was over. I had missed out. Now I was really pissed off. When I heard my name over the Public Address system I tuned in but was none the wiser as to where I had to go. Cyril came along and showed me the way to the physiotherapy centre adjacent to the gym.

Mrs Berwick, the senior physiotherapist, greeted me warmly and made me feel very much at ease. Two other physiotherapists, the blonde I had seen in the dining room and another woman more Mrs Berwick's age (and who looked like she had just swallowed a lemon) were treating other residents. I was invited to sit on a workbench while Mrs Berwick explained how I was to have daily physio and receive training in the use of my artificial arm and leg. I was wearing my arm, which appeared to please her. When asked where my leg was I told her it was still at the limb factory.

After lunch I was called to Matron Smith's office. She told me that Doctor Boutcher had requested that every effort be made to have me fitted and walking on an artificial leg. He also wanted me to receive educational coaching in preparation for starting full time studies the following year. I was going to be busy five days a week. On the weekend I could rest. The next morning I was determined not to miss out on morning tea and arrived before the main crowd. Cyril was sitting at the front of the room and beckoned me over. Residents helped themselves to one piece of toast smeared with Vegemite from a large galvanised washing tub placed on the counter and a choice of tea or coffee was available. As I drank my tea, I was told it was the same everyday.

The weekend gave me an opportunity to explore the grounds. I looked through any building that was unlocked and walked down the hill to the beach. Returning up the hill almost had me beaten but I managed by taking many short breaks. Eventually, I made it back to my room totally stuffed. By Sunday evening I had met many of the residents and played ping-pong after a slight adjustment to the way I served. A number of teenage girls and older women were in residence and I even met two blokes who were completing prison sentences and receiving remedial medical treatment before being released. Many residents had physical disabilities as a result of an accident or birth defect; others were stroke victims. On the centre notice board I read an article complete with photo that had recently been in the daily papers. It was about a bloke with an eye patch whom I had seen around the centre. In the photo, he was sitting in a wheelchair with a bow and arrow and assisted by the young lady who led the morning exercise routine. He had been a promising jockey until he was injured falling from a horse. The lady was Peggy, a remedial gymnast.

By Monday morning, I felt quite settled in and looked forward to getting stuck into a daily routine, particularly my schooling. Within minutes of meeting the teacher Mrs Webb, a serious looking woman in her late forties, I had doubts about how well we would get on. The mood in the classroom was far too staid for my liking. It was definitely not a fun place. About fifteen students were present. Three were pursuing higher education via correspondence, while the rest were working their way through arithmetic and English grammar questions on the blackboard. Mrs Webb directed me to a seat at the rear of the classroom. An exercise book, biro and a ruler were handed to me. I was to complete the work on the board. With the exception of the first four or five English grammar questions the rest was way over my head. Mrs Webb then handed me an arithmetic paper to complete. It was not long before Mrs Webb noticed me staring off into space. Standing close to my desk and in a low voice she said, 'We have a lot of work to do John.' I could only sit and look forlornly at her and as I did, I was surprised by the warmth and compassion in her eyes.

More schoolwork was soon added to my daily program and homework became a regular task after dinner. Returning to full time study was out of the question until I improved my basic reading, writing and arithmetic ability. Writing short essays about things I knew was an enjoyable way to spend my evenings. Memories of my time in the Army, early school days and friends gave me much to write about. Spelling was my greatest difficulty and a dictionary became a constant companion. Mrs Webb's encouragement helped me maintain my desire to work hard.

Weekend leave was available however, I was not too eager to go home without the sanctuary of the hospital nearby if Mum got too much for me. But I felt compelled to make the effort. On the second Saturday morning Dad called for me. By Sunday afternoon I had made arrangements to buy a car. With the benefit of sales tax exemption as I had lost a leg as a result of war service, I was able to pay for the latest model Ford Falcon Fairmont and still have a grand or two left in my bank account. Money is not everything but having no financial problems was boosting me along the road towards freedom and independence.

25
Hurt Pride

Leonie, the young blonde physio, picked up my 'work book'. I watched her reading my stories. They represented over two weeks of struggle and effort on my behalf. I noticed her smiling as she read. I was certain she liked what I had written and was impressed with my ability to write. After hours of practise, my writing with the hook was legible if not too neat. As Leonie returned my book to where I had left it, I saw her shaking her head as she walked away. Puzzled by her reaction, I waited for an opportunity to ask what she thought of my work. Leonie said she remembered writing essays like that when she was in Sixth Grade. I turned red with embarrassment as a feeling of loathing surged within me. I could only think what an ignorant insensitive bitch she was. I wanted to crawl away and hide.

Nursing my wounded pride I returned to Mrs Webb's classroom. My enthusiasm to work had vanished. Images of Leonie sitting around with other staff members talking and laughing about my essays troubled me for days. They were essays that had taken a lot of hard work; it wasn't easy writing with an artificial arm.

Mrs Webb noticed my change in attitude towards schooling and asked if there was a problem. I told her I was too far behind to ever catch up enough to pursue a reasonable education.

'No, that's not so. Once you learn the basic rules of English expression and arithmetic, you will progress rapidly,' Mrs Webb assured me.

In my third week I had a meeting with Doctor Boutcher. He gave no indication that he was aware of my recent setback. All reports were favourable and he was confident that by the end of the year I would be walking and well on my way to living independently in the community. I no longer shared a room with Ray. Matron had moved me to a single room that had access to the fire escape. I was told as a soldier and familiar with self-discipline I was being trusted to occupy this particular room. Single rooms were few and I felt privileged. Now I was able to sit up and read or do my homework late into the night. The fire escape provided me with a cosy place to sit and enjoy fresh air, leaving the door open cooled the room. Sitting outside I was able to greet many of the domestic staff. With the exception of the staff in the dining room, very few domestics were encountered during the day.

At lunchtime, it was announced that we would be going down to the beach later in the afternoon. Peggy, the remedial gymnast, would drive me and another resident; the rest would walk down under supervision. At the beach Leonie and Margaret the tall dark haired OT, were parading around in their bikinis, a sight much appreciated by most of the blokes. Leonie's generous boobs adequately compensated for her slight broadness through the hips. Her long blonde hair flowing freely half way down her back created a very sexy image. Margaret's tall lean figure had a fragile appearance. Her smallish boobs didn't do justice to her long brown shapely legs and pretty face and long curly dark hair. The water was inviting and I needed to cool down after my brief but delightful moments of perving. Cyril walked out into the water with me until our bums were wet. Handing him my crutches I plunged into the small waves and swam parallel to the beach. Unburdened by my inability to walk, I felt relaxed, oblivious to everything and everyone around me. Saltwater buoyancy and sunshine on my back encouraged me to swim further. There were no obstacles to my progress as I swam with only my thoughts for company.

Hearing my name called, I looked towards the beach. The group was getting ready to head back up the hill. Allowing the waves to propel me gently towards the beach, I perved on Margaret and Leonie again. They looked different. Wet straggly hair added heaps to their sexy, dishevelled appearance, more than worthy of a long lingering look. Some blokes commented on my ability to swim. Others asked crudely what I thought of the girls in their bathers. I appreciated the compliments and ignored the other remarks.

The centre's visiting driving instructor advised me that although I had a driver's licence I would need to be re-tested owing to my disabilities. Also a couple of modifications to my vehicle would be required; the headlights dipswitch would have to be repositioned from the floor to the steering column so I could operate it by hand. A steer-easy knob would give me a more secure grip on the steering wheel, and a way to hold the wheel with my hook was needed. I thought he was talking through his hat about the hook but as I needed his assistance I kept quiet. We went for a test drive in his specially fitted out vehicle. I drove around the local area executing a hand brake start, three-point turns and even parallel parking. It was difficult but I satisfied the instructor. He agreed to set up an official test at the Mornington Police Station once I had my own vehicle fitted out.

On Saturday 9 March my new car was ready for me to collect. Its 'Stratosphere Grey' duco was gleaming and the burgundy trim smelt rich and warm. I handed over a bank cheque, signed a few papers and the car was mine. I declined a look under the bonnet. I didn't see any point. *What could I do under there with my hands?*

With my brother-in-law Keith driving we headed for home. Along the way we passed the Repatriation Hospital. It was hard to believe that after all I had been through I was now passing by in my own car. Most of the weekend I drove around with anyone who had a licence and a little spare time - not going anywhere just getting the practice I desperately needed. Dad had manufactured and fitted three steel lugs to the outside of the steering wheel. They would assist steering with my hook. My official test was on Wednesday.

On Monday, Mrs Berwick suggested we walk to my car and see how I managed getting in and out wearing my wooden leg. I was trying a leg with further modifications to the shoulder strap. The walk from physio to the car park was painful and slow. With the driver's side door wide open and the seat pushed all the way back, I lifted my leg to place it in the car. That's all it took for the suction grip to give way and separate from my stump. Walking back to physio, I was ready to abandon my desire to wear a leg. Mrs Berwick was even more determined to succeed.

The driving instructor arrived early on Wednesday morning. He examined the steering wheel modifications then we went for a drive. He asked me a few road rules, not that he expected me to be tested on them. I had taken the precaution of brushing up on the rules over the last few days. After morning tea we headed off to Mornington Police Station. Luck was with me. The young constable detailed to take me for a test drive was very interested in my situation and showed a real willingness to assist me. He told me that he had a friend serving in Vietnam as a Nasho infantry platoon commander; I was more than happy to milk the situation. Sitting behind the wheel with the helpful constable beside me and the instructor in the back seat, I demonstrated my ability to operate all controls. Once around the block and it was done. My licence would be amended accordingly.

As I parked my car back at Maryport the manager stopped me and asked how I had got on. Enthusiastically, I told him all went well.

'That's great news John,' he said. 'You will have to leave your keys with me and you are not to give anyone from the centre a ride in your vehicle.'

'But I'll want to drive my car when I'm not on program,' I said.

'That's fine. Just come to the office and ask for keys,' he replied.

That did not sound too bad. Being able to drive was my main concern I wasn't that interested in giving anyone a ride. Over lunch I shared my morning experience with Cyril who had now become a regular companion. He suggested we pop down to the pub that afternoon. A celebratory drink before dinner appealed to me. Then I remembered what the manager had said about giving anyone a ride. Cyril offered to wait down the road while I collected the keys. The manager was not in his office when I went there. I had to wait for him to return but he didn't return that afternoon. Cyril walked back up the hill after waiting for almost an hour. He figured something had gone wrong. We tried to go to the pub on Friday afternoon. Again, the manager was not to be found. He arrived just before dinner and handed me the keys. He was of the opinion I would be going home on weekend leave. When I told him I wasn't going home he asked for the keys back. Suppressing rapidly developing anger and frustration based on the belief he was deliberately stifling my plans, I refused and told him I would be heading off after breakfast. Without comment he walked away. I didn't go home.

On Saturday afternoon I drove to Balcombe Army camp with Cyril and David Dwyer, a patient recovering from a broken neck. We were not going to get into the booze, just look around. At the canteen we played a game of carpet bowls as we drank a beer. We were back in time for dinner. Nurse Pat was on duty and requested my keys. I refused to hand them over telling her that I might want to go out again. Nurse Pat asked me to call into the office after dinner. I had heard that she was a former army nurse and had served in the Victorian Police. Pat, in a very stern tone, invited me to sit. It looked like we were in for a serious talk. She told me her cousin, Sister Walsh, had also served in the Army and was also an ex-police officer. I was not sure where this conversation was going but suspected I was to be either impressed or intimidated.

We chatted about our time in the Army. Pat described herself as being one of the 'blokes' in the Sergeants' Mess at Puckapunyal. She liked to drink beer, play snooker and make love. At first I did not believe my ears. In response, I mumbled something about her being an all-right type of sheila. Drinking, snooker and shagging would have made her very popular in any mess. Unable to resist the temptation I told her I would be happy to join her in all three activities. With just a wisp of a smile Pat told me she thought I was too young for her. Then I was dismissed. Sitting alone on the fire escape steps, I reflected on our chat. Pat had not called me into the office to discuss her sex life. She really did want to say something to me but I did not know what. On Monday morning I handed my keys in, thinking I'd better not push my luck.

Mrs Berwick conceded that it was not possible for me to wear a normal suction type leg. I was pleased she had reached that decision and heard her say that she would prepare a report for Doctor Boutcher, recommending that a Canadian Hip was the only chance I would have of walking with an artificial leg. I continued to practise walking on the suction socket leg each day to prevent deterioration of the muscles in my stump. Mrs Berwick, like Mrs Webb had that special ability to keep me motivated and determined to succeed.

Home for the weekend, I arranged to meet Fay on Saturday morning. Despite her romance being back on track, we arranged to go for a short drive. She liked my car and more importantly felt comfortable with my driving. She was rostered on the afternoon shift, so we only had a short time together, but enough for me to appreciate her willingness to continue our friendship. As I watched her walk back into the Nurses' Quarters, I could not have been more confident of our friendship.

Too early to go home, I went up to Ward West 2. It was well before visiting hours but Harry Jenkins would not object. My old roommate Kevin had been assured his leg would recover and that was good news, however, it would require much more surgery over the next few months. As I was leaving the hospital I met two student nurses with nothing but spare time on their hands. They were aware of who I was, although I didn't recall seeing them around the hospital while I was a patient. Rather boldly, I suggested that I could round up a mate and we could go to the Drive-In that evening. To my surprise, they agreed. Now I had to find a mate not doing anything on a Saturday night willing to go on a blind date.

After phoning around, I found a mate willing to join me as long as I was paying. We headed off to the hospital and waited out the front of the Nurses' Quarters. Many nurses came out but not the two we were waiting for. Fearing that we had been stood up, I suggested we go in and ask for them. They'd had a little difficulty getting a leave pass at such short notice. We gave our names and my car registration number to the elderly Sister on duty and hurried out. The shorter of the two, Kate, was rather cute with light brown hair. Sue was taller with long, black curly hair and a wickedly mischievous smile. I invited Kate to sit in the front with me. Sue got in the back with my mate, Arthur. It was only a short drive to the Drive-In. Just enough time to learn that Kate was a country girl and Sue a city girl. The line of cars waiting to enter went a long way down Murray Road. I made a snap decision and headed for the Tower Hotel. It was crowded and too noisy to have a reasonable conversation, so after one drink we drove to a park near the river. Time to try a little canoodling; Kate and I, although slow to start, were enjoying our moment of closeness in the front seat. Sue and Arthur failed to spark and kept their distance. As we parted back at the Nurses' Quarters I asked Kate if she would like to go out again next weekend. We had a date. On Sunday I went back to the hospital to see Kevin and caught up with David Byrne, an army trumpet player, who had lost a leg as a result of a blood disease. He was being discharged from the hospital the next day. He would be staying with his sister and asked if I could call in on my way home next Friday.

With an early morning appointment at the limb factory on Monday morning, I had arranged for an extended weekend leave pass that allowed me to stay home on Sunday and drive myself to the limb factory on Monday. Driving home on Friday evening I called in on David, he too was having difficulty being fitted with a wooden leg. He asked if I would like to go to the Drive-In on Saturday with him and his girlfriend Ann. I was not that interested until he mentioned Ann had a girlfriend who would most likely be available to join us.

I felt eager to experience a date with a girl who was not a nurse – one, who had no medical involvement at all, someone not familiar with disabled people, disfigurement and artificial limbs. On the understanding that my disabilities were explained to the girl and she was still willing to go out with me, I would go with them. Early Saturday morning David rang me at Mum's and said we had a date. Immediately following the call I had an anxiety attack. I started shaking and sweating whenever I thought about going on the blind date. I did not particularly care what the girl looked like. *Would it be a case of shock, horror?* I would not blame her, but how would I react? *Would I handle the situation calmly or would I get angry?* Memories of Leonie laughing at my writing came flooding back. *Why must I put myself through this anxiety?* The temptation to ring and call the date off was increasing. If I did, I'd either have to face it again sometime or resign myself to avoiding mixing and socialising in the general community. After a lot of thinking about what I should do, I convinced myself that my only option was to face the consequences.

The girl I was about to meet had been friends with David and Ann for some time. David described her as being a good-looking sheila. My guts were all stirred up and I felt clammy as I waited in the car while Ann went to fetch her. Watching her approach the car I quickly checked her out. My first impression was that she was a little short, but slim and shapely with a pleasant face. I got out of the car as Ann brought her around to my door to meet me. Diane displayed no awkwardness as we said hello. At the Drive-In, David and Ann got down to some serious canoodling while Diane and I sat and talked. We had moved just a little closer by the end of the movie. David suggested we meet again next weekend and when Diane agreed, I felt so much better. However, as I had a date with Kate the next day, I responded cautiously. David was not someone I knew well so I had not mentioned Kate to him. I slept well that night. My date had turned out as good as I could have hoped for.

I woke refreshed and looking forward to my date with Kate. When I arrived at the Nurses' Quarters, Sue and Kate were out the front, and I thought Sue was going to join us, then she turned and went inside. I drove to Elwood Beach, a nice long drive, once there we sat and watched the sun set over Port Phillip. It was a romantic setting but I let it slide. *It was too early in the evening.* We headed into the city. Melbourne RSL club was in the *Duckboard House* building where the Limbless Soldiers' Office was located in Flinders Lane. I knew the club would be open and that I'd feel comfortable there.

The doorman recognised me and welcomed us in. I was not wearing a tie and he produced one from a small collection. It was pre-tied with an elastic neckband so I had no difficulty placing it around my neck after Kate did the top button up for me. Once I had conformed to club dress rules we went into the main clubroom. A small group of middle-aged couples were dancing; music was coming from a piano played by an elderly bloke who I gathered was a member of the club. We looked for a table; most were occupied either by patrons, or their drinks while their owners danced. The patrons might have been a lot older than us but they were certainly enjoying themselves. While we sat and waited for our dinner to arrive Kate declined several requests to dance, opting to sit and talk as we soaked up the friendly atmosphere. Back at the Nurses' Quarters we parked and snuggled into each other. As my excitement started to grow, we heard the time announced on the car radio. It was time for Kate to check in, but not before we agreed to meet again. *Two good nights, not too bad at all,* I thought as I drove home.

My Monday morning appointment at the limb factory was the only disappointment for the weekend. It was officially agreed my stump was too short for a suction style leg however, Doctor Hughes still insisted that my stump was too long to try a Canadian Hip style of leg. I suggested that we could shorten it, if that was the case. He promptly told me that surgery was not performed so readily.

Easter 1968

I received a phone call from my mate Butch Carman, who was now posted to 21 Construction Squadron at Puckapunyal camp. He was going to be in Melbourne over Easter as his girlfriend was a nursing sister and had to work. We arranged to spend some time together. I would have to juggle my time as once again I had two potential girlfriends to date over the Easter break. On Good Friday evening David Byrne and I were at a loss as to how to entertain the girls, because nothing was open. We settled for parking in a secluded spot along the Yarra riverbank. Diane was more than ready for some serious canoodling but I found my artificial arm an impediment, as I had earlier discovered, it was not something you could caress your girlfriends' thigh with, and its rigidness made it difficult to comfortably position out of harm's way. Diane appeared not too concerned and happily positioned herself to snuggle into me.

26
ANZAC Day 1968

Butch Carman met me at the Tower Hotel in Ivanhoe on Saturday afternoon. He had a girl with him, not his girlfriend but one of her flatmates. While Butch and I talked about our mates, his friend Pam and David Byrne (who had come along with me) happily chatted away. Hearing that most of my mates were back at Enoggera with 24 Construction Squadron I thought it would be good to drive up and join them for ANZAC Day. Overhearing my conversation, David said he'd like to go with me. We headed north on Friday evening with a leave pass issued from *Maryport* to keep everything in order with the Army.

The miles were rolling by and we were well up into northern New South Wales on the New England Highway. Apart from me getting a ticket for speeding just before dawn, the drive had gone smoothly. Once we crossed the border into Queensland we pulled over and slept. There was no point arriving in Brisbane too early on a Sunday morning. The Brook Hotel/Motel was close to the Enoggera Army camp. We headed there first and booked in for the night. David rang some friends to call for him. I rang Mr Brooks,

Dennis's dad who had called in on me at Heidelberg hospital last year, to arrange catching up on ANZAC Day. It was getting close to the first anniversary of my mate's death.

I headed over to 24 Construction Squadron at Enoggera. Very few sappers were at the unit boozer. I was told that on Sunday most blokes went over to the new Diggers' boozer. I felt rather self-conscious as I entered the very new Diggers' Club. Then I heard, 'Jethro, you old bastard get over here.' It was my old mate Charlie McKay calling me towards a group of old mates. Remarks were made about how well I looked and how many could not believe that in less than twelve months I had returned to Enoggera. It was disappointing to discover that most of the squadron were working up at Shoalwater Bay.

When David returned, I asked him how he felt about driving up to Shoalwater Bay, which is a little further north than Rockhampton. He was more than agreeable, as he had not been north of Brisbane. We could drive up Monday and be back late Wednesday. We booked a room at the Brook Hotel in advance for Wednesday and Thursday night before heading off. An early start had us in Rockhampton late on Monday afternoon. After checking into a motel and having a short nap, I rang a girl who used to write to me while I was in Vietnam. I had met Jane at the Bouldercombe dance hall one Saturday night when I was up in Rockhampton on Exercise *Barrawinga* in 1966. Although she was never my girlfriend, with each letter I received from her I became more determined to win her heart on my return from Vietnam. Getting blown up quickly put an end to that plan. Jane's mother invited us round for dinner and we jumped at the invitation. Jane was now a student nurse and had a steady boyfriend however, she agreed to join us in the morning for the drive to Shoalwater Bay.

The track from Yeppoon was dusty but not too rough. I spotted Sapper George White. After a few words of greeting he hopped into my car and showed me to the main camp. Captain Bielenberg came over and said hello, he told me he had reservations about Jane being at the camp. I understood his position and suggested that David drive Jane home. I had been invited to stay the night and have a few beers with my mates once they were stood down. I arranged to meet David back in the Yeppoon pub in the morning. He seemed happy to be alone with Jane but she appeared very annoyed with me preferring the company of a bunch of blokes to her.

My old Troop Sergeant and mate Harry Webb joined me in the Diggers' boozer after dinner. An impromptu party got underway. Beer and tales from the past started flowing with 'dirty ditties' and boozy singing thrown in for good measure. Around midnight Jack Doohan picked me up several times as I made my way to bed. A most uncomfortable Land Rover ride next morning into Yeppoon punished me for drinking excessively the night before. A long cold shower in the park across from the beach was my haven as I tried to sober up for the trip back to Brisbane.

25 April 1968

The sound of rain on the roof woke us nice and early. Radio reports were predicting the march through Brisbane would be cancelled. The crowd that braved the weather for the traditional Dawn Service were drenched. Over coffee we listened to the radio and considered our options. David borrowed the car and went visiting friends. I only had a short walk over to the pub where my mates would eventually turn up. When I heard that the decision to cancel the march had been made, I went back to bed.

Mr and Mrs Brooks knocked on my door and woke me just before midday. We went to the pub for a drink. I did not particularly enjoy their company; it was not their fault. The terrible burden of guilt was weighing me down. *How could I have a drink with them and enjoy myself?* Mrs Brooks looked so sad. Memories of that terrible morning in May began to swamp my every thought. *What can I say? How can I ease their pain? I can't!* I felt *guilty* was written across my forehead in large letters. I wanted to be somewhere else.

Then I heard Charlie McKay's voice. He was coming towards us. After introductions, Mr Brooks encouraged me to go catch up with my mates.

Sitting around a table having a beer with my mates was just what I needed. Compliments about my survival and recovery were accompanied by unflattering derogatory remarks about my many stuff ups in the past. By early evening many of the blokes had drifted off home. Rather unwisely, I stayed longer than I should have. I had had very little food and too many beers, the walk to my room was quite an effort. Once I was safely on my bed, I crashed. Waking early, I reflected on the previous day. It had been good catching up with old mates and meeting new members of the squadron. Mr and Mrs Brooks were heavy going but I was pleased we had a little time together. I remembered I was going to their place for lunch later that day. ANZAC Day was a great day, well worth the time and effort. All I needed now was a way to ditch the hangover.

'Jethro, are you awake?' I heard Mr Brooks, calling. He had come to take me home for lunch; David would meet me there. With some difficulty, I packed our bags and paid the bill. The Brooks' house was not a happy place to be. A recently sketched drawing of Dennis was hung on a wall in the lounge room. Its likeness was remarkable. They asked if I had any photos of him, I didn't. The pain of their loss had not diminished and was bound to get worse with the first anniversary of the tragedy looming. Although I did not feel totally responsible for their grief, it was me who stood on the mine. As we prepared to leave, I feared how my parting gesture would be accepted. Slowly and with a heavy heart, I embraced Mrs Brooks.

The drive home went smoothly until we got to the 'Fruit Fly' inspection point just inside the Victorian border. We sat waiting to be checked.

'Any fruit in the vehicle?' the inspector asked.

'No, nothing we shouldn't have,' I replied.

'I'll be the judge of that,' he said.

Smart arse, I thought.

'Open the boot,' he demanded. I handed him the keys. The boot was opened and instantly slammed shut again, he was saying something but we did not know what. We both got out to see what his problem was. Then the penny dropped. We had our wooden legs in the boot! One look at us explained everything as he recovered from the shock of discovering two artificial legs in the boot.

27
First Anniversary

Monday 29 April 1968
I had no difficulty getting back into routine after my trip up to Queensland. Meeting up with army mates and being treated so well by them helped me put a few demons to bed. I had harboured the view that some of my mates would have held me totally responsible for the accident that resulted in the deaths of two of our mates. No animosity was detected. Having Mr Brooks say, 'I know you didn't step on the mine deliberately,' was an enormous relief to me.

With renewed enthusiasm I applied myself to my schoolwork. Writing about my week attracted praise from Mrs Webb although she was disappointed to read I'd been booked for speeding. I coped well with Mrs Berwick's reprimand for failing to wear my leg as requested and decided that I would no longer hand my car keys to the manager. It was Friday afternoon before he got round to asking me for them. Politely, I explained that I failed to see why I should; after all, I had driven to Queensland quite legally and back. The manager's response was simple: if I didn't hand over my keys I'd be forbidden to bring my car on to centre property. My response was even simpler: I'd park my car on the street by the front gate.

Sleep was becoming elusive once again, as I tossed and turned night after night. The sound of an exploding land mine would wake me and then I would hear the noise of the Dustoff choppers coming. I felt a need to talk about my dreams to someone but as Doctor Boutcher only called in every fortnight, I started drinking a bottle of beer each night on the steps outside my room and not caring about the consequences if discovered. The beer helped me sleep. I had befriended one of the ladies working around the centre whose husband was serving in Vietnam and had asked her to buy the beer and sneak it into my room. She did, and removed the empty bottles for me.

The first anniversary of my wounding was approaching. I was going to drive up to Mildura and visit Ray Deed's grave on the weekend. I rang both Diane and Kate and told them what I was going to do. Both were understanding and appreciated my desire to be alone. Sister Walsh however, hearing that I was going to Mildura asked if I would give another resident who came from Mildura a ride home. I was familiar with the resident; a tall red headed bloke about eighteen years old who was in Mrs Webb's small group of correspondence students. I agreed once I knew it was a one-way ride. I could not resist pointing out the Centre's rule about giving another resident a ride in my car. Sister Walsh said occasionally rules were broken for good reasons. I figured it depended on who was breaking the rules.

We headed off immediately after breakfast. Talk was slow as I concentrated on finding my way. Once on the highway to Mildura I relaxed and started to talk. His name was John also, and as we drove along he told me how he suffered from a condition known as dyslexia. Broken bones I understood, appendix and heart attacks

I was familiar with – dyslexia, I didn't have a clue. John explained his difficulties and I quickly understood that it would be best not to ask him for directions. With John safely delivered to his family, I found myself a motel for the night and freshened up.

I went to the Police Station and asked if they could help me locate Ray's parents or his widow's address. A helpful constable located Ray's mother's address for me and gave me instructions on how to find my way there. Sitting outside the house I questioned what I was about to do. I did not want to bring further pain to the family. I wouldn't identify myself as the bloke who had stood on the mine. I knocked on the door and a frail, elderly looking lady I thought must have been Ray's grandmother opened it. She was his mother. I identified myself as one of the soldiers wounded in the incident that had cost Ray his life. As a mate, I had come to visit his grave to mark the first anniversary of that fateful day. I followed Mrs Deed into the lounge room where we sat and talked for a while. Her sadness was so visible. I was hurting too and feared that I would lose control over my emotions. I felt vulnerable and fragile and I wanted to be away from this house of sadness, but until I learnt where Ray was buried I had to stay. Without prompting, I heard about Ray's love of trees and how Mrs Deed had managed to have Ray buried near a large tree. That was my moment; I asked where exactly was Ray's grave.

Returning to the motel I bought two bottles of beer. One helped me sleep, the other I shared with Ray the following morning. Sitting by the grave in the deserted cemetery I talked to Ray. I assured him it was an accident and asked for his forgiveness. With the sound of cars arriving to visit other graves, I said I'd return one day and headed back to Melbourne. As I drove, I reflected on the previous year. So much had happened. My recovery had been almost miraculous. Mates had continued to support me. I had attracted new friends and girls. My successes had boosted my self-confidence and taught me some valuable lessons. Physically, I was doing well, but emotionally, I was still searching for happiness.

The long lonely drive to Melbourne was nearly over. Soul searching had helped pass the time.

From that point onwards, I saw less of Diane and more of Kate. Each day passed slowly regardless of how busy I kept myself. Completing work for Mrs Webb had become particularly difficult as I had trouble concentrating. Images of Vietnam, land mines and my mates, kept invading my thoughts at all hours of the day and night. I felt the first anniversary of my wounding was stimulating my memory excessively. Physio was about the only place I gained some relief. The sound of constant activity was a great barrier to daydreaming.

On his way back to Portsea, my old mate Charlie Lynn took a slight detour and called in to see me. We settled on the veranda and talked, oblivious to where I should have been. Matron Smith appeared on the scene and wanted to know what I was doing. Surprisingly, I received her approval to stay were I was and continue talking. Explaining her past military experience in the Korean War to Charlie, we agreed she fully appreciated what 'mateship' was all about. Charlie had been doing it hard at OCS; I was not surprised to hear he had an accumulation of demerit points that had to be redeemed by the time he graduated. Our time together was short but satisfying.

When Friday afternoon arrived, I was keen to get up to Melbourne. I had ideas about persuading Kate to spend a night with me. She would need an overnight leave pass from the Nurses' Quarters and a reasonable excuse – such as going home for the weekend. Kate had an early start the next day so we did not have a late night. I told her that on Sunday I was driving David Young to Kyabram to visit his father. I asked Kate if she would like to come with us and visit her parents, who also lived near Kyabram. She told me that would be great. I suggested she try and get an overnight leave pass. Kate said she was looking forward to meeting my mum. I said nothing to dissuade her from thinking that was to be the case.

Late Saturday afternoon I saw Kate coming out carrying a small overnight bag. Things were looking good. Driving towards the city Kate asked where we were going. Caught a little by surprise, I said that I needed to meet David, who was at his girlfriend's place in South Yarra and arrange a suitable departure time. After talking with David briefly we went for dinner at McClure's Restaurant in St Kilda Road. I asked Kate if she would rather go to a motel with me for the night than go to my parents' home. My request appeared to stun her. She sat quietly for an embarrassingly long time. I certainly had surprised her. The silence had me concerned. *Had I misread the signs?* A heated cuddle in my car is a long way from actually going to bed. In anticipation of Kate agreeing to spend the night with me, I had driven down the Nepean Highway earlier in the afternoon and booked a room. The silence was broken when Kate said, 'I thought you were up to something.' Without a yes or no, I drove towards the motel.

After a few minutes Kate appeared quite comfortable alone in the room with me. When I suggested it would be fun to shower together the idea was rejected. The bathroom was small and accessing the shower itself provided me with a major problem. It had three sliding panels across the front and a step. I placed a towel over the step then sat on my bum and crawled into the cubicle. Not the most graceful entry, I was pleased Kate was not watching. Taking advantage of my absence from the bedroom, Kate undressed and got into bed. Without the obstructive awkwardness of my artificial arm, we were able to embrace more intimately.

When we arrived in Kyabram I dropped David and his girlfriend off at his dad's place and Kate guided me to her family's property. Kate received a warm welcome from her parents as I stood nervously on my crutches beside the car. Country hospitality was punctuated with probing questions ranging from how long had we known each other to how did my artificial arm work. It was obvious to me that her parents were looking at my suitability, or lack of it, to be their daughter's boyfriend.

28
A Birthday Party

I had arranged to join some friends for an afternoon of fun on snow covered Mount Donna Buang east of Melbourne. Sunday traffic was heavy as Kate and I drove towards Healesville and it was bitterly cold. Hopefully, someone would have established a decent campfire before we arrived. On the road to the summit traffic was crawling. Our plan was to meet at the first official car park. The mountain is not particularly high but the crawling pace of the traffic made it a very long journey. Cars were parked along the side of the road and people were walking uphill. Many were playfully throwing snowballs at each other and passing cars. Seeing David Dwyer my mate from *Maryport*, was a lucky break, otherwise I would not have noticed the group huddled around a pitifully small campfire. He guided me into a tight parking spot.

When I stepped out of the car the cold was breathtaking. I quickly discovered my crutches were not designed for walking in snow. I went no more than a few feet then splat! I was on my face licking snow. I found the going a little easier off the roadway and out of the slush. We were introduced to a group of blokes and sheilas from the Army who worked with David Young. He was serving out the remainder of his National Service at Albert Park barracks Melbourne. He had also invited along a few friends from his civilian employment in an insurance office. David Dwyer had brought another resident from *Maryport* a bloke called Ian, and my least favourite physiotherapist, Leonie.

I wasn't really enjoying myself, as I was unable to move around freely and freezing my tits off. Many in the group were happily throwing snowballs or posing for photos. Ian sat and talked with me for a while. I heard about his muscle wasting disease, which is why he was at *Maryport*. He and David had invited Leonie to come to the snow rather half-heartedly and were surprised when she accepted.

At physio on Monday, Mrs Berwick was aware that my 23rd birthday was not far off and invited me to her home to meet her husband and have a home-cooked dinner. She cleared it with Matron Smith for me to be excused from the dining room and stay out a little later. I had to admit that I felt rather privileged. Cyril had been at the Centre for nearly a year and was not aware of anyone being invited home by a staff member. It was arranged for Wednesday, exactly one week before my birthday. On the day, Mrs Berwick asked if I could arrive about six o'clock and would I mind giving Leonie a lift. Ostensibly, Leonie was to balance the numbers. I suspected Mrs Berwick was aware that I harboured ill feelings towards Leonie but did not know why.

'I'll pick her up at five-thirty out the front of her cottage,' I said reluctantly before heading off to Mrs Webb's class.

Dressing in my best clothes was no easy task. This was the first time I was dressing up without any assistance. Normally, I dressed in shorts with my shirt hanging out. On this occasion however, as a mark of respect, it was going to be long trousers with my shirt tucked in and a tie. Tucking my shirt into my trousers was a real challenge with only a partial hand. Holding my trousers up with my hook and pushing my shirttail in, with my only finger, while balancing on one leg, tested my ability and patience. A pair of braces holding up my pants would have been helpful. Eventually, I had my shirt tucked in and trousers belted. I went to the bathroom, as I needed a mirror to tie my preferred Windsor knot in my only necktie. Smartly dressed, I collected Leonie. We made our way up into the hills behind Mornington. On arrival I saw Margaret's car in the driveway. Margaret was the tall slim occupational therapist at Maryport. *Had she also been invited?* If so, why hadn't Leonie come with her?

'Margaret must be still out riding,' Leonie said. Noticing my confused look, Leonie told me how Margaret was a country girl and regularly rode Mrs Berwick's polo horses. Listening to Leonie talk, I became even more confused. I could not imagine Mrs Berwick's dumpy figure perched on a horse galloping around a polo field! Before we entered, I was told the horses belonged to her son.

We were shown into a warm, cosy lounge room. A variety of dainty looking canapés and cold drinks were presented. I was in all sorts of bother trying to lift one from the serving tray. My stiff finger and thumb were not suited for this delicate form of eating. Miraculously, I avoided sticking my finger into anything other than the piece I was trying to lift. I also avoided spilling any drink or food on the very expensive looking carpet or myself. With an overwhelming feeling that I was being scrutinised by everyone around the table, I managed to eat dinner without any mishaps. Sipping a very fine brandy back in the lounge certainly helped me relax. I had avoided joining in much of the conversation at the table, needing every ounce of concentration to successfully use the variety of cutlery displayed before me.

Relaxed and relieved that dinner was over and I had not made a goose of myself, I was able to tune into the conversation. Mr and Mrs Berwick had lived and worked in Canada for a number of years. Leonie was heading to Canada shortly. She was only filling in time at *Maryport*. We talked about what I might like to do in the future. Meaningful suggestions were forthcoming but my lack of education and not my physical disabilities was my stumbling block to almost every suggestion. Jokingly, I suggested I had aspirations of becoming an elevator driver at Myer's department store. Taking my remarks seriously, Mr Berwick suggested I should aim to gain a better education before thinking about employment. Sitting comfortably across from Leonie I looked her over more closely than I had previously. Her light blue eyes appeared to sparkle as they moved around the room. She had a bright toothy smile and her beautifully long blonde hair was flowing freely over her shoulders and down her back. An eye-catching bust line complemented her skirt and blouse and added to her physical attractiveness.

We thanked the Berwick's for a delightful dinner and their most enjoyable company. Driving along the Esplanade towards Mount Martha I was feeling good and a little forgiving towards Leonie. *How could I not like a good–looking sheila who drank beer?* We talked about our evening and found we both enjoyed the dinner. Like me, Leonie floundered a little when it came to the merits of the wine we were drinking. Otherwise, she found the stimulating conversation provided her with more knowledge about working in Canada.

I saw the sign pointing to the beach and turned in. Leonie said nothing as I parked. When Leonie lit up a cigarette, I stepped out of the car and was surprised when she followed me out into the cold. Feeling the cold a little myself, I put a protective arm around her then said, 'Nights like this are designed for romance.' I don't know if it was the booze or the fresh air, but we got into the back of the car and quickly got into a little body warming canoodling.

After a very disturbed sleep reliving my sudden good fortune, I made it to breakfast. Leonie was not to be seen. She walked into the dining room a little later. Our eyes met briefly and I noticed her cheeks go a little red. I wondered if she was blushing or having regrets. Throughout the day she maintained a 'business only' attitude towards me. At physio on Friday, I quietly asked if she would like a ride home to Melbourne. She already had a ride but would be happy to have a ride back on Sunday night. With her address in my pocket, I attacked the remainder of my day with renewed vigour.

I wouldn't be able to catch up with Kate until Sunday owing to her shifts, which was just as well as I was in a quandary about endeavouring to date two girls simultaneously again. I knew in my head that it was wrong but I had an overwhelming desire to grab everything that came my way. I felt an urgent need to make up for all the lost opportunities while I languished in my hospital bed last year. I didn't want to hurt anybody, but I continued to put myself first.

On Saturday afternoon I went over to the hospital. Two more Diggers had arrived from Vietnam and both had lost limbs. David McKenzie lost his legs, one below the knee and the other above, and also an arm above the elbow. Johnny Richardson lost both legs below the knee and his arms were broken. They had been with the Third Battalion pursuing the enemy up in the mountains known as the Long Hais in late March.

Sitting in a pub later downing a few beers with Butch Carman my mate, who had sat next to Jack and me when we flew to Vietnam, provided a most welcome relief from the horrors of war. Butch reminded me that he and a few other mates would be down next weekend to celebrate my birthday. Hell! I had completely forgotten about having a party. I'd been too busy chasing skirt. My mates would be more than happy about my success but they'd be very pissed off if they turned up and I wasn't around.

Sunday afternoon I took Kate for a drive. I felt like a real heel as I only had thoughts about meeting Leonie later that evening. I liked Kate a lot and valued our time together but her submissive and timid personality lacked excitement: I wanted to be challenged. With so much still to be achieved, I needed someone to push me and challenge me to conquer all obstacles that were likely to be encountered. My immediate dilemma was that I knew my time with Leonie would be limited to a few short months. It would not be worthy of me or possible to deceive Kate for that long. Once Leonie had left where would that leave me? 'A tit in the mitt is worth all your scrub turkeys in the bush' was an appropriate old saying that sprung to mind but I discarded the wisdom of the message.

As I drove Leonie back to *Maryport* I invited her home to help celebrate my birthday on Saturday. She accepted. The pressure was now on me to let Kate down gently. Rather cowardly, I rang her on Monday evening to tell her, but before I could say much, she told me she would be working the late shift over the weekend. We would not be able to have any time together. I gutlessly promised to call her the following week.

Wednesday 3 July 1968
My birthday. I would rather be going to the pub than getting ready for another busy day on program! As I was finishing my lunch Ruth, my helpful domestic, whispered that she would leave my beer outside the door before she went home. I slipped her the money to cover its purchase. I had invited Cyril, David and Ian to join me in a drink after dinner. The night air was cool but not unpleasant, containing our laughter was difficult, we had to keep the noise down to avoid discovery. Nurse Pat was on duty and she had noticed my guests heading towards my room. She became suspicious when she could not hear any noise. When she opened the door and found the room empty, her suspicions were confirmed. Opening the fire escape door she discovered the four of us sitting, quietly chatting. Cyril had taken the empties to the bin just in the nick of time. I really enjoyed my clandestine drinking sessions in defiance of the pompous little manager, but more importantly, the alcohol helped me sleep.

My sleep continued to be invaded by terrible dreams involving many of my mates. Happy memories of past occasions in the Army constantly turned into tragedy. Images of my mates being killed or maimed by exploding land mines kept encroaching into my thoughts. At night, the noise of the explosion would wake me. Each time I would be staring at my mutilated hands.

I recalled an occasion the year before in Ward West 2: a World War Two Digger was having dreams about the war and asked for something to help him sleep. The Sister on duty rather insensitively told him the war had been over for twenty years so he should put it behind him. That answer did not help the poor bloke. Remembering the occasion did not help me either. I could not and would not talk about my dreams. Drinking a bottle of beer was much easier.

The ease with which a person could become addicted to alcohol was not lost on me. I had known many blokes in the Army who could not get through the day without a beer. Mindful of the danger I endeavoured not to drink excessively. More importantly, I remembered the Sister's rather blunt remark to the old Digger, I was determined to put the past behind me, and only look forward, be grateful to be alive.

On Saturday night, Mum and my sisters had prepared a mountain of food and the bathtub was filled with bottles of beer and ice. I must have invited almost everyone I knew. People just kept coming and it was not long before a cloud of cigarette smoke engulfed almost every room. A few blokes from 1 Field Squadron were present. Butch and I were introduced to Kevin Smith's fiancée, Jackie, and now we understood why he tried to write to her at every opportunity. Kevin and Jackie were dressed in matching clothing and looked a picture of health and happiness. They mixed well but stayed close together.

Kevin Stephens and David Young appeared to be enjoying listening to many yarns being told by my army mates, especially the ones that were not too flattering. Dad had set up his movie projector and was showing a movie taken while on my plant operators' course at Greenbank camp near Brisbane. Roars of laughter could be heard whenever the footage of me driving a D-pull scraper too fast and nearly bouncing completely out of the machine was shown. A friendly wrestle between Charlie Lynn and I on a stockpile of gravel attracted even more derogatory comments.

Around two o'clock the place was quiet as almost everyone had left. I had not drank too much having spent most of my time talking with friends. Leonie had gone to sleep in the spare room. Mum and my sisters were finishing off the dishes. Hardly any food was left but a load of grog was still in the bathtub. Most of the guests had brought grog with them. Dad was going to be pleased with the leftovers.

Waking to the smell of eggs and bacon wafting out from the kitchen, I went looking for coffee. Mum and Leonie were sitting at the kitchen table chatting about some of the characters present at the party. My mates appeared to have made a good impression with Leonie, except for David Byrne. Although he amused the crowd with his enthusiastic trumpet playing, he appeared to lapse into periods of moodiness and did not mix well. We felt that he was a little out of place not having been to Vietnam, as almost every other bloke had. After a long shower, I was eager to be off and spend some time alone with Leonie.

Back in my bed at *Maryport*, I knew I'd made the right decision. Remembering how Leonie laughed at my writing still hurt, but she had redeemed herself by offering to help me whenever she could. *How good can it get?* I had my own physiotherapist providing free therapy whenever we were away from *Maryport* together and my own remedial English and arithmetic coach. To top it all off, she enjoyed a beer or two. Maintaining our distance during the week was the only problem. The testy little manager would not have viewed too kindly a member of staff fraternizing with a resident.

29
A New Leg

On a visit to the limb factory I was introduced to Fred Hinde. He had the reputation of being one of the best limb makers in the trade. I liked him immediately. Fred explained how my new leg would function and what was involved in its making. It would be a more complicated leg than the previous ones I had been trying to use. He showed me through the Centre's workshop; starting with blocks of seasoned willow that would be shaped into a thigh or lower leg section. I would need one of each. Once fitted to a metal knee joint they were coated in skin-colored fiberglass. A suitable sized rubber foot would be attached and an aluminum cast hip joint would attach the fiberglass bucket to the top part of the leg.

    Stripped naked, holding on to a support bar I stood still while Fred wrapped me in cold wet Plaster of Paris bandages from my navel down and over my bum. Only the family jewels were spared. Once the plaster dried, Fred used a large pair of shears to crunch his way down the right side of the cast. Fearing an accidental slip may achieve what the landmine blast didn't was all the incentive needed to stand perfectly still! Once the cast was removed I had a bath and cleaned away any residual plaster.

My next appointment was on the following Friday so I arranged an extended weekend leave pass. I would go home Thursday evening. I could go to the limb factory early and have the rest of Friday to myself. It also gave me an extra night with Leonie. We drove into Frankston for dinner together and then before I took her home we parked at Mount Martha Beach for a little canoodling.

It started to rain heavily as I headed home after dropping Leonie off. Not concentrating as well as I should have been, I went into a long, sweeping, right hand curve too fast and lost control. As the car spun around, I had visions of plummeting over the cliff to a watery end in Port Phillip. When the car stopped rolling, I was still in the upside down car but unhurt. I could move quite freely, so I crawled out. As I made my way clear I felt pieces of wood everywhere, then wet grass. The rain was still coming down hard. I made my way towards a wooden fence. Sitting up against it, I could see my car on its roof. My crutches were nowhere to be seen. I crawled along the fence line until I came to a gate. A light had been turned on. Expecting the front door to open in response to the noise of the crash, I waited but the door remained closed. I stood up and cautiously hopped towards the door. My knock was answered by a male voice.

'What do you want?'

'I've had a crash and need to ring a tow truck,' I said.

'I'll call one for you,' was the reply. I stood and waited. The door still did not open. Whoever was inside was not opening the door to strangers.

My crutches were retrieved from my wrecked car before it was towed away. The tow truck driver estimated it would be at least ten weeks before I got it back. A cab was called and I headed for David Young's, he lived nearby in Frankston. It was around one o'clock when I knocked on David's front door. I was cold and wet. As I explained what had happened he handed me a large brandy and guided me to the spare bedroom. Next morning I rang David Byrne and asked if he could drive down and collect me. We headed to the nearest branch office of my insurer to lodge my claim. A helpful claims officer sat patiently listening to my slightly modified version of how the crash happened. He suggested I claim it was caused by a front tyre blowout.

I was in no mood to attend the limb factory so I rang and cancelled my appointment. While David was driving me home I decided I'd buy a replacement car, as I did not like the idea of being without a car for so long. My time with Leonie was running out fast, I needed a car if I wanted to spend time with her. Courtney and Patterson (the company where I bought the Ford Fairmont from) had a used car yard. We agreed I would sell the replacement car back to them once repairs were completed, I bought an older model blue automatic Holden. Mum was confused when I arrived home. I told her I had been in a minor accident and the car was at the panel beaters. She would have had a heart attack if I had told her the truth. Dad wanted to know about my steering accessories. I said I would buy a new steer-easy knob and convince the police that I really did not need the lugs attached to the steering wheel. When I went over to Leonie's she was flabbergasted to hear that after crashing one car, I went out and bought another.

The following week Fred had my stump bucket ready for fitting. It looked like a misshapen ball made out of fiberglass. Fred explained how the interior would be lined in kangaroo hide as its supple texture made it suitable for use with artificial limbs. Fred was happy to proceed to the next and final stage. He would build a leg onto the bucket.

Looking forward to another weekend away from *Maryport* with Leonie I was heading to my car when Nurse Pat called me into the office. She suggested I might like to take home some of my personal belongings. Curious to say the least, I asked why. She closed the door behind me. My behavior had been under close scrutiny and was on the agenda for next week's staff meeting with Doctor Boutcher. My removal from *Maryport* was going to be discussed, she told me.

'Well, that's fine with me,' I replied. Cyril helped me clear out my room. As we drove towards Melbourne, Leonie told me one of her colleagues had been complaining about me breaking the rules and getting away with it. She refused to tell me who it was but Doctor Boutcher did not appreciate me walking away from *Maryport*. He wasted no time bringing my army career to an inglorious end. I was now classified as being medically unfit for service in the Military Forces and discharged from the Army on Monday 9 September 1968.

Seeing my completed leg for the first time shocked me. The bucket was big, cumbersome and although reasonably comfortable to wear, the top edge poked me in the ribs. Walking with it required a lot of practice, an action that could be described as an *exaggerated pelvic thrust* to swing the leg forward. As I walked with the leg I found it hard to let go of the parallel rails I was using for support. Remembering that Douglas Bader with two artificial legs refused to use a walking stick, I took a few steps unaided before crashing to the floor. Fred explained how my leg with two joints was a lot more difficult to use than what Bader had. He recommended I use a walking stick for safety until I became fully accustomed to the leg. I took his advice.

Leonie was leaving for Canada at the end of the week. Deep within me, I had harbored the thought she was attracted to me enough to abandon her trip but that was not going to happen. Our last night out together was to the theatre to see Barry Humphries waving gladioli everywhere. Leonie wanted me to wear my leg but I didn't feel confident enough. Also, I felt self conscious about walking with a limp. Leonie could not understand how I was prepared to be seen on crutches with only one leg but did not want to be seen walking with a limp. Our night out was a little frosty.

We'd had our first bad moment. Driving home in silence, I reflected on our short time together. Feebly, I hoped that she would return sooner rather than later, to me. But in reality I accepted that at the end of the day I could offer her very little. Physical attraction between two people might create a memorable sensual experience however, it did not necessarily contribute to long-term compatibility. I was seriously disabled, uneducated, unemployed and had no career prospects. In summary: not much of a catch for an attractive well-educated, professional young lady. Now all I wanted was to shut her out of my life, but the torch I carried was not ready to be extinguished. On Sunday afternoon I drove her and her parents to Essendon airport. As I watched her walk towards the aircraft, I could only think how lucky I had been to know such a wonderful woman.

Within weeks I was walking reasonably well on the Canadian Hip and despite frequently falling over I gained confidence. Fred told me the foot was catching on uneven surfaces stopping it from swinging forward into the correct position. He suggested that the leg be shortened a little to give me more ground clearance. The downside was it would it enhance my limp, but not falling was without doubt my preferred option. Preventing the top rim of the bucket poking me in the ribs was more difficult to remedy. Doctor Hughes had refused to allow it to be lowered, as it had been made according to specifications available to him. I asked him to show me the specifications for making a leg for John Thompson. He was offended by my remarks. I felt as an able-bodied person, he failed to appreciate the associated discomfort of the prosthesis. Unable to persuade Doctor Hughes to at least try a little adjustment, I bluntly told him that I would have Dad cut it down. My raised voice attracted the attention of the factory foreman. Ivor Appleton supported my suggestion and convinced Doctor Hughes that my idea was reasonable. When Fred was asked for his opinion he also agreed.

With the modifications completed my walking improved and I was soon wearing the leg for many hours each day around the house. Angie, now my brother-in-law, offered to go buy me a pair of trousers that would fit when I was wearing the leg. He ran a tape measure around my middle and bum and came home with a pair of trousers that fitted reasonably well.

I required a lounge suit as I had been invited to Kevin Smith's wedding in late November. David Young suggested I try Fletcher Jones in the city, explaining how they meticulously measured clients and I would only need to try on the finished product once. Large spacious change rooms were also available. Margaret, the occupational therapist at *Maryport,* was going to be in Melbourne on the weekend, so I asked if she would assist me choose the material. Given the number of samples produced, I was grateful for her help. When I returned to try the suit on, staff helped me remove and replace my trousers over my legs without undue attention to my artificial leg. The suit fitted well and the left trouser leg had been lined to protect it from excessive wear by rubbing on the hard surface of the artificial leg. I was so impressed by the service, I ordered a new sports coat and two extra pairs of trousers.

It was early November. My Ford Fairmont was back on the road and the Holden had been sold back to the car yard. On my way to an appointment with Mrs McLeod at the hospital I met Doctor Benson, the rehabilitation specialist who had spoken to me on many occasions while I was in hospital. He was pleased to see me walking and on hearing about my appointment with Mrs McLeod invited himself along. David Young had suggested I enrol at Taylor's Coaching College. Mrs McLeod and Doctor Benson were well aware of the college and its excellent reputation. However, they had reservations about my access to its location in Little Collins Street in Melbourne's Central Business District. Personally, I had serious doubts about my ability to study at matriculation level considering I had only attended school to year nine. I suggested I study for the Leaving Certificate. We agreed I would arrange a meeting with the College Principal and discuss my options and check out access at the same time. Mrs McLeod would initiate the appropriate paperwork with the Department.

A photo of David McKenzie taken from the Melbourne *Herald* was shown to me. David had passed his driving test nine months after losing three limbs in Vietnam. We were all happy to see him making such good progress. Mrs McLeod told me he was now waiting to receive his Repatriation Gift Car. A Hillman Hunter was given to eligible veterans every two years. An application submitted on my behalf last year had been rejected on the grounds I had not lost three limbs. After a brief discussion it was agreed that a fresh application should be lodged, citing my mutilated left hand as being the appropriate third limb.

Driving home I could not help but think about all the wonderful people who were willing to help me. From the moment I regained consciousness in hospital, total strangers had been willing to steer me in the right direction. Now I felt I must honour their support by making every effort to succeed. Studying for the Leaving Certificate might not be that big a deal for the average student, but for me, a bloke who had flunked school at almost every level, it would be a challenge. Life for me had been one long challenge. Being wounded and seriously disabled increased the intensity of the challenge. If I wanted to continue moving forward I had to give it a go.

30
Independence and Avoiding Reality

My meeting with Mr George Taylor the principal of the college was encouraging. We agreed that I should limit myself to four subjects: English Expression was compulsory, Economics, Social Studies and Geography were more than enough and would keep me busy. I couldn't help but question my ability to study at such a high level. Previous schooling achievements had done nothing for my confidence. Seeing the book list added to my apprehension: Economics? I had not the faintest idea about the subject.

Dressing for college next year was going to be a real chore – a suit and tie was the required dress for male students. Feeling totally bewildered, I wanted to sit and cry. If I had not been in such a public place I think I would have. Wearing my leg brought a whole load of new difficulties. Fitting socks and shoes to my wooden leg was not easy. Changing my trousers took some time to master. Regularly I fed the wrong trouser leg onto my wooden leg. Tying a neat Windsor knot after doing up my top button with the aid of a 'button hook' was a major achievement. The temptation to return to the college and tell them I'd changed my mind was very strong. However, conceding defeat without first having a go was not in my nature.

I went to the local branch of the State Savings Bank of Victoria and enquired about a cheque account. Standing patiently in line I eventually reached the teller and was handed a number of forms to fill in. With the forms completed, I again joined a queue. After looking at my signature, the young female teller held up a form and told me that my signature was different on each form. Feeling the stares of the people queuing behind me burning into the back of my neck – I explained that writing with an artificial arm was new to me and I was still trying to develop a signature. Her reply that I would have to speak with the manager left me feeling embarrassed and angry.

I moved to a shorter queue at the Enquiries counter. When I asked to see the manager, the bank officer began telling me how it was necessary to make an appointment. As I was about to abandon my quest for a cheque account the manager came out of his office and asked how he could help. After introductions I explained how difficult it was to have two signatures look similar. My writing varied substantially between writing sitting down or standing, whether I was wearing my leg or using crutches. All had an effect on my writing ability. I was invited into his office and we discussed the merits of using a password or a thumbprint. Neither option had any appeal to me. All I needed was a little appreciation of my situation by the bank staff. He accepted my position and assured me I would have no further difficulties but I should try and stabilise my signature.

I decided to trade my Fairmont in on a new V8 Fairlane but I had a small problem owing to purchasing my car without paying Sales Tax. I was obligated to keep it for two years or twenty five thousand miles (40,000 kilometres) and I was well short of meeting either condition. My mate Kevin Smith was a panel beater and said he might know someone who could advance the odometer. He did. I returned to Courtney and Patterson and bought a white Fairlane with power steering.

Dear John

In the afternoon mail I received a letter from Leonie. It was brief and to the point. She would not be writing anymore and asked that I didn't write to her. It was all over between us. Although I had expected it would come to this, it was still a hard blow to take. The bluntness of the letter was what really hurt. Leonie would quickly become a pleasant memory. There was no value in beating myself up over something that was out of my control.

It was getting close to Kevin Smith's wedding and I was starting to feel uncomfortable about going. I would be alone and apart from Kevin's brother Ray, I would not know anyone else. The invitation was for me alone so I really could not take Fay or anyone else with me. I had bought a present and had my new suit. My walking was coming along although I had some difficulty accepting my limp, which was very noticeable, and the wooden leg was so much thinner than my own leg. I still felt very self-conscious walking in public. Also, for some inexplicable reason, the appearance of my hook and left hand that looked more like a chicken's foot had started to bother me now that I was wearing the leg. I felt I'd be an object of either pity or curiosity at the wedding. I could not go. While visiting Fay I told her about my intention to go to Queensland for a visit but I didn't mentioned why. I could not believe my luck when she said she'd like to go with me. Her romance had come off the rails again. We agreed to leave the next Sunday.

17 November 1968

I woke early, eager to be away and alone with Fay. By midday we were on our way. The sound of the V8 engine was music to my ears as we raced up the Hume Highway. Our first stop was Fay's parents' at Benalla. Under close scrutiny from her mother I managed to enjoy a feed of scones with strawberry jam and cream while delicately fielding questions about why we were heading to Queensland together. Fay was equally evasive about falling out with her boyfriend.

On reaching Gundagai I pulled into the first motel I saw with a vacancy sign on. As I walked back from handing in our breakfast menus at the office, I wondered if our time away was going to be as fulfilling as I was hoping. Fay's convincing explanation to her mum about our friendship being platonic may have been genuine, I would soon find out. Again, I was faced with the perils of showering in a strange bathroom. A wet bathroom floor is a hazard for most people, but for a bloke with only one leg and no hands to support himself, it's like skating on thin ice. I placed towels on the floor and managed to shower without mishap. Fay was unbelievably welcoming as we snuggled up together. Our passion was ignited by our long absence from each other. Alone in a large double bed, with no fear of being disturbed, we slept soundly. On hearing the breakfast tray being pushed through the service opening Fay sprang out of bed and brought it over. As we enjoyed our breakfast in bed together, I could not recall breakfast ever being so good.

North of Newcastle the smell of smoke had our attention. We saw the smoke-filled sky in the distance and then fires burning on both sides of the highway. We reached a police roadblock and found the highway was closed. We had the option to park and wait indefinitely or backtrack and head up the New England Highway to Brisbane. Backtracking appeared to be our best option. Sleeping in the car had no appeal. Carefully driving through smoke we saw many soldiers fighting the fires as we headed south. After two days on the road we finally arrived in Brisbane. I caught up with many mates and Mr and Mrs Brooks. Memories of my past had quite an impact on me but fortunately, Fay coped well with my changing moods and most of our time was packed with fun.

23 November 1968

Kevin Smith's wedding day. I lay in bed feeling like a first class louse. I had run away rather than attend a mate's wedding. What was wrong with me? Was being looked at, that big a problem? If it is was, I needed to get over it. It was an issue that wouldn't be going away. I decided to ring Kevin and tell him I was stuck in Brisbane and unable to attend. Then I felt even more disappointed in myself. I couldn't believe that I could lie to a mate about why I wouldn't be turning up at his wedding. *Why can't I just tell him the truth?* As a mate he would understand. When I rang Kevin's home his mother answered. Feeling relieved that I was not lying to Kevin I told her that I had car trouble and was waiting on spare parts.

My delightfully intimate holiday with Fay was coming to an end. I listened as Fay said how she wished we could just keep driving. She had enjoyed herself and my ego was soaring to new heights. I could not imagine what life with Fay would be like. We were not in love with each other. We satisfied each other's physical needs and were there for each other. How long our unique friendship would be permitted to endure was subject to many other influences. *Should Fay marry her boyfriend?* At the moment, he did not appear to mind that we were away together, probably because he was pursuing other girls.

31

Leaving the Nest

The Limbless Soldiers' Association's annual dinner was on in Melbourne on Friday night. I had bought a fine new shirt with double cuffs that required cuff links and a button down collar for the occasion. With the shirt laid out on my bed, the cuff links were placed into position. Then I threaded my tie around the collar. A little pressure was needed to get my left hand squeezed through the cuff. Doing up buttons was slow but no longer beyond me, not even the top button. I used a buttonhook to fasten it. Positioned in front of a mirror, I tied an excellent Windsor knot in my tie. Fully assembled and dressed, I didn't look too bad but felt terrible. My stomach was churning with anxiety, I had not been out to a formal function dressed up in my Sunday best since I was wounded and I was developing a phobia about crowds. The dinner was a grand affair with many guests. Toasts and speeches went on a little too long as I sat in a cloud of cigarette smoke. When it was necessary to applaud, I banged my hook on the tabletop to contribute to the noise of appreciation.

Saturday morning I drove over to talk with Pam, the nurse

I had met earlier in the year with Butch Carman. She had been sharing a two-bedroom flat with a couple of girlfriends and they had all decided to head home to Queensland. If the flat was suitable, I was prepared to take over their lease. The flat turned out to be ideal, being on the ground floor with only a small step to negotiate. It had ample parking and was just up the road from the Repatriation Hospital. I did not hesitate accepting and we agreed that I would move in the week before Christmas.

With help from my two brother-in-laws, who could see an opportunity to visit and have a few drinks occasionally, I was quickly settled in by 18 December. Second-hand furniture was easily found. Mum was not too pleased that I had moved out of home again. She was concerned I would be alone. Being *alone* was not my plan. Apart from entertaining visitors, I was hopeful of finding someone suitable to share the place. I had already received word that my mate Jack Campbell would be down over Christmas and New Year. He would appreciate having a place to stay when not staying at his sisters. Patrick, another mate languishing in the hospital with a broken leg, had also expressed an interest in sharing with me. Although I had only known him a short time I was confident we would get along.

David McKenzie had become romantically linked to Flip, a physiotherapist at the hospital, and I had started keeping company with her colleague Robyn. The two shared a flat. Regularly we made a foursome and went out for dinner. Robyn and I had even developed and practiced a few basic dance steps. Keeping my left leg turned slightly out and behind me prevented me from falling over. Together in the dimmed lighting, we could shuffle cheek-to-cheek around restaurant dance floors. It was a big step in the right direction!

I took Jack and Robyn to David Young's New Years' Eve party. I was keen for Jack to meet a girl. He had spent a quiet Christmas with his sister and had now moved into my spare bedroom. At the party there were many unaccompanied girls but Jack showed no interest. He was content to sit and drink. At midnight we all sang 'Auld Lang Syne' then headed for home. I did not feel too bad being out in a crowd, considering most of the crowd were total strangers. Being with Jack and Robyn had given me a feeling of security. As we enjoyed a nightcap, I asked Jack why he was so disinterested in the girls at the party.

'They were all too young for me,' he replied.

1 January 1969

Jack and I called in at the hospital to visit Kevin Stephens. Head Nurse Harry Jenkins, was on duty and as Jack and I entered the ward Harry rushed towards us thrusting out both hands. Most of the Vietnam War wounded had been released to go home for Christmas. My mate Kevin was back recovering from further surgery on his left leg. He would be in hospital for a long time, but at least his leg would be saved. Kevin had been advised at his last army medical board that his period of National Service had been extended to allow for his recovery. Another 7 RAR bloke who had been shot in the right leg was sitting up in bed. He was so long his bed had to be extended. Barry O'Dea told us he was six feet six inches tall (1.98 metres).

Unfortunately, a misunderstanding between Robyn and I about where our friendship was heading resulted in us drifting apart. We only saw each other whenever we met at the hospital. Over the last couple of months Robyn had taught me much by example and explanation. No longer was I overawed when entering a flash restaurant that had tabletops covered with cutlery and glasses of every shape and size. Wine lists were not flippantly dismissed as I endeavored to conceal my awkwardness. I could order the popular French dish *Chateaubriand* with the confidence of a seasoned diner.

Patrick agreed to share my flat once he was discharged from hospital. When he settled in our social activity quickly moved up a notch or two. Barry O'Dea had started to call in frequently with his girlfriend Sue, who I had met last year with Kate. He brought his cousin Marcia around on one occasion and she and Jack hit it off really well. Marcia became a regular visitor to the flat even after Jack returned to Queensland. Patrick and I were happy to have her around. We appreciated her company and her willingness to tidy up after us was very much appreciated. Kate started to come around with Sue. I felt she was trying to resurrect our romance however, I was ashamed of the way I had treated her and wanted to keep my distance to avoid repeating my past behavior.

Applying myself to achieving a successful result at the end of the year was my single driving ambition. Attending college and completing assignments was going to challenge every ounce of self-discipline I possessed. Not that I had intentions of hibernating! With more than enough friends to socialise with whenever I needed the diversion from studying, I could manage my time according to my needs. That was the plan I intended to follow and maintain.

Back to the books

The books recommended by Mr Taylor remained unread despite all my good intensions and assurances I had given him to prepare for the start of the school year. A desire to let my hair down once too often left no time for book reading. Foolishly, I had made very little effort preparing myself to undertake what was going to be one of the most difficult and challenging episodes in my life. In anticipation of driving in peak hour traffic each day, I took a test drive. Getting up early and dressing in a new grey suit I drove into Little Collins Street in the city. It took 30 minutes to reach the car park that I would be using while attending classes. The publican of the Arcade Hotel had agreed to let me park behind the pub providing I left my car keys in the bottle shop. In my new suit I felt more like a young man on his way to work in a city office than a schoolboy. Coffee and toast for breakfast at the restaurant opposite the college was enhanced by an endless stream of nicely dressed girls on their way to the bank on the opposite corner. I headed home satisfied I would cope.

Monday 3 February 1969
Full of apprehension, I headed off to college. As I walked up the Causeway towards the college entrance I saw young blokes dressed in lounge suits and nicely dressed girls chatting in groups along the footpath. Cautiously, I negotiated my way through the crowded entrance and headed towards the elevator. A bloke, who was either a member of the college staff or a member of the building management, asked if I was a student. Answering that I was, he officiously told me that students were not permitted to use the elevator. Stepping up close to him I suggested he might like to make an exception on this occasion as I had only one leg - he allowed me to enter the elevator.

The end of my first day was a welcome relief. I had sat around for hours waiting to be enrolled in my chosen subjects. Wednesday was an early start but with only two classes I'd finish no later than ten-thirty allowing the rest of the day to be free. The other four days classes did not start until nine o'clock or later. Mid-afternoon finishing was more than acceptable to me. Changing class between each subject caused me a few hassles as I tried to avoid students rushing between floors to their next subject.

By the end of the first week my confidence was shattered when I received my first English Expression test paper back. It looked like the teacher had slashed his throat and bled all over it. Corrections and remarks were written in red biro all over the page. As I was leaving, the teacher asked if I had time to talk. With mounting anxiety I waited for the last of the other students to clear the room.

'You are well below standard John,' he said. 'When did you leave school?'

I provided as much detail as I could in the time available. We discussed my chances of getting up to standard.

'With additional coaching and some hard work, you have a chance,' he said. Additional remedial coaching was available at the college for a fee. I assured him that I would follow up that option with the Repatriation Department. I did, and the Department agreed to pick up the additional expense.

32

Distractions

I put in many hours trying to get into a study routine. It was difficult to stick to the task but motivation kept driving me onwards despite floundering when asked a question in class. It was not so much a case of not knowing the answer but lacking the confidence to express myself adequately. I felt so out of place. I really appreciated the meaning of being 'a fish out of water'.

A party at the flat created a wonderful diversion. Studies went on the back burner for the weekend. The crowd was much larger than I'd expected it to be. David Young always managed to gather a crowd. He regularly boasted that working in an office with lots of girls guaranteed he had a very full little black book. One girl attracted my attention. Margot looked like a sheila I could happily spend time with. As the night wore on I was able to corner her and arranged to take her home after the party. Feeling confident about my chances with Margot, I went to my bedroom and removed my arm and leg. When asked why I had done so by the partygoers I explained that wearing the artificial limbs chafed me after a while, especially in hot weather. This was true but not why

I had removed them on this occasion. Parked out the front of Margot's I was able to comfortably engage in a little canoodling.

I returned to college on Monday feeling much happier and relaxed about being there. All four teachers had now spoken to me about the standard of my work. Although highlighting my weaknesses, other remarks were encouraging. My social life had to be curtailed even more. I could not afford to be chasing girls at the expense of ignoring my studies. I hoped it was all going to be worth it in the end.

Chris Sallmann introduced himself as we sat next to each other in English class. He invited me to join him for coffee afterwards, where I met his friend Ian Hamilton. Both were about 17 years of age. They had been students at St Kevin's College Toorak before attending Taylor's College. I also became friendly with two young girls, Joanne Carter was at least 18 and Donna Curran was only 17, who were also in three of my classes. Having someone to talk to between classes helped pass the time. My four young friends provided me not only with company but guidance about studying and completing my assignments. I also met two other Vietnam veterans: Barry Heard had served with 7 Battalion and Anthony James had served with the artillery. Both were National Servicemen and had known each other in Vietnam. They were studying for their Matriculation Certificate.

Friday after college I drove to the RSL Club in Duckboard House for a drink before heading home. Parking in Flinders Lane on Friday evening was never easy but I was lucky, there was a space at the front door. The bar area was crowded with smartly dressed blokes. Almost all were involved with the clothing industry: Flinders Lane had been associated with the garment industry for over 100 years. Young ladies accompanied older looking blokes and I figured it must be a perk of the industry. Journalists and staff from *The Herald* and *The Sun* newspapers located around the corner in Flinders Street also gathered at the club.

A photo of a girl wearing a fur bikini was being passed around. It was a good look but not very practical. The model in the photo was present in the club and I managed a quick look at the photo then checked out the girl as she moved between tables. She was about 25, slim with short blonde hair and a pleasant smile. I figured she was well out of my league and continued chatting at the bar.

Wanting quiet time to get into my studies I went home early. I had a couple of novels to read. Patrick however, was eager to go for a drink but I'd already had my fill for the evening. I started reading a book called *My Crowded Solitude* by Jack McLaren. After a few pages it became obvious that sleep was what I needed. Reading was a waste of time.

On Saturday morning I made a fresh start. It was not a book I would have chosen but I didn't have any choice in the matter. Late in the afternoon I was happy to put the book aside and prepare for my date with Margot. Sunday morning I was up early determined to finish reading the book. When Patrick asked what the book was about I scratched my head and said it was about a bloke who chose to live in isolation up on Cape York Peninsula and establish a coconut plantation. I struggled to provide any more detail. Now it was obvious how much more work I had to do. My English teacher would not be satisfied with such a brief explanation.

A small crowd including Dad and my brother-in-law Keith had turned up for a Sunday morning drinking session that would soon become a regular event. My studies were shelved for the rest of the day. However, I avoided drinking too much as I had an early start in the morning with my English tutor, Mrs Arnott, an elderly lady who had been assigned to assist me. She had asked me to read the book and be ready to answer questions. I got up early on Monday to finish reading before heading off to college. With an earlier start I encountered more peak hour traffic adding an extra five minutes to the journey. Answering questions about what I had read gave me a greater understanding into what was required when studying a book, as opposed to simply reading for pleasure.

Again, I opted to conclude my week with a few drinks at Duckboard House. While talking with the Corps of Commissionaires officer at the front door, the girl who had posed in the fur bikini the week before came into the foyer from the bar. She said hello and I said hello back. She asked if I knew Bob Henriksen from Mackay in Queensland. I remembered a bloke by that name. He was one of the reinforcements for Vietnam assembled at SME in December 1966 with me. He was a stocky blond haired Nasho, posted to 17 Construction Squadron at Vung Tau and he regularly visited me in hospital. The girl then introduced herself as Maree and asked me to follow her. I happily followed! Bob was sitting at a table with three other girls. When he shook my hand, I feared he would break it with his enthusiastic handshake.

Bob had hitched down from Mackay to Melbourne and was looking for work and a place to live. Staying with the four girls he knew from Mackay was straining their friendship. In reply to whether I could help Bob out I mentioned that maybe I could. First, I would have to discuss it with Patrick. With Bob's problem in hand I turned my attention to the four girls. I had been invited to an engagement party the following night. Margot unfortunately was not available to go with me. I figured that out of four girls I should be able to get one to step out with me. If not, I'd better change my technique. Maree was sitting next to me so I asked her first, she accepted without hesitation. With a promise to have an answer for Bob the next night, I excused myself and headed home.

Patrick had gone home to Bendigo for the weekend so I rang him and asked how he felt about sharing his room with Bob, halving his share of the rent. I did not particularly want to share a room as I was regularly staying up late with my books. Patrick was happy to share on the understanding that Bob pulled his weight.

I was confronted by four flights of stairs to climb when I called for Maree. I recalled how in *Reach For the Sky* Douglas Bader had to climb up six flights, a total of ninety-six stairs, when courting his wife. It did not make my climb any easier; I made it to the top breathless. I knocked on the door and Bob answered eager to know what news I had for him. He was delighted and we agreed I'd call for him tomorrow afternoon. I was not expecting to have a late night as I thought Maree had only agreed to go out with me to influence my decision about Bob. From what I had seen and observed at Duckboard House, the garment industry may be glamorous but I felt it was awfully fickle as those involved maneuvered for an advantage over their competitors.

Arriving at the party, I met David McKenzie at the front door. He too was familiar with the photo of the fur bikini. He couldn't stop grinning as I introduced him to Maree. As David and I stood alone while Maree went to get more drinks he looked at me with a mischievous, 'I know you Thompson' look, and muttered something about my deviousness. The party was a fun night and I appreciated being out with a bunch of mates celebrating the engagement of two friends.

Parked out the front of Maree's flat, I was not too keen on climbing up and down all the steps. So I asked if she would excuse me from the climb.

'With no privacy upstairs it's best we say goodnight here,' she said in a rather sexy tone and moved closer to me. Instinctively, I pulled her even closer. Fully assembled I'm limited in my ability to become too physical. Fearing she might take my reluctance to engage with her more intimately as a rejection, I asked if she would like to go to the beach tomorrow. She liked the idea. I sat and watched her walk safely into the hallway and disappear as she climbed the stairs.

The weather was still hot enough for a trip to the beach in early March. I headed out on my crutches dressed in shorts and tee shirt. Mindful of Maree's working environment, I started to think about how she would react to my missing limbs. Bob answered the door also dressed for the beach. Melbourne bayside beaches are rather tame compared to the surf beaches Bob and Maree were accustomed to and they soon lost interest splashing around the calm waters of Elwood Beach. They opted to sun bake while I enjoyed the freedom of movement swimming gave me. I saw Bob sitting a little behind Maree. No doubt he was admiring her near-naked body, as she lay flat on her back in a very brief bikini. I suspected that Maree was admiring the many sun tanned able-bodied males strutting up and down the beach. While I remained in the water, I felt relaxed, but I soon became anxious when I clumsily left the water. My ravaged body was now on display for everyone to see and compare. As much as I loved the beach I doubted it was a wise choice when trying to impress a sheila.

As we drove back to her flat, Maree surprised me when she whipped off her bikini top and rummaged around in her bag for a tee shirt, obviously quite accustomed to rapid changes of clothing in front of others. Apart from her rather sexy wink she didn't say a word. While Bob went upstairs to collect his gear, we remained in the car and had a brief kiss-n-cuddle. We arranged to meet on Friday at Duckboard House.

Bob was more than pleased with the flat and after a quick drive around the area felt confident he'd be happy living in Heidelberg. Patrick got home early and over a couple of beers we shared our accumulated local knowledge with Bob. On Monday he looked for a job. Wednesday he began work as a general handyman at the nearby Austin Hospital. We were confident of our compatibility considering none of us had known each other too well prior to sharing the flat.

With two flat mates temptations were plentiful. Recognising the danger signs that could derail my study plans was not too difficult. I had to establish an understanding that my studies were very important to me; weeknights were study nights. I broke that rule within days when I had a date with Margot, who I was still very much interested in.

My four new college friends had displayed a real willingness to help me and I genuinely appreciated and needed their assistance. Chris suggested we have a study group on Sunday morning at his home. I was the only one able to attend but that was fine with Chris. I looked on my new friends as joining forces with my old friends who had persistently supported me and prevented me from falling into an abyss of misery. Succeeding would be the only way I could ever acknowledge their efforts and honour my mates who had perished in Vietnam.

A few drinks and dinner with Maree before tumbling into bed with her would be an absolute perfect finish to my first month as a student. Then I remembered the house rules I saw on the girls' kitchen cupboard. For all to see in bold writing it said, 'Boys are forbidden in Bedrooms'. When I read the rule I thought it was a good rule, as two girls shared each bedroom. But on this occasion I was not too keen on the rule. I doubted that Maree would be too keen to come home to my bedroom now that Bob had moved in.

A good crowd had gathered at Duckboard House. I found a seat at a table and waited for Maree to turn up. After a while I started to think she had stood me up. When she arrived it was obvious she had been drinking elsewhere. She'd had drinks at the office to celebrate the signing of some big deal. We did not stick around for long, Maree was eager to go home. I suspected I'd be getting the arse once I drove her home but I was wrong. The flat was empty and Maree changed into casual street clothes. Talking and watching TV looked as good as it was going to get for a while. Not exactly the romantic fun-filled Friday night date I had envisaged.

When we were in the kitchen, I pointed to the house rule. 'Yes, we'll have to wait until the others are home, then we can turn down the couch,' was her very encouraging response. Patiently, we continued to watch TV as we waited. When one of her flat mates arrived home she told us the other two wouldn't be coming home. I watched as Maree prepared our bed for the night. I splashed a little water over my face in the bathroom to freshen up a little before we snuggled up nice and close. Maree was interested in my arm and leg that now rested on the adjacent couch and asked lots of questions about how my arm worked and how difficult was it to walk with such a bulky looking leg. Eager for more than close cuddling I assured her I'd explain in the morning, she could watch me put myself together again as I dressed. Any fears I had about Maree being repulsed by my heavily scarred body and amputations were rapidly dismissed.

As non-medically oriented people both Margot and Maree had shown absolutely no discomfort with my battered body and artificial limbs. Both were patient with my slowness as I walked and my need to disassemble myself occasionally. I had worried needlessly about a problem that only existed in my mind.

Driving home wearing yesterday's clothes and in need of a shower and a shave I had plenty to think about. I was foolishly ignoring the known dangers involved with dating two girls at the same time. My earlier fears that I would be rejected because of my disabilities could not justify my duplicitous behavior. With work to complete I showered and put the night behind me. I was going to the Drive-In with Margot, David Young and his friend Elizabeth later that evening. They would arrive together allowing me an extra hour of study time. Four assignments had to be completed by Easter. Engrossed in my studies, I did not notice the time. David and the girls arrived and still, I had not shaved. Margot did not care for the look but we did not have time to spare.

Margot and I sat close but didn't embrace. I feigned a headache brought on by all the studying I'd been doing. The real reason was I felt a compelling need to consider my recent behavior before I got myself into another convoluted juggling act. When we got home, I maintained my charade and went straight to bed. After David finished having a shot about 'Isn't it the women who are supposed to have the headache?' he offered to take Margot home.

Bob woke me with the smell of burning toast and coffee. Surprisingly, I had slept well. As we enjoyed breakfast I remembered I had agreed to join Chris for a study session that morning. It was 9.00 am. Grabbing my books, I raced out to the car and looked up his address in my directory; Burke Road turn right into Toorak Road, left into Irving Road. *Holy shit! What a mansion.* I had never before ventured into this posh part of Melbourne. As I parked the car I caught a glimpse of myself in the rear view mirror. A three-day beard was not a good look. My trousers had a hole in the knee from a recent fall. I made a hasty retreat and headed home. Along the way I rang Chris from a phone box to say I would be a little late. Showered, shaved and dressed in my newest casual clothes, I headed back to Irving Road, Toorak.

Chris greeted me at the door. He was not quite 18 but had stubble covering his face and was dressed more like the gardener. We worked diligently completing our outstanding assignments before his mother called us for lunch.

33

Tarnishing My Ego

With no outstanding assignments I eased back a little with my studies. Patrick and I took Bob to the movies at the hospital. As it was free, Bob was eager to attend. I remembered he was known for having deep pockets and short arms when we were at SME. Whatever was showing had attracted a large crowd. We made our way into the theatre and I heard a familiar voice behind me. It was Elaine, the nurse who had accompanied me to the theatre for the first time about two years before. Elaine appeared as delighted to see me, as I was to see her. After a quick chat we agreed to meet after the movie. I sat through the movie thinking about the time she wheeled me down to the theatre and all the good times I'd enjoyed since. I really did have a lot to be thankful for. My opportunity to reward Elaine for her kindness had arrived. I would take her out to dinner soon.

Fay called in for a chat after a day of lectures at the hospital. Rather than have coffee at home we headed down Bell Street to a recently opened coffee lounge. It was becoming popular with nurses from the two hospitals in the area. Bob was keen to check it out but Patrick went off to bed. We found a table and ordered. The crowd was mostly girls who were smoking something more than cigarettes by their stony-eyed look. Anti-war badges were worn proudly or defiantly by many of the young crowd. One badge said, 'Make Love Not War', Bob ambitiously suggested to almost every girl in the place that he would be happy to assist them achieve their objective. A female vocalist was singing anti-war songs in a corner, her unrestrained boobs swaying in harmony beneath a shapeless dress. Her maudlin song had me even wanting to smoke some funny tobacco! When Fay and I were ready to leave, Bob happily stayed behind. He must have thought he had a chance of helping at least one girl make love not war…

Arab Avotins my mate from the Army, whom I last saw in Vietnam, was in town. He was attending the Language School at RAAF Base Point Cook. He turned up regularly on the weekend, another major threat to my studies, looking for a beer, a bed and a shower. Arab had complained he had not found a girl willing to join him in bed recently. He seemed not to appreciate that you had to stay a little sober if seduction was your ambition. He could dance as well as anyone I knew and was entertaining when sober. Several girls who visited the flat, initially showed interest in him, even Barry O'Dea's girlfriend Sue - much to Barry's annoyance. Arab was either not interested or too honorable to move in on another bloke's girl.

Easter 1969

Easter was not far off and Maree suggested we drive to Adelaide. Four days alone with her appealed to me. Immediately I started plotting a little deception to cover my absence from Margot for four days. I fabricated a boring study tour to some uninteresting location as part of my Geography studies. Margot was such a fun girl I felt she would have happily joined me on an excursion if I made it sound remotely interesting.

I arrived at Maree's flat around seven o'clock on Good Friday but my knock on the door was not answered. *Maybe the girls are still asleep?* I knocked a little harder, but still no answer. Was it possible that they had got up early and gone to church? I sat on the steps and waited for over an hour before heading back down to my car. After waiting another hour I headed for home. Bob was surprised to see me. No sooner had I explained that not one of the girls was home then he said, 'You've been stood up mate.' I did not accept that Maree would have done that to me. After all it had been her suggestion. I returned to the flat later in the afternoon. Still no answer. Bob continued to make disparaging remarks about Maree. I rang Maree at work after class on Wednesday. Maree told me all four girls had been invited to spend Easter at a holiday house in the hills near Healesville. Accepting the invitation was helpful to her career she added. When I told Bob what Maree had said he thought it was vintage Maree.

'She would not give a stuff about who she inconvenienced,' he said offhandedly. *Well, that's justice. I've been shafted,* I thought. When I rang Margot at work I got another unpleasant surprise. Margot asked how did Maree enjoy Adelaide? I was dumbfounded. I had no answer for Margot. My silence meant guilt. I heard the phone click. I had been well and truly knocked off my pedestal.

Sitting in the near empty RSL Club I allowed myself to drift into a period of quiet reflection. Again I came to the realisation that my social life was interfering with my studies. *Maybe I should abandon the study after all, what was I trying to achieve?* My ego was all that was driving me. Maybe I should let it tarnish a little. Maree and Margot had certainly started the tarnishing process. Admitting that my crusade to conquer my fear of being left on the shelf had got out of hand was not easy. I was still a young man with a lot of living ahead of me. I had certainly been able to attract girls. Holding on to them was my problem – either through being too greedy or by being too insensitive. I was getting on top of my physical disabilities and my emotional problems were diminishing even though I had not sought any professional help so far. Accepting what I couldn't change had to be put to one side to allow me to actively pursue what I could improve. I doubted that anything so disastrous could happen again. Having focused on the wrong issues was my downfall. Studies must come first, even if I only learnt how to confidently write a letter that would be an achievement. The crowd in the club started to build and brought an end to my soul searching.

The next Sunday morning I let my hair down and joined in more enthusiastically with my mates who had gathered for a beer drinking session. Nick – one of the regulars – announced that he was getting married next month, as his girlfriend was pregnant. Arab was to be best man. The wedding would be on Saturday 10 May. My second anniversary of being blown up was the day before but I planned to keep quiet about that. Nick's wedding would provide more than enough reasons for everyone to get on the grog.

April 25, ANZAC Day 1969

As the day for all veterans to commemorate their mates who had perished in active service fell on a Friday, the long weekend would provide plenty of recovery time. *Should I overindulge?* I got up early and attended the Dawn Service at the Melbourne Shrine of Remembrance. I did not go to the morning march through the city, opting to have a few more hours sleep in anticipation of a big day out. When I arrived at Duckboard House the place was packed. Diggers young and old, smartly dressed with their medals proudly displayed were drinking and yarning shoulder to shoulder. Not a safe place for me. I retreated upstairs and joined in the activities there. Two Up and Crown and Anchor were in full swing with no shortage of gamblers willing to wager a handful of dollars on their fancy.

Lady Luck was with me. A successful throw of the dice rolled three diamonds rewarding me with a return of three to one. I accumulated a small pile of dollars and held them firmly in my hook. The bloke handing over the cash asked me if my name was

John Thompson. Before answering I looked at him, but he did not look familiar to me. When I said yes, he said that I would know his fiancée.

'Who would that be?' I asked.

'Jill, a nurse who looked after you in hospital,' he said.

Feeling myself turning red I asked him to extend my compliments to her and wished him well. Knowing that Jill had found happiness was genuinely pleasing.

The Sunday after ANZAC Day Nick turned up at the flat alone and regretfully told his friends enjoying a few beers that we would not be able to attend his wedding. He explained how his girlfriend's parents were putting on a small reception at their family home. Arab as the best man would be the only one going. Nick's mum however, had invited us all to turn up at her place later in the afternoon.

On the Friday before the wedding Nick and Arab arrived at the flat to stay overnight. Both were rather drunk. They had gone to collect hired dinner suits to wear to the wedding. After a few more beers Nick decided to try his suit on and treat the rest of us to his impersonation of a 'male model' and parade around for our amusement. Unfortunately, not even a nice black suit and white shirt could improve his appearance. A missing front tooth did not help either. As he paraded around, we noticed that he was still wearing his concrete covered work boots. When asked to change his boots, he realised he had not bothered to buy a new pair of shoes. No one in the room had a pair of shoes that would fit him. Nick's remedy was to step into the shower with his boots on and try to scrub them clean. His boots did not dry overnight but he wore them anyway. I drove Nick and Arab into the Registry Office. I left Nick sitting in the gutter with a brush and tin of Kiwi shoe polish trying to swish up his wet boots.

That evening I joined a group of his mates at his mother's place to celebrate his wedding. An impressive collection of presents, were stacked on the kitchen table. When Nick's mother suggested he should open his presents, Nick grabbed his bride and started to tear away her clothing. It required a firm whack on the head from his mother to make him behave. Arab was looking rather pleased with himself too. The happiest I'd seen him for a long time. He was getting along really well with Nick's sister…

17 May
I drove down to Longwarry about eighty kilometres south east of Melbourne to attended my mate Kevin Stephens' wedding. I'd arranged to meet a few friends also attending at the Longwarry pub for lunch. Despite the Saturday morning crowd we managed to find a table. As the church and the local hall were not far away we would be able to walk to both venues. While we sat around chatting, David Young asked about my trip to Adelaide. Immediately, I was suspicious. *Was he the one who shafted me with Margot?* It turned out that he had but not with any malicious intent. David was of the opinion that I was no longer seeing Margot. At a recent gathering I had arrived with Maree and we had talked openly about heading to Adelaide for Easter. Not aware of my duplicity, he had mentioned my trip to Adelaide when Margot had asked about my study trip. At least I could stop doubting my friend's loyalty.

The wedding was an enjoyable occasion, family and friends filled the little Catholic Church. Afterwards invited guests assembled in the local hall. As an outsider, it looked to me as if most of the population of Longwarry and Druin were present along with the local football team that Kevin had played with prior to being called up. Country hospitality was amply displayed with an endless supply of drinks and food. A group of Kevin's mates surrounded him intending to perform some traditional local ritual of entry to married life. Kevin, aware of his mates' intention, put up a futile resistance as he was carted out of the building.

Kevin had recovered well from his surgery earlier in the year, not well enough to return to the family dairy farm, he accepted an administrative position in his cousins transport business in nearby Warragul.

34
Quieter Times

Towards the end of June, Patrick and I decided to move closer to the city. Bob had returned to Queensland with a substantial wad of cash he had saved. Arab had quit his language course, eager to return to Vietnam. My studies were progressing well, thanks to my four young friends to whom I had become very attached. With their combined help I was achieving a pass mark in all subjects, admittedly only by the skin of my teeth but a pass nonetheless.

I spent Saturday morning looking through the classifieds section of the paper. A small ground floor one bedroom flat was available in South Yarra only minutes from the city. It had easy access, ample car parking and was close to everything we wanted, pubs, public transport and shops it was ideal. We entered into a 12-month lease and moved in the next weekend. We also agreed not to advertise our whereabouts. My application for a Gift Car had been successful. The Hillman Hunter was much easier to park in the very small car park behind the pub while attending college.

Time spent traveling into college was more than halved. Chris regularly hopped off the tram at the end of the street on his way to college and rode in with me. At the end of the day I would give him and Donna a ride home. It was the least I could do in return for the help they were giving me. Occasionally, Donna and Joanne would come home with me between classes and over coffee we would talk about our assignments. All was above board, but one afternoon our Geography teacher asked me how I was getting on with the girls. Not certain about the thrust of his question, I told him how helpful the girls had been to me.

'How helpful are you to them?' he asked. Before I could determine exactly what he was getting at, students started to enter the room. Later I was telling the girls about his remark and Donna told me how he had asked her out a number of times.

September was gone. The school year was now racing towards exam time. My social life had become almost non-existent and I had started to have difficulty suppressing my desire to bust out and have some fun but that would have put my studies in real jeopardy. Even my feckless womanizing had been curtailed. My determination was tested when Jack Campbell called in on his way back to Brisbane with his very young new bride. Fortunately, they only had a few hours to fill before their train left.

Exam Nerves

Just passing by the skin of my teeth when I had unlimited time to complete my assignments made me have serious doubts about my ability in the exam room. *Was I kidding myself? Did I really think I had half a chance of passing?* I thought about putting in a big final effort shutting myself off completely, but why? I had really enjoyed letting my hair down from the moment I first got out of my hospital bed. *Did I really need to work?* Money was no problem; I had more than enough to keep me out of the poor house. A disability pension cheque from the Repatriation Department arrived each fortnight. A superannuation cheque from the Army also arrived each fortnight.

As I pondered my next move I felt deep within me an urge to call for help. Doctor Benson at Heidelberg had always invited me to call should I ever need to and now was the time. I went to see him the next day after class. He greeted me warmly and wasted no time getting down to business. With tears welling up I told him about my doubts and the voice within that kept telling me to abandon my studies. I had no need to subject myself to the anxiety associated with exams. Get out and have fun, one voice was saying, while another told me to stick it out as I'd almost finished the year and I owed it to everyone who had helped me cope with my determination to honour my mates and not let the feeling of guilt derail my progress.

'John, John! You have been so determined in your quest for forgiveness, you are wearing yourself out,' he said. 'You continue to struggle under the burden of guilt. It's unnecessary John. Let go and accept that it was an accident,' he said in his calm voice. He had always been a man I trusted and felt good about. I listened as he suggested I put the books away for the weekend and have a little fun.

'You should reward yourself after the exams. Regardless of the results, don't wait for the results. You deserve a reward for the effort you have made to get this far.' A reward sounded good to me but what about actually doing the exams? The time available wouldn't be enough: I wrote too slowly. Doctor Benson rang a colleague and then assured me that additional time would be made available. However, I needed to nominate an acceptable alternative venue. He suggested I visit Miss Nolan at the Red Cross Centre.

'This should be ideal for you,' Miss Nolan said as we looked into the centre's library. She also volunteered to supervise me during the actual exams.

Over dinner I considered how I would reward myself. Peter Dixon, who I met when I was in the 36 Evacuation Hospital and with whom I had maintained contact with in the US and had regularly suggested I visit him when I was up to it. Peter was now flying commercial airlines all over the US with PAN AM, so I thought I would check with him if Christmas was a suitable time for me to go over for a couple of weeks.

With only four weeks to go until the exams I was determined to put in a big final effort by waking early and studying at least two hours before heading off to college. In the evening I also made an extra effort. However, interruptions in the evening were hard to avoid. I was delighted to receive a reply from Peter so quickly, inviting me to stay with his family at New Canaan, in Connecticut. He warned me that it could be cold and most likely snowing.

I needed a passport and wrote letters to relatives in England, as I had decided to go there as well, and Robyn, who I still thought fondly of, was now working in London. I wrote to her hopeful she would want to catch up. I made plans to stay in Singapore as well as many of my army mates were now based there. Also Janice Webb (my favorite Red Cross lady) had married a British Army officer and was also living in Singapore. On a recent visit to Melbourne, she too had invited me to call in if I was ever in her part of the world. I wrote and told her I would be heading to Singapore in late January.

I drove to the Commonwealth Centre at the top of Spring Street to apply for a passport. A bloke behind the counter asked how he could help me. He presented me with a number of forms and asked me to fill them in. A quick glance at the forms and I knew I would have trouble trying to write in the small spaces. I asked if there was someone who could help me.

'What's the matter can't you write?' the bloke asked in a voice loud enough for everyone around to hear. As others nearby looked at me, I held up my arms and explained that writing was a little difficult. Abruptly, he summoned another bloke to assist me. The crap was about to hit the fan.

Noting my date of birth, I was asked for my clearance from the Department of National Service and Labour. I produced my Discharge Certificate, clearly stating that I was no longer fit for military service.

'No, that's not acceptable, you'll need a Clearance Certificate,'

I started to get hot under the collar. The certificate was only available from the Department's Melbourne office, which was in the Gas and Fuel building in Flinders Street. Great! It was at the other end of the city. He looked at my birth certificate and said, 'What's this, you're not an Australian.'

Now I was boiling under the collar. 'What do you mean I'm not Australian?' I tersely asked. I had served in the Australian Army for four years, been on active service on two occasions and this prick wanted to tell me I was not Australian. Good enough to go off to war but can't have an Australian passport! I was now well and truly pissed off.

'No point going any further with your application,' I heard the bloke saying as he walked towards the back of the office and picked up a phone. When he came back he told me an official would be down shortly to assist me make an application for Australian citizenship. With no real option but to sit and wait I tried to control my mounting anger. I really did not need any more anxiety so close to sitting my exams. A short bald-headed bloke walked in and introduced himself in a heavy European accent. I was not remotely interested in his name, catching only that it ended with a ski. I was more concerned about the way he had thrust out his right hand and awkwardly shook my left hand. I was amused that a 'wog' had been sent to help me become an Australian.

More forms were produced as I listened to Mr Baldhedski tell me that I could apply for a 'Certificate of Registration as an Australian Citizen' and it would be granted in about four weeks.

'Well we better get started,' was all I could say. We were into the questions when he asked about my injuries. Naturally, I thought it was a legitimate question and responded with a brief description. Questions about my views on the Moratorium marches followed. I answered again believing all questions were relevant to my application. When it came to providing a sample of signatures he asked how my hook worked. I had reached the end of my patience by then and asked as calmly as I could where that question was written. He said that he was curious and wanted to know how it worked. Well, I'd had enough by then.

'Stuff you and your paperwork. You can stick the lot up your arse,' I yelled. I got up and stormed out of the office. I drove down to Duckboard House and got into a few beers.

Well, that's blown that idea, I thought to myself as I downed another beer. When the bloke next to me asked how things were going, I told him. I knew him casually from drinking at the club on Friday evenings. He was a journalist with the *Herald* newspaper. He was listening to me rant on about my frustrating afternoon. The next morning a much younger journalist and a photographer arrived at home as I was getting ready to head into college with Chris. The journalist had heard about my experience at the passport office and wanted to interview me.

At the first break Chris suggested I should try and obtain a British passport.

'How would I do that?' I asked. As I was born in Malta and my father was English it would qualify me to make an application, he explained. He suggested we walk up to the British Consular office at lunchtime. Once there I explained my circumstances and Chris assisted me in filling out an application. Birth certificate and photos were needed to accompany the application. Walking back to college we stopped off at a photographer's shop offering a next day passport photo service. Chris offered to pick the photos up for me in the morning.

Later that afternoon, the *Herald* printed my photo and story. It was accurate and had a response from a department spokesman. He was quoted as saying that I would not be refused a passport if I made an application. I had no doubt about that. My bitch was about the hoops I was expected to jump through to get the passport. On the Friday afternoon I was able to return my completed application. A staff member looked through it and told me I should have my passport within fourteen days. Confident that my plans were back on track, I went home with every intention of studying for my exams.

35
The year is almost over

A phone call from my mate John 'Pom' Passant interrupted me; he wanted to come over to the flat. I tried to tell him that my exams were getting close and I still had a lot of work to do. He said it was urgent and he needed to talk to me. I relented and said he could come over but I would not be getting on the grog. When he arrived his toothy grin was a fair indication that whatever was so urgent was not too serious. He wanted me to be best man at his wedding. I was not his first choice, our mate Ron Beveridge was, but he was now in Singapore with the Engineer Malay Troop and would not be able to attend the wedding. Despite being second choice, I was flattered to be asked, although I was not too keen about having to make a speech. The wedding date was 6 December – a week after my last exam and two days before I flew to the United States. Pom suggested we go together to hire a dinner suit but with my bits and pieces, I thought it best to get a dinner suit made for the occasion.

Last minute cramming for the exams had not improved my confidence. I had almost reached saturation point and could absorb no more information. My first exam was English Expression and I feared my spelling and punctuation was going to sink me despite my best efforts. Any correct use of punctuation when writing my assignments had been more luck than knowledge. At least I felt confident about the content of all four subjects. With the assistance of my young team of helpers I had read all the compulsory books, dissected them and formed an opinion of each book and characters mentioned. I could do no more. *Or could I?* The humiliation associated with failing encroached on my thoughts. For the remainder of my time, I made lists of words that I anticipated could be used in the exam and would give the impression I had a greater knowledge of the subject than I really had. Words that I doubted my ability to spell went on a list. Not that I was going to squander time trying to learn how to spell them; I concentrated on learning the meaning of many of the multi-syllable words. I hoped a comprehensive list in alphabetical order would compensate for my lack of ability to write satisfactorily.

I planned to smuggle the list into the exam room tucked down the inside of the bucket of my wooden leg. My confidence lifted. I was giving myself every chance of getting a pass mark. Occasionally, I wrestled with my conscience about the right and wrong of what I was going to do. Without a little skullduggery I had no chance. *Was anyone going to be hurt by my action?* I didn't think so. The other three subjects did not have the same emphasis on spelling and punctuation; subject knowledge was the main requirement.

English Expression was the first exam. I drove over to Heidelberg Hospital and parked near the Red Cross Centre. Miss Nolan was waiting for me and we went straight to the library. Immediately, I saw a problem. The table and chair were in the middle of the room and anyone passing the glass door could see me. I suggested we move the table to one side, ostensibly to allow for more light across the table. Now I was out of sight of anyone approaching the door. Miss Nolan was keeping a close eye on the time. She was under strict instructions not to let me access the exam papers until one o'clock. When I took my seat she asked if I would like a glass of water. I used her absence to check how out of sight I was.

At one o'clock I was handed my exam envelope and I was free to start. Miss Nolan took a seat at the end of the room. *Stuff it. I had not counted on her remaining in the room.* I laid the contents of the envelope out before me and carefully I read the instructions and then the questions. Taylor's College had prepared me well; I was familiar with almost everything in the questions. That was a good start. If I could minimise my spelling and punctuation mistakes I had a chance. As I sat with my biro poised a knock on the door broke the silence. Miss Nolan was wanted on the phone. *Great!* I made the most of her absence to get my cheat sheet out and concealed amongst the official papers on the table.

With my head down, I was frantically writing my first essay when Miss Nolan returned. Then there was a second knock on the door. I put on quite a show of being piqued about the disturbance. It worked. Leaving the room she said she would bring me a cup of tea later. Accessing my cheat sheets was now a lot easier. I wrote confidently but not believing I would overly impress anyone. Once finished and packed up, I wondered what my mates would think of my behavior. A superb example of sappers' initiative I thought. The next three exams went as smoothly.

Relieved that the school year was behind me I was able to relax and finalise my trip. I now had a British passport.

Pom's wedding was only a few days away so we had a pub-crawl around St Kilda but behaved ourselves. We did have a couple of sheilas hanging around us for a while. When one went to sit on my leg she got such a fright at the hardness she fell off and we laughed too loudly.

The bouncers had us out the door real fast. Once we got home Pom listed all that he did NOT want me to mention in my speech. 'What about the time your fat girlfriend got stuck in the fire escape?' I said.

'Don't you dare,' he hollered.

As we talked it became obvious, he was not trying to conceal his past from his future wife it was from his parents.

The big day arrived. It was not too hot for December. I'd driven to the church and waited for Pom to arrive. Giving a speech continued to cause me a load of anxiety but not as much as the fear that I would fall over in the church or dropping the wedding ring. Visions of me lying flat on my face in the aisle as everyone rushed to help had disturbed my sleep. My dinner suit fitted really well. I fantasized that I looked more like James Bond standing round a roulette wheel in a casino, than the best man at a wedding.

The Pom arrived. His perpetual toothy grin never faded as he entered the church. We sat in the front pew, as the crowd assembled behind us. I felt beads of sweat running down my face and neck. I was getting nervous. When the music announcing the arrival of the bride started, I felt some relief. Everyone would be looking at Jeanette now. Helen, Jeanette's sister was one of two bridesmaids and stayed protectively close by my side as we walked slowly down the aisle. Once wedding photos were completed I relaxed with a cold beer. Family and friends tucked into a fine meal with plenty of wine and beer loosening up their inhibitions. I was drinking very slowly until I had delivered my speech. When the time came for me to honour my good friend I took a deep breath and did my best. The applause at the finish was too sustained to be simply polite.

John and Jeanette showed no eagerness to leave the reception. Jeanette's laughter was heard around the room and the Pom's smile had not diminished one iota as he circulated among the guests. When they eventually departed to start their honeymoon. I felt a growing sadness: I could never see myself experiencing their type of happiness.

That night alone in my bed I reflected on all the good times the Pom and I had shared over the last five years together. To suppress the envy that was engulfing me, I turned my thoughts to my overseas trip that was now only a day away. I would not be back until late March and return to college after the Easter break. Patrick would have the use of my car and I had handed over my contribution to the rent. David Young had offered to drive me to Essendon airport after lunch on Monday. All that was left for me to do was visit Mum and Dad to say goodbye.

Around midday friends started calling in to say goodbye. Many brought food and booze. Chris, Ian, Joanne and Donna, my very own coaching team arrived. Together, they had lifted my spirits on so many occasions. A party atmosphere developed very quickly. I felt totally flattered by all the attention. Very few of my guests had travelled outside of Australia with the exception of my army mates who had been to Vietnam. Friends expressed their concerns about me travelling so far by myself. I did my best to allay their fears telling them that I would be in the company of friends most of the time.

As stragglers at the party cleaned up for me I headed to the bathroom. Getting into the shower I slipped and crashed into the glass screen then fell onto the bathroom floor. Friends, fearing the worst, raced to my assistance. Not only was the shower screen broken, my pride took a blow as I lay naked on the floor. Friends helped me to my bedroom and dried me off. What a timely reminder of the dangers of wet bathrooms for amputees!

Monday morning I woke to the sound of Patrick getting ready for work. Hearing the shower running reminded me of my fall. Immediately, I felt pain in my right shoulder. In the mirror, I saw the yellowing signs of bruising developing. After swallowing a couple of pills for pain, I set about my final preparations. Nothing was going to interfere with my holiday.

I treated David and Elizabeth to a farewell drink as we waited for my flight to Sydney to be called. Climbing the steep stairway into the aircraft required my full attention. I sat next to a young man heading to Los Angeles from Sydney. He assisted me to the International Airport and safely aboard my BOAC flight to New York.

36
Epilogue

Christmas morning 1969

New Canaan Connecticut was covered in snow. Peter Dixon's father woke me early to join the family riding sleds down a nearby hill. I climbed to the top on my crutches; they had been modified so that I could fold them to fit in my overnight bag. Climbing snow-covered hills was a struggle but with assistance from Peter's brothers Eddy and Lucian, I made it. The exhilaration of speeding down on the sled lying flat on my stomach only inches from the snow was repeated over and over again. Exhaustion eventually brought the fun-filled morning to an end.

Christmas dinner was a feast fit for a king. Mr Dixon sat at the head of the table with the largest turkey I had ever seen in front of him. With the skill of a surgeon, he delicately sliced meat off the bird for everyone then he presented me with one of the legs. After three weeks of living with snow I was mastering a new range of difficulties. Whether I was on my crutches or my leg the potential to fall was so much greater as I walked on slippery pathways.

In London, whatever flame Robyn may have carried for me last year had been well and truly extinguished. Although I stayed at her place and we went out together we really had nothing going between us and I did feel a little disappointed. On a visit to Australia House in London I met Captain Graham Hellyer who had flown home from Vietnam on the same flight as me in June 1967. He had made a very good recovery from his spinal injuries and was now posted to the UK. Together with his wife we enjoyed a fine meal one evening before I headed to Singapore.

Janice Webb and her husband were living in a beautiful big house in Orchard Road and made me welcome. Within days of my arrival I received a letter from David Young with my exam results. I had passed all four subjects. Surprisingly I felt no guilt; although I was sure some people would be disappointed if they knew about my cheat sheet. I felt I had worked hard and learned the subjects well, I had not cheated on actual answers to questions. My difficulty was with transferring the knowledge to the exam paper and that was where my cheat list had assisted me.

Many of my army mates who I had served with in Borneo and Vietnam were now married and had joined the Malay Troop. The Troop had recently been relocated to Singapore for a two-year posting; the married blokes were able to take their wives with them. They were living in army married quarters at Nee Soon, about a twenty-minute taxi ride from Janice Webb's place. After a week of travelling out by taxi each afternoon I accepted an offer by Nev Bartells and his wife Kathy to move into their spare bedroom. Nev was the only one on leave at the time. While the rest fronted up on parade each weekday, we roamed all over the island on Nev's motorbike. I rode pillion, my crutches tucked under my left arm with my shortened arm around Nev's ample waistline. We attracted many long lingering looks from other road users and pedestrians.

April 1970

Returning to college in early April, I discovered that Chris Sallmann and Ian Hamilton were still willing to assist me. Joanne Carter and Donna Curran had not returned but both remained in close contact with me and became supportive friends for many years.

The two ex-Nasho's, Barry Heard and Anthony James, who I had met the year before were continuing their studies. I started seeing more of them around the college. Settling in to study after my extended holiday was difficult and not only did I lack motivation, I knew that I was no scholar. With help from Chris and Ian I caught up with all the outstanding assignments that I had missed. I desperately tried to develop a study routine that would get me through the year.

Rather than renew the lease on the flat in June, I purchased a one-bedroom apartment in Canterbury Road, Middle Park. Not long after my twenty-fifth birthday in July, I terminated my studies and joined the Victorian Public Service as a clerk with the State Rivers' and Water Supply Commission. The daily grind of an eight-hour day tested my self-discipline. I toned down my lifestyle and discovered I enjoyed staying home, reading books of my choice, listening to music and entertaining friends. I was reasonably happy with life but I still felt I was ambling along without direction or any real purpose.

Barry Heard lived about half a mile away and we regularly got together. Barry was from the Omeo Valley district and knew many girls from the area that were working or studying in Melbourne. I appreciated meeting and dating several of his lady friends. I accepted an invitation to Barry's New Year's Eve party at the beach house he had built near Lake Tyers, east of Lakes Entrance. There I met Michael Hosking, who was also a former Nasho with 7 Battalion in Vietnam at the party. He too, lived within walking distance to my apartment. Back in Melbourne, Michael introduced me to his widowed sister Judy, a mother of two young children, three year old Dominic and Justine, who was born four weeks after her father had passed away two years earlier. I took an immediate shine to Judy.

We started dating regularly and in September we married. The following year my request for a transfer to Geelong, where Judy's parents and many of her friends lived was approved. Our family grew rapidly after the birth of our first child Danielle. Deirdre came along then Judith; three babies in three years. We settled into our new home and were enjoying our life together. I had even managed to kick a football around with Dominic and play ball games in the backyard with the girls. Working at a job that was not terribly exciting became more tolerable as I had a whole new purpose and direction in my life. My fears about never marrying and having a family of my own were totally wiped from my thoughts. I was the happiest man in town.

Whenever we had an opportunity my army mates: John 'The Pom' Passant and Kevin Smith regularly took Dominic and me away on camping and fishing trips. Sitting round a campfire reminiscing about our time together reminded me of the value of friendship. Chris and Ian my two young friends who had helped so much while I was at college were more than willing to drive down to Geelong and assist me with the physical work required to develop the garden around our new home.

In July 1974, Judy was diagnosed with terminal bowel cancer and given only two months to live. It was just two weeks after our youngest child Judith was born; I was a shattered man once again. With my disabilities, I knew I would not be able to perform my duties at the office and care for my children at home. I resigned and I applied for a Totally and Permanently Incapacitated Pension, (TPI). Friends and neighbours, many we had only known for a short time were unbelievably helpful, cooking meals and helping look after the children. The Pom (now out of the Army and working as an electrical goods salesman) asked for leave. When leave was denied he told his boss to shove his job and came down to Geelong anyway. While I visited Judy, he looked after the kids. When I returned home we sat in the kitchen for hours drinking coffee, talking about the future, and how I was going to cope.

Judy held on for 359 days. Long enough to celebrate Judith's first birthday. As I walked away from her grave after the funeral my eyes were dry, I had no more tears left. Judy was gone and she took with her a huge chunk of my heart. My grieving was coming to an end, it had started the moment I received the terrible news a year before. Now, I had a family of five children to care for. I had given Judy my word that I would keep all five children together. However, caring for a twelve-month baby was physically beyond my ability. Baby Judith had been taken in and cared for by many friends and family over the last twelve months. Michele and John Eldridge, long time friends of Judy's, agreed to take Judith into their home and care for her along with their own three children. There was hardly a day that I didn't call in to spend some time with my baby daughter. Looking after the other four was not easy on them or me. Cooking and washing I could manage but ironing was beyond me. I had no option but to pay a lady to iron a basket of washing each week and another to help with the house keeping. The nappies that had to be changed several times a day almost had me beaten too but with teamwork we managed. It was necessary for me to remove my leg and arm and get down on the floor. The older children would hold the folded nappy in place as I carefully inserted the safety pins. Unfortunately, I often heard a little whimper as I accidently pricked their little bums.

To ease my burden I worked out a signal system with my neighbour across the road Mrs Lorna Eaton. When I needed assistance, especially with nappies, one of the kids would stand on the toy box in front of the lounge room window and wave a nappy. Lorna would see the waving from her kitchen window and come across to help. Once I had made it through the first year, Judith came home.

JOHN 'JETHRO' THOMPSON

The Legacy Club of Geelong became aware of my predicament and had invited Dominic and Justine to join the club's Saturday morning youth group. While attending the groups' Christmas party I observed an attractive young widow watching her two boys, Ian and Anthony participating in a gymnastic routine. Fate unbelievably brought the two of us together a couple of weeks later. My mate Patrick had returned from Western Australia and married the young niece of the widow's late husband. Rob Butler had served in Vietnam with 7 Battalion and was killed in a motor vehicle accident three years later. Patrick urged me to make myself known to Rob's widow, a shy, slim girl called Perle.

Although I had only been widowed for six months, I was eager to have the company of an adult female friend to partner me whenever I was invited to a social function. Together with our seven children tagging along, we started dating. As the children grew, I delighted in walking around the block with them. The girls displayed no aversion to holding my hook as we walked and talked about their mum who had gone to heaven and the new mum who would love and care for them. In December 1978, Perle and I married and moved to Queensland. We figured that with so many in-laws between us, we needed some space.

We settled in Ormeau south of Beenleigh and built a family home on acreage. Ray Brooks, the father of my mate Dennis who had perished in Vietnam, was an architect and readily offered to draw plans and supervise the building of our house once he heard we were moving.

Life as a blended family was not easy, but we managed to overcome most hurdles. The girls were a lot happier having a mother. Once we had established our home I looked for something to occupy myself outside of the family. I enrolled in a TAFE course to become a Welfare Officer. On completion of the course I became involved with the Beenleigh RSL Sub-Branch assisting war veterans apply for pensions for their war-caused disabilities and committed myself to assisting The Limbless Soldiers' Association and Legacy, in appreciation of the assistance they had provided to me. When the Vietnam Veterans' Association was formed I did not hesitate to join their cause.

In 1989 I received an Australia Day award for service to war veterans and in 1992 was awarded Honorary Life Membership of the Vietnam Veterans' Association of Australia. In the 2006 Queen's Birthday Honours' List I was awarded an Order of Australia Medal (OAM), for service to war veterans and war widows. I appreciated this recognition and proudly display my OAM with the rest of my gongs awarded for my military service.

My greatest reward however, is Perle's love, companionship and devotion to assisting me travel life's uncertain path. Perle had her work cut out for her looking after seven children and did a sterling job. Living with a disabled husband, I'm sure has not been easy but thirty-four years later we are still happily married and enjoy being Nan and Pa to ten grandchildren.

My wounds have healed: both physically and mentally. However, as a consequence of wearing my artificial leg for over twenty years I developed lower back problems. Walking on crutches to ease the discomfort of wearing my leg eventually affected my shoulders, further increasing Perle's burden; a burden she never complains about or avoids.

Following emergency open-heart surgery on the morning of Australia Day 2007 my mate Charlie Lynn was again present by my bedside in the Intensive Care Unit. It was forty years after he had stood beside my hospital bed in Vietnam. Not only was my hospital room regularly filled with visitors, mates who had been with me in the minefield: Brett Nolen, Kevin Smith, Max Staggard and Ivan Scully flew from Melbourne to Brisbane to support me once again.

Of all I have learned in my life maybe it is the lesson of friendship that comes through loudest. Mates: people who stand by me, encouraging, supporting, and challenging me when I need to be challenged, and at the end of the day can have a good laugh with me, that's what friends are for.

Acknowledgment

I have not mentioned everyone who assisted with my recovery and rehabilitation, nor the many friends and family who helped me cope with the loss of Judy, they know who they are and how much I appreciated their help at the time and continue to do so.

ORDER

		QTY
A Vietnam Vet's Remarkable Life	$26.99	....
Postage within Australia (1 book)	$5.00	....
Postage within Australia (2 or more books)	$9.00	....

TOTAL* $_____

* All prices include GST

Name: ....

Address: ....

....

Phone: ....

Email Address: ....

Payment:

❑ Money Order ❑ Cheque ❑ Amex ❑ MasterCard ❑ Visa

Cardholder's Name: ....

Credit Card Number: ....

Signature: ....

Expiry Date: ....

Allow 21 days for delivery.

Payment to: Brolga Publishing (ABN: 46 063 962 443)
PO Box 12544
A'Beckett Street, Melbourne, 8006
Victoria, Australia
admin@brolgapublishing.com.au

BE PUBLISHED

Publishing through a successful Australian publisher. Brolga provides:
- Editorial appraisal
- Cover design
- Typesetting
- Printing
- Author promotion
- National book trade distribution, including sales, marketing and distribution through Macmillan Australia.
- International book trade distribution
- World-wide e-Book distribution

For details and inquiries, contact:
Brolga Publishing Pty Ltd
PO Box 12544
A'Beckett St VIC 8006

Phone: 0414 608 494
admin@brolgapublishing.com.au
markzocchi@brolgapublishing.com.a
ABN: 46 063 962 443